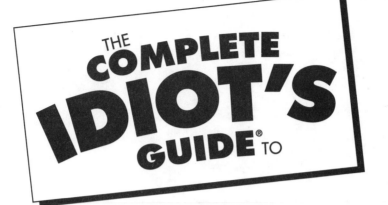

THE COMPLETE IDIOT'S GUIDE® TO

Dating

Third Edition

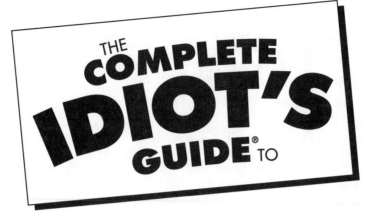

THE COMPLETE IDIOT'S GUIDE® TO

Dating

Third Edition

by Dr. Judy Kuriansky

ALPHA

A member of Penguin Group (USA) Inc.

Dedicated with love and appreciation to my family and friends who support me and all those who trust me to share their inner feelings.

International Standard Book Number: 1-59257-153-0
Library of Congress Catalog Card Number: 2003112967

05   04   03   8   7   6   5   4   3   2   1

Interpretation of the printing code: The rightmost number of the first series of numbers is the year of the book's printing; the rightmost number of the second series of numbers is the number of the book's printing. For example, a printing code of 03-1 shows that the first printing occurred in 2003.

Printed in the United States of America

Note: This publication contains the opinions and ideas of its author. It is intended to provide helpful and informative material on the subject matter covered. It is sold with the understanding that the author and publisher are not engaged in rendering professional services in the book. If the reader requires personal assistance or advice, a competent professional should be consulted.

The author and publisher specifically disclaim any responsibility for any liability, loss, or risk, personal or otherwise, which is incurred as a consequence, directly or indirectly, of the use and application of any of the contents of this book.

Most Alpha books are available at special quantity discounts for bulk purchases for sales promotions, premiums, fund-raising, or educational use. Special books, or book excerpts, can also be created to fit specific needs.

For details, write: Special Markets, Alpha Books, 375 Hudson Street, New York, NY 10014.

Publisher: *Marie Butler-Knight*
Product Manager: *Phil Kitchel*
Senior Managing Editor: *Jennifer Chisholm*
Senior Acquisitions Editor: *Randy Ladenheim-Gil*
Development Editor: *Lynn Northrup*
Production Editor: *Megan Douglass*
Copy Editor: *Molly Schaller*
Illustrator: *Jody Schaeffer*
Cover/Book Designer: *Trina Wurst*
Indexer: *Tonya Heard*
Layout/Proofreading: *Becky Harmon, Mary Hunt*

Contents at a Glance

Contents

Introduction

This book is intended for everyone looking for love—whatever your age, background, dating history, or sexual preferences or intentions.

Now you have an excellent, thorough, and useful guide to dating at every stage—from meeting and starting a relationship to making a commitment. You'll know how to make a date work out, and even what to do if it doesn't. As you read on, you'll get so many helpful hints about things you can do right away to up your chances of finding fulfillment in dating; exercises that are fun for you and a date to do; and important facts you need to know. Some tips are simple and some are quite sophisticated (based on solid psychological principles), but all you can put into practice right away to enhance your understanding of yourself and others, to know how and why people feel and do what they do, so you are prepared to get what you want in dating—and in life!

Life has become so complicated these days, of course you have less time and more stress. That's why this new edition had to be done, to give you not just the basics, but everything that's up-to-date about dating that you need to know.

In the search for love, fears can come up—like feeling hopeless, or that you "failed" before. Frustrations about others' behavior also arise. Men and women alike ask me, "Why did she say that?" "What does he mean by that?" "How can she do this to me?" When you understand what motivates or immobilizes others and yourself, as I help you to do in this book, you'll feel more empowered and in control. All of this will increase your self-esteem and therefore your chances of dating success. I've seen it happen in so many workshops on dating I've done, and through so many years giving advice: your dream can come true. What you want can come to you.

How to Use This Book

Treat this book as a good friend who supports you at any time and in many situations, who calms you down and peps you up. Many people have told me how helpful it has been to them, so I pass the suggestions on:

- ◆ Keep it by your bedside to read before you go to bed.

- ◆ Discuss what you've read in various chapters with your friends.

- ◆ Refer to a relevant chapter before a date.

- ◆ Read sections and do the quizzes *with* a date.

◆ Use it as a great conversation opener and way to learn about each other in a nonthreatening way—since I often advise starting a conversation with something you've read or seen. You can say something like, "I was reading Dr. Judy's *Idiot's Guide to Dating* and she said …. What do you think?" This can give you a boost to ask some tough but revealing questions like: "What are we each looking for?" "When do you think people should have sex?" "Are you into commitment or just having a good time?"

To help you get the most out of this book, you'll see the following information boxes scattered throughout:

Dating Data

These boxes offer research and statistics relating to dating behavior and relationships.

Dr. Judy's Dating Do's

These boxes give you good advice on dating know-how so you can capture and keep your newfound love interest.

Woo Warning

These boxes help you steer clear of potential pitfalls so you don't do something that would make you feel bad or lower your chances of getting what you really want!

This book is chock full of advice you can put to use right away. It draws on my many years of experience as a love coach, professor, and workshop leader. Read through a chapter quickly when you feel like it, or at other times, go slowly and thoughtfully, as there are some deep messages that can deserve some profound reflection and can really change the way you see yourself and the world.

Throughout this book you'll find some fun and simple exercises designed to reveal aspects of your personality and love matches. Some are based on more extensive and even scientific methods that I have simplified here to make them easier to do and interpret. I have used many of these exercises in my many workshops, seminars, lectures, therapy sessions, and classes over the years, so I know you can learn from them and enjoy them. Use them to gain a little knowledge about yourself and your date, and as a stimulus to get you to talk about yourselves, your interests, feelings, and needs.

Every situation can have many variations. So keep in mind the following guidelines:

♦ The situations and advice apply to men and women alike, even though a question or example may refer to one sex or the other. In some cases, women or men may more commonly have that issue, but the differences between the sexes are melting.

♦ Cultural differences play a role in some aspects of dating. For that reason, I included a whole new chapter on dating diversity. But my extensive work throughout the world shows me there are more similarities than differences among people than we think. So the situations in this book can more often than not easily apply whether a person is Caucasian, African American, Asian, Hispanic, Indian, African, Latin, or from any other cultural or ethnic group.

♦ The situations and advice apply equally to gays as well as straights. I've included some examples from gays who have asked me questions, but you can easily substitute the pronouns at any place in this book! I've learned from so many years of experience that the issues, questions, and challenges may have some specifics, but in general there are so many similarities that people face, regardless of sexual preference.

♦ Shyness is a big issue in dating. If some suggestions sound too bold, tone them down to suit your comfort level.

♦ In various places in this book, I refer to three A's: *acceptance*, *appreciation*, and *adjustment*. When you're feeling you're having trouble in the relationship, the three A's can help restore your focus. You'll find them helpful in all kinds of situations—whether you're ready to make a commitment or trying to resolve an argument.

Being Single Today

You may think there's no one out there for you. But the number of singles is large—there are over 80 million unmarried adults in the United States these days. Singles constitute more than 40 percent of the population, and make up the majority of the adult population in many major metropolitan areas, according to recent reports from the American Association for Single People. That's a lot of people to reassure you that you are not alone, and that there are many possible mates for you!

Here are some other relevant and reassuring facts—the number of singles is increasing, in the United States and around the world, and singles are getting married at older ages. According to the Census Bureau, the average age of those getting married for the first time is 25.1 years, an increase of 4.2 years in the past three decades; for men the average age is 26.8 years, an increase by 3.6 years. "The postponement of marriage has led to a substantial increase in the proportion of young, never-married adults," said Jason Fields, author of the Census Bureau's "America's Families and Living Arrangements." By 2000, nearly three out of four 20-24 year old women had never married, double the number in the past three decades; and over two in ten 30-34 year old women were similarly single, a number that had more than tripled over thirty years. The numbers for men were even higher: about eight in ten men age 20 to 24, nearly half of men age 25 to 29, and about one third of men in their thirties, had never been married.

Despite complaints about the lack of eligible men, in fact by the turn of this century, the female population in the United States was only 6 million higher than the male population. Among the group under age 20, there were 105 boys for every 100 girls. As you might expect, the male-to-female ratio declined as age increased, so that for men and women aged 20 to 44, the ratio was 98 to 100—but even that is *almost* equal, and likely higher than you expected. True indeed, by age 85 and older, there were only 50 men to every 100 women—but even one man to every two women may be higher odds than you thought.

While being strong in numbers, singles also have to become increasingly strong in attitude and coping these days—despite the fact that life has become ever more stressful on every level, practically, emotionally, financially and spiritually. This book will help you develop that strength even more, and address those challenges.

My Philosophy of Life

It is my intention that as you read this book, you gain trust that you can have what you want and need in life. This message came across to me powerfully during a trip to India's Taj Mahal, where our guide ended up taking us to a carpet store. Initially, I had no desire to buy carpets, but the owner spread them out, inviting me to "just appreciate the *art*." Surprise, I ended up buying several rugs to the tune of several thousand dollars. I asked him, "How did you get me to buy these when I had no intention of buying carpets, much less spending so much money?" What he said rings in my ears (in his Indian accent): "Whatever is yours will come to you." It makes me smile to think about it. And it's a wise statement that applies to all the messages in this book (and for all of life for that matter!): The love that is yours will come to you.

Of course, not all is fate. *You* are in control—by your thoughts and actions. One of my favorite phrases is: Whatever you believe and conceive, you can achieve. A fundamental message in *The Complete Idiot's Guide to Dating, Third Edition*, is that the key to success is to be happy with *yourself*. Happiness is not just the fulfillment of needs; it's how you choose to think and feel every second. Make each second count by thinking good thoughts and feeling good about yourself!

This book is unique and different from other dating guides, as you will see. For one, it's an entire encyclopedia of what you need to know! In addition, I give you more useful advice than other guides that tell you to play games in dating (to hold out, or maintain mystery). I do not believe in game-playing. Real love comes from being appreciated for who you are—not who you pretend to be. And importantly, because I am on my own course to be completely authentic and more spiritual in life, I encourage you through this book to consider dating as meeting kindred souls, teaching and supporting each other in life's journey. There's a wonderful Sufi principle that says this succinctly: Show up, pay attention, tell the truth, and don't be attached to the outcome. Trust and value yourself, with few demands or expectations on others, to bring you truer love.

Acknowledgments

This book continues to be the result of sharing from thousands of amazing, wonderful men and women of all ages who have trusted me and sought my advice at my many workshops, seminars, and speeches, or on radio or TV, or through letters or e-mails from my various columns in newspapers and magazines around the world. My blessings and thanks go to you all who have revealed such open hearts. Gratitude, too, to so many colleagues who created these opportunities, and especially everyone at my inimitable "LovePhones" radio show that aired for so many years resulting in so much fun and growth. So many people come up to me remembering that show or even a specific call. I sometimes refer to my co-host Chris Jagger and producer Scott "Badger" Hodges, or a special caller. I further acknowledge everyone I've worked with on all the editions of *The Complete Idiot's Guide to Dating*, and the staff at Alpha Books for their continued enthusiasm and support, and with whom I've worked for so many years, including publisher Marie Butler-Knight, editors Mike Sanders and Randy Ladenheim-Gil, development editor Lynn Northrup, publicists Gardi Ipena Wilkes and Vicki Skelton, and marketing manager Dawn Werk. Thanks to the new team, too, including copy editor Molly Schaller and production editor Megan Douglass who showed such care in this manuscript.

Special soul-felt gratitude to the angels in my life—mother Sylvia; father Abe in spirit; brother Robert; sister Barbara; soul mate Edward; soul sisters Rhea Ross, Jill Marti, Edie Hand, Laurie Handlers, Lucille Luongo and Voltage; soul brothers Joshua Smith and Brian Courtney; LovePhones radio family and "the King" Steve Kingston and Sam Milkman who started it all; cherished friends Allan Rose and Maxine Figatner, Teri Whitcraft and Fred Barron; healer Carole Maracle; Louise Koeghan and everyone at E! Entertainment; my fellow "goddesses" Carla Tarantola, Laurie Sue Brockway, Jaiia Earthschild, and Marci Javril; my students and assistants who offered valuable suggestions and contributions like my amazing class at Yeshiva, and Columbia grad students

Ben Adams and Sara Brubacker, Wang Yi, my assistant and world travel buddy Deborah Schoenblum and my T.A., Rachel Snyder, whose devotion and intelligence I cherish and whose insightful suggestions for this edition I greatly value; and my "second family" Sandy and Jay Pollack—for their ever-present love and devotion, and for giving birth to Alissa , my most trusted, cherished, and beloved friend, "daughter," soul sister, assistant and advisor, and inspiration throughout this project and all my life.

NOTE: Some names in examples in this book have been changed and details adjusted in order to honor people's confidentiality, while the essence of the messages holds true.

Trademarks

All terms mentioned in this book that are known to be or are suspected of being trademarks or service marks have been appropriately capitalized. Alpha Books and Penguin Group (USA) Inc., cannot attest to the accuracy of this information. Use of a term in this book should not be regarded as affecting the validity of any trademark or service mark.

Part 1

A New View on Where to Go and Who's "the One"

The world has changed in so many ways that affect dating—which is exactly why this new edition is necessary. In this part, I'll go over those trends, and tell you how you can take advantage of these changes to make your dating experiences more successful and fulfilling.

Although you might feel overwhelmed, don't give up! In this section, I'll give you many helpful ideas about where to meet people, as well as fun and helpful exercises to do. You'll feel refreshed and renewed about your next steps, and enthusiastic about what you're going to do to meet someone. Despite the complications of life today, you can take advantage of these opportunities—once they are pointed out to you, and once you open your heart and mind. That's what I'll help you do in this part, so read on and get ready to grow, be inspired, and enjoy!

Dating Today in the New Century and Beyond

In This Chapter

- ◆ The two basic rules of dating
- ◆ How dating has changed in recent years
- ◆ Putting a new focus on health and spiritual connections
- ◆ What dating is—and what it's not
- ◆ Special issues for special interest groups

The times they certainly are a-changing. Many events have happened in recent times, and many influences promise to keep changing life today; the world of meeting your match, falling in love, and making it work is also changing. *Fast!* That's why this new edition of *The Complete Idiot's Guide to Dating* is necessary! You need to be totally up-to-date on how things like new technology, globalization, the economy, war, the threat of terrorism, spirituality, bisexuality, diversity, globalization, and mass media affect your world, and the world of love. I've noticed it, and no doubt, so have you— there's a shift in the way people behave and the way they seek—and express—love. And there are shifts that are also *necessary* to make. Through these chapters, we'll examine these major events and trends, to refine the best approach for dating today.

While so much is changing in our world, my 30 years of experience as a psychologist, conducting call-in advice on the radio, answering letters through various columns and articles, and doing television shows on dating have proven that some popular problems and questions still persist in the world of dating. Among the top 10: "Where do I go to meet a good person?" "What do I say?" "Why haven't I found anyone?" "What's wrong with me?" Others still despair, "There's nobody good left out there for me" or "I have no time to look." But some questions are more pressing, or new, like whether long-distance relationships can work, and how to use the Internet for finding love.

There's plenty of stress in dating. But there's also good news: I've witnessed a greater desire for openness, and more yearning for intimacy—in men, as well as women. More good news is that dating is experiencing a surge of popularity with many TV shows, Internet sites, books, and events. Everywhere you look, there seems to be talk about dating. That makes it easier for you to be open and to feel no shame about being single. Better yet, it spells hope and lots of opportunities!

My Two Basic Rules of Dating

Over time, I have become even more convinced of the validity of the two basic principles about dating that I've developed during my many years as a therapist and relationship advisor. Keep these principles in mind as you read this book and as you go through your dating experiences:

1. Your ultimate goal—and the goal of this book—is not about dating, per se. It's about being happy with yourself, getting to know yourself and someone else, and enjoying yourselves individually and together. Take the pressure off and stop worrying about "dating" or "getting a date" or about being single! Enjoying who you are will lead to relationships more naturally working out!

2. Dating is not about playing games. It's about being yourself. Put aside the fear of being foolish. If you're shy, that's okay. If someone is going to love you, they'll love you as you are, not as something (cool or suave) you're trying to be.

How the Dating Scene Has Changed

Here's a review of major trends that have changed dating habits today—and that continue to affect how men and women behave.

Love Online

With the advent of the computer age, increasing technological gadgets and ever-expanding presences on the Internet, information for singles and possibilities for connection abound! You cannot log on to the net without coming across some online article about singles or dating, or advertisement about some personals site. There's such a plethora of online dating services, one reporter called them the "ebay for people" and a "human shopping mall." Meeting online has become the new means of meeting people. Read Chapter 6 for all the ins and outs and etiquette of computer dating and finding "e-love."

The TV Dating Show Explosion

Sex and the City has become a seminal television show, exposing the world of being single to all of America and countries around the world, as it followed four female friends exploring all the trendiest and most troublesome angles of finding men and deciding about sex. Then came a flood of singles shows, far-racier and sexier versions of *The Dating Game* of years ago, with every combination of dating problems in dating, and titles from *The Bachelor* and *The Bachelorette* to *Blind Date, Elimidate, Fifth Wheel*, and *For Love or Money*. While these dating shows expose some not-so-admirable dating behaviors and dating horrors (plots usually involve competition and being eliminated in a contest), at least you get to see that whatever you're going through in the single world is either normal, or not *that* bad!

Fast, Faster, and Faster Yet

Speed is the operative word for these new times. There are faster connections to the Internet. No sooner do you get one electronic toy than the next generation with improvements comes out. Everything is going wireless. And everything must be "extreme" as in extreme sports, indicative of how people are pushing themselves to the limit. All this emphasis on speed makes dating rushed, too, including pressures about how to meet people and decide where the relationship is going—quickly.

The faster you go online, fly around the world, or get anything delivered, the faster you have to decide on Mr. or Ms. Right. A good reflection of that is the dating craze currently sweeping the world called speed dating, where you get less than 10 minutes to chat up a stranger, then quickly switch attention to a new partner. It's like square dancing meets musical chairs, and I'll tell you more about that in Chapter 5.

The most defining aspect of life today is fast-changing and advancing technology. In this communication age of beepers, fax, e-mail, the Internet, cell phones, and web cams, technology offers more ways to start a relationship, more opportunities to develop a relationship, and more possibilities to make a long-distance relationship last! More about this in Chapter 6.

The Threat of Terrorism and Realities of War

There's no doubt about it, the tragic attacks on September 11, Anthrax scares, the SARS epidemic, war in Iraq, and tensions in the Middle East, have gravely affected all aspects of our lives. In the face of the black cloud of such terror, there are some silver linings. Research shows that people take stock of their love life, and either hook up or break up. While a few people withdraw, most seek more meaningful relationships. This is the case with Kevin, a typical commitment-phobic guy who resisted his girlfriend's pressure to marry for five years, until the 9/11 terror attacks. "I realized I better stop thinking that there's some other woman around the corner who could be better than the woman I have," he told me. Facing tragedy also teaches that real men *do* cry. And women become more open to nice guys, who treat them well, like Theresa, who finally dumped the guy she had been dating who was cheating on her. "Life is short," she told me, "and I finally realized I shouldn't waste my time in pain over this guy who treats me so bad." Terror also affects people's sex drive; while a few become irresponsible, imagining the "end of the world," most want to solve any sexual problems and make life and love the most fulfilling it can be.

Dating Data

Studies show that in spite of stress that strained relationships post 9/11, couples generally became closer and more committed. One online survey of responses before and after the attacks, done by the Universities of Michigan and Pennsylvania, showed an increase in character traits such as faith, hope, and love, all positive for healthy relationships. Responses to another online survey, replicated by my own studies and my students' studies at Columbia University Teachers College, revealed that up to two-thirds of women and men wanted more connection with their partners. *Brides' Magazine* editors noted a surge in wedding enthusiasm, and a survey by the Jewelers of America found diamond engagement ring sales increased 20 percent compared to the previous year.

Show Me the Money ...

Today most singles are more savvy about finances, but also wary (what with Bullish times and the dot.com boom behind us), weary (given high unemployment and business downsizing), and worried (about what to spend on a date and how to handle finances for their future).

With more women working, more questions about money in dating arise. Who pays for the date? What happens to his ego when she earns more than he? All these issues about money matters required that I add a special chapter on this subject for this new edition of this book, Chapter 14.

Less Pressure to Marry

Statistics show that people in this country, and around the world, are getting married later. My mother's generation dreaded being the "old maid," and even in my college days, you had to graduate with an engagement ring and an "MRS." degree or you were looked upon askance. But times have changed; more people now spend their 20s and 30s focusing on career instead of commitment. The results are mixed; some singles feel pressured and lonely, but they also have more time to develop themselves and go slowly in finding the right partner.

Sexual Matters

Making wise decisions about sex is crucial in dating. Knowing that I'm a sex therapist as well as a clinical psychologist, many people ask me about when's the right time to have sex in a relationship, and how to keep the excitement going. Some factors that have changed the dating scene forever, and impact singles in these new times, have to be taken into account, such as sexually transmitted diseases, increased sexual choices, and an ongoing rage to find the latest aphrodisiac or love drug. I'll discuss sexual matters in Chapter 24.

A New Focus on Health

It's the rage of our current times: health. It affects the physical, emotional, and spiritual dimensions of our relationships. "Everyone these days wants to have a healthy mind, body, and spirit," says Mark Becker, who runs New Life health expos around the country. This quest has led to many services and opportunities to meet other health-seeking singles along the way.

A Rise in Spirituality

In these new times, many men and women (regardless of formal religion) are becoming more conscious of becoming spiritual as a way to feel more love in their lives. The desire for someone who touches—and connects with—their soul, has created more interest in the concept of finding a "soul mate." There's more about this in Chapter 2.

Conscious Dating

"Conscious dating" is a new term derived from a wonderful concept called "conscious loving" whereby couples put as much thoughtfulness, attention, and nurturing into their relationship (and lovemaking) as they would into a career, family, or cause. You can tell from the word itself that being "conscious" requires being aware of who you are, and appreciating who you are. This is consistent with my major point in this book: In finding companionship you need to be yourself and love yourself, and love will find you.

Dr. Judy's Dating Do's

Meditation is becoming increasingly popular to help reduce stress and express who you are without fear. Yoga also helps quiet the mind and stretch the body, for ease of breathing that is essential for confidence and openness to intimacy and love.

Conscious dating involves getting deeply into one another's soul. You can do this with the following exercises that can also help delay sex in dating, because you end up connecting on a deep spiritual level:

◆ **Conscious touching.** You can "run energy" between the two of you by resting your hands upon each other body on nonsexual parts, without moving. Face each other and place your right hand on each other's heart space (near or touching the chest, as you feel comfortable), and cover that hand with your other hand. Imagine energy flowing through your hands into each other's heart (like a game of catch).

◆ **Eye gazing.** Since the eyes are the window to the soul, face each other and look into each other's eyes, without speaking. Let your eyes communicate what you feel.

◆ **Massaging.** Rub each other's shoulders or other nonsexual body part, without any intention to arouse sexually. Take turns. Give in to receiving and practice totally giving. Experiment with different touches (long strokes, tapping, squeezing, pinching), directions (lengthwise, circles, zigzags), and pressures (from light to firm).

Other activities to do together consciously: sing or chant, play musical instruments, build something, fix something in your home, make a flower arrangement, do puzzles, read a book aloud, or compose poetry.

If you follow the principle of conscious dating, you never experience the desperation of losing love. Why? Because love is always *inside* you. You created it and keep love inside even if a lover goes away.

These techniques are part of the latest craze sweeping the country and parts of the world that come from ancient Eastern practices over three thousand years ago, but have been adapted by Westerners like myself and others, to apply to more modern times. Average couples from all walks of life are coming to tantra seminars to learn these new secrets to loving. And many singles are finding new love partners on the same spiritual path. Read my book, *The Complete Idiot's Guide to Tantric Sex* (see Appendix A), for more about how learning these techniques can help singles find wonderful new dates, as well as enlightenment and ecstasy.

Dr. Judy's Dating Do's

Use my favorite words to refer to your date: See the *Goddess* in her and the *God* in him. Sweep her off her feet by asking her, "What can I do to please my Goddess?"

Other Eastern Concepts Applied to Dating

With globalization and increased spirituality, more people have opened their minds to new concepts of dating and mating that are more traditional to the Eastern rather than the Western world. You may not believe in reincarnation, but if you've ever experienced feeling you've known someone before whom you've just met, you'd be more open to believe that past lives are possible and that they affect dating choices. Angela is one powerful example of this. During an intimate kiss with her new boyfriend, Angie whispered in his ear that she felt like Guinevere from medieval times. Astounded, her boyfriend said how he was thinking the exact thing at that moment, and that as a child he had listened to the music of the play *Camelot* over and over, imagining that he was Lancelot. You might call this coincidence, but the experience brought the two lovers closer.

Appreciation for Intuition

Being rational about dating certainly helps you pick the "right" person, make compromises, and deal reasonably with outcomes. But modern times have brought a new appreciation for intuition, and more men and women are trusting their instinct and their "sixth sense" that tells them what to do without thinking it through.

Woo Warning

You might feel drawn to a particular person like a moth to flame if you have deeper, unresolved issues (called "karma") with that person or within yourself.

Intuition helps you sense when someone needs "more space." (That used to be such a dreaded request to hear!) Practice becoming increasingly good at sensing when you need to back off from a relationship to give it time to grow more slowly, when to end it entirely, or when to go full steam ahead because the promise of real love is there.

Energetics

The word "energetics" emerges from the language of holistic relationship counselors and guides. It refers to the ways people are attracted to one another. I use this term a lot in my counseling work, considering, "What are the energetics between these two people?" or "They have positive energetics." I'll explain more in the next chapter.

Be a Straight Shooter: No More Games in Dating

Don't listen to any "retro" advice to play games or "hard to get" in dating, purposefully turning down dates, pretending not to care or that you're busy. If you're interested, show it. True enough, some research showed that guys liked women who initially presented a little challenge, but then gave in. And they wanted the girls to play hard to get with *other* guys, not with them.

Woo Warning

Always playing at "pursuit" reveals problems. Knowing that you're wanted makes both men and women more confident and happy.

Over the years of responding to so many people's dating questions, and lecturing about *The Complete Idiot's Guide to Dating* at bookstore signings and workshops all over the world, I have pointed out what dating is—and what it is not:

◆ Dating is not a game. There are no winners or losers. Dating is a learning experience that should allow both people to grow.

◆ Dating is not just about "looking for love." The truth is, dating should not be a desperate search for the perfect mate who will make you feel loved. Instead, you need to find love inside you and let that radiate outward. That's why you often find love when you're *not* specifically looking, since those are the times you are most naturally yourself.

◆ Dating is not about complaining about who you're with (he doesn't bring flowers or she never calls back). Instead, it's about whom you *choose* to be with. There is a world of people out there and whomever you choose reflects what you need to learn. Imagine yourself as a gate, with lots of people walking by, but only those you invite being allowed in.

Review these changes in the old rules versus what dating is in these new times:

Passé:	Now:
The man has to love a woman more than she loves him.	Both people should love each other equally.
You need someone to date to validate your worth.	You are fine on your own; a date merely annotates.
Play games.	Be yourself.
Play hard to get or pretend you're not interested.	Show interest when you feel it.
Withhold details about yourself to keep the mystery.	Reveal yourself to be intriguing.

As you will see as you read through these chapters, I make reference to some useful metaphors about dating and mating, since the mastery of aspects of life are similar. Here are metaphors that are helpful to keep in mind:

- **Dating is art.** You start out with an empty canvas and then layer on the shapes and colors. The details are all of your choosing. What picture are you painting of your dating life? Who's in it? What are you doing?

- **Dating is a play.** As Shakespeare said, "All the world's a stage and we are but players on it, who strut and fret their hour upon the stage." You create your own play of your dating life, writing the script and casting the leading characters. What have you been putting on your love screen? Is it a romantic drama where the two people fall deeply in love and live happily ever after, or is it an action adventure where they encounter violence, enemies, and end up alone? There's a fun and helpful exercise about this in the next chapter, and lots more exercises in the coming chapters.

- **Dating is about selling.** Put aside cynicism; the truth is that, in dating, you're selling yourself to others. Follow certain tried-and-true rules of selling that you'll read more about in Chapter 11. Go after your prospects. Make cold calls (without needing formal introductions). Don't be discouraged by a "no," but see each as an opportunity to get to a "yes."

- **Dating is like a deal.** Suspend how unromantic this sounds for a moment and consider that you each bring something to the table when you meet. This analogy is useful in these days when so much attention is paid to the economy, business mergers, and the market. As you evaluate your assets, think about what you need, and what a date offers that is valuable in the merger.

◆ **Dating is an adventure.** This is my most favorite—and fun—analogy of all. When you are feeling "lost" in the dating world, desperate, or frustrated with rejections, reframe your situation to feeling awe over interesting challenges in those twists and turns on your journey to love.

Dating is fun! The word doesn't necessarily have to give you butterflies, sweaty palms, or heart palpitations. Instead, when you think of the word D-A-T-I-N-G, think of it as a way to meet people, learn about yourself, and, if all goes well, experience love. Most importantly, it's time to be yourself. To help you with your search, here are some tips:

◆ Let people know you're available.

◆ Know—but be flexible about—your "love criteria" (described in the next chapter).

◆ Accept "no" and let go.

◆ Go to places and see things that you enjoy.

◆ Boost your self-esteem and mates will flock to you.

◆ Remember that you have the power to get what you want.

◆ Always have hope—you can meet someone special anytime and anywhere.

◆ Meet as many people as you can.

◆ Be ready and open for love.

Each one of us has responsibility to set the trends for these new times in how we think and behave. Contribute to a better age by ...

◆ Respecting what feels right for you.

◆ Getting rid of fear—or feeling it and acting anyway.

◆ Relying on your intuition as well as logic.

◆ Re-evaluating and starting afresh in patterns; giving up what doesn't work and having courage to step into the unknown.

Special Issues Depending on Your Background

All the issues in this book apply to everybody, of every age, cultural background, religious upbringing, socio-economic status, and even sexual preference (I've paid particular attention to that). But, of course, there may also be special issues you face dependent on your lifestyle and background. Think about whether any particular "circumstances" about your present or past affect your dating—to whom you get attracted and how the relationships work out.

Consider how your roots, your parents and grandparents, affect your decisions about dating. How do their stories change how you feel, think, and behave? What did they teach you? What traditions did they follow that they want you to carry on? Parents from a Middle Eastern or Fundamentalist background may have strict rules about "dating," and certain cultures still have distinct attitudes toward homosexuality (although even countries like China have begun to recognize homosexuality as they are forced to address the threat of AIDS). Mothers who have been abused can give messages to their daughters about men being untrustworthy. Build on positive influences. For example, even if your father didn't give you enough attention or approval, pick partners now who appreciate and support you.

Dating for All Ages

While all the advice in this book applies to all ages, at certain stages in life, there are particular issues associated with certain ages and stages. The pressures on teens in dating are intense, with self-consciousness about appearance, insecurities, and challenges in developing friendships. As life becomes more complicated, these anxieties only increase, demanding that much more support from friends, parents, and advisors about all the ins and outs of asking someone out, falling in love, and dealing with rejection.

Teens have asked me whether they can "fall in love" at their age. Of course they can, but lasting love takes time to grow and prove to be lasting! Innumerable teens ask me about when to have sex, with some girls giving in to pressure in order to keep their boyfriends. An unfortunate number of teens ask me about what I call "double betrayals," an exceptionally painful experience, where you find out about your best friend hitting on your girlfriend or having sex with your girlfriend (my advice: consider a break-up with both!). Another common dilemma for teens is like Max's: "I'm still in high school and my girlfriend went off to college this year and I'm worried that she's dating other guys." The truth is that going away to school often spells the end of committed relationships, as both male and female coeds have innumerable opportunities for meeting others—making it wise not to have grand expectations that a love will last. But, of course, your relationship can survive, if you both want it to.

The still-single 20-somethings get frustrated over the dating scene, and pressures to get their career going, while those in their 30s worry even more about finding Mr./Ms. Right. Dating in mid-life brings many fears and insecurities, and a smaller pool of eligible mates, not to mention questions about how children will react. While the over 60s singles are keeping more fit and looking better than ever, they need reassurance of being desirable, deserving of dating pleasures, and staying optimistic.

From Me to You ...

It has been heartening for me to see over these past years since earlier editions of *The Complete Idiot's Guide to Dating*, how much appreciation there has been for this book. Men and women alike have told me, "I read your book cover to cover," "I used your advice and found a wonderful woman," or "I keep your book by my bedside." I am grateful because I put my heart and soul into these pages, and have reflected the hearts and souls of many who have asked my advice over the years. I have reviewed each section to include the most up-to-date information so you can have the most fulfilled love life! I invite you to learn, grow, and enjoy.

The Least You Need to Know

- Changes in people's habits and philosophies, as well as current events and advancing technology, require you to rethink dating strategies.

- Dating should not be about playing games or the hunt for the perfect mate, but about enjoying yourself—and others.

- Many new trends in dating include a focus on health, a rise in spirituality, and the influence of being closer in touch through technology.

- Always remember that being yourself is the best guiding principle.

2

Unraveling the Mystery of Attraction

In This Chapter

- ◆ The meaning of attraction and chemistry
- ◆ Increasing your chances of finding a partner
- ◆ Who's right for you? Identifying your "love criteria"
- ◆ Debunking the myths about dating
- ◆ Do nice guys (and gals) really finish last?
- ◆ Test your compatibility

"It ain't gonna be no pickle man!"
—Amy Irving's character in *Crossing Delancey*

Of course you want to fall in love, but, like many singles, you despair of finding that "right" one. You may have that traditional idea of your perfect mate—he should be good-looking, rich, and powerful; she should be beautiful, sexy, and smart. Or you want someone who can "be it all"—a good provider, parent, professional, and passionate to boot.

A single guy in one of my workshops complained, "In real estate you look for three things: location, location, location. But in the dating market, women look for three things: cash, cash, cash." A woman answered him, saying, "But all that men care about is a woman's body, body, body." In this chapter I'll go over just what qualities men and women look for.

Indeed, as the free love of the 1970s emerged into high commercialism of this new century, dates got judged by the "BBD"—the "Bigger Better Deal." But the "right" one for you could be a surprise. For Amy Irving's character in the movie *Crossing Delancey*, the pickle man she first dismissed turned out to be just the Mr. Right she needed. Similarly for Meg Ryan's character in *When Harry Met Sally*, the best friend she complained to about all her other dates ended up capturing her heart.

Understanding Attraction

In many ways, attraction is a mystery, but there are some principles to help you understand the process. I'll share my favorites with you in this chapter.

First off, I'd like to introduce you to my concept of "The Mirror Law of Attraction." According to this principle, we attract, and are attracted to, those people who have something we desire, deny, or wish to defy. For example, people who have commitment problems end up attracting unavailable types. In another example, those who are insecure about their appearance can become obsessed with finding the most attractive dates, to compensate for what they consider their own lack of good looks.

Another one of my favorite and useful concepts that I'd like to introduce to you is what I call "love antennae." It's like we are each a radio station or satellite dish, sending out and receiving signals that tune us into certain types of people. But beware, your love antennae may be improperly programmed, leading you to make choices that end up making you unhappy.

Your love antennae get tuned by your particular "love criteria"—things you think you must have in a partner. But on closer examination, searching for someone with those qualities may not work for you, and you may have to change your criteria to find a relationship that lasts. (I'll outline an exercise to help you identify this in the next section.) Michelle, a radio DJ from Duluth, dated a string of "losers" until I explained the concept of love antennae to her. She realized what she was broadcasting and said, "I see—I have to change my signal!"

The frequency of your love antennae is affected by what's called an "eligibility score," by which we assess our "market" worth, and that of potential mates. To understand how we assess our worth, do this exercise. Think of the top three qualities you think you have (looks, intelligence, sense of humor, and so on). Assess each quality from 0 (weakest) to 10 (strongest) by putting a check in the appropriate column. Now do the same for what you are looking for in a mate.

My Qualities	0	1	2	3	4	5	6	7	8	9	10
1. _____	—	—	—	—	—	—	—	—	—	—	—
2. _____	—	—	—	—	—	—	—	—	—	—	—
3. _____	—	—	—	—	—	—	—	—	—	—	—
	—	—	—	—	—	—	—	—	—	—	—
Qualities I Look for in Someone	0	1	2	3	4	5	6	7	8	9	10
1. _____	—	—	—	—	—	—	—	—	—	—	—
2. _____	—	—	—	—	—	—	—	—	—	—	—
3. _____	—	—	—	—	—	—	—	—	—	—	—
	—	—	—	—	—	—	—	—	—	—	—

Notice how your qualities and those of an ideal mate compare. If you rate yourself a "9" in looks but a "4" in intelligence, see if you look for someone who ranks a "4" in looks but a "9" in smarts—so your scores even out. If you feel you have a quality "covered" (with a high score), you may find yourself going after someone who offers something that you don't quite have (a high score in a different quality) but admire. No scoring is "right" or "wrong;" the exercise just helps you get an idea of your dating choices.

Making Your Love Deal

Of course it's best to let love happen naturally. You'll notice throughout this book, I encourage you to keep an open mind, follow your heart, and go with your instincts in responding to people. But realistically, we do make assessments about people. Picking a mate can be like the art of the deal. There are qualities you definitely want ("deal points"), conditions that you won't accept under any circumstances ("deal-breakers"), and points you are willing to negotiate.

Look back over the list of qualities you're looking for in a mate that you rated in the previous exercise. Circle the qualities that are non-negotiable—the deal-breakers for you—that are an absolute "must-have." Put a question mark next to the ones that are negotiable—things you are willing to compromise on, or could learn to live without. Put an "x" next to any qualities that have caused trouble in relationships—these may be things you should consider giving up when looking for a mate.

Dating Data

Research indicates that 8 out of 10 men rate "looks" high on their list of attractive qualities. In comparison, women value personality characteristics such as sensitivity and caring. Studies show that physical attractiveness does affect how people react. In one study, people at the controls of a vibrating chair that created pleasurable sensations gave more vibrations to the people they rated as attractive.

While traditionally men have rated physical beauty as important, my research over the years indicates more men are putting increased value on personality characteristics. This is good news! Both sexes rate intelligence high. You'll be happy to know that the one quality that has crept into the top three for both men and women is sense of humor. As long as you make someone laugh, they'll overlook other things and want to be in your company.

Money does matter, and though people don't usually put that on a questionnaire, they will talk about it in discussion groups (more about that in Chapter 14). But I'm sure you also know stories of the beautiful girl who doesn't have a date on Saturday night— because men are too intimidated to ask her!

My friend Laurie Handlers has always been good at connecting people (even now through her tantra seminars at www.butterflyworkshops.com) and once was a professional matchmaker. She had people be very specific—even picky—listing all the qualities of the person they were looking for, like "owns a tux" or "gives wet kisses." Her own list had "has done transformational work" and "appreciates diversity more than just eating at ethnic restaurants." She asked clients to code "M" for must and "P" for prefer. Her list had "M" next to "non-smoker" and "loves to dance," and "P" next to "plays tennis" and "loves skiing." Her beloved Joshua had 38 of the 40 things on her "M" list, but he does not play tennis or ski. Does she miss doing these things with her partner? Yes. Are they deal breakers? No. As a matchmaker, Laurie would encourage clients to *purposefully* go out with five people who were not compatible, just to become at ease with dating and clear about qualities they want. When she talked with them after the date, she'd invariably find that their criteria changed a little, so then she'd make the next match closer to what they really wanted.

Identifying Your "Type" by Your Love Criteria

Even if you try to be open-minded about who interests you, you likely have some "type" you are attracted to. Mr. or Ms. Right likely looks a certain way to turn you on. Do you know what that type exactly is? And are you willing to change it, to be open to a wider variety of potential mates?

Do this exercise to help identify your "love criteria"—the picture of who you are looking for, and the qualities to which your love antennae are tuned. This expands on the previous exercise, to identify qualities of past or present love interests to see any patterns. Fill in their names and check off qualities they have. Are they intelligent, pretty, or funny? Write in others that are not listed.

My "Type" History

Qualities	My Past Loves Were:			
	Date 1:	*Date 2:*	*Date 3:*	*Date 4:*
Sensitive, caring				
Thoughtful				
Adventurous				
Honest				
Easy-going				
Fun to be with				
Flirtatious				
Affectionate				
Uncommunicative				
Bossy				
Shy				
Sexy				
Outgoing				
Smart				
Specify:_____				
Specify:_____				

Notice the qualities you like and don't like. Are those similar qualities you like or dislike in yourself?

Romantic Resumé

Create a "romantic resumé" just like you would a job resumé, advises another of my friends, Laurie Sue Brockway. List your qualifications, as you would your job skills, and your past relationships as you would previous jobs. Writing out your own qualifications helps you reassess, and affirm, your good qualities, and stating your desires helps you focus on what you want, describes Brockway in her "30-Day Program to Transform Your Romantic Destiny" (www.selfhealingexpressions.com).

Blind Date

Imagine you are waiting for your blind date to arrive. What do you picture the person looking like? What do you imagine talking about? How do you imagine feeling? Now put that image out of your mind, and open the door with a blank slate, prepared and open to anything.

What Is Chemistry (and Does It Really Exist?)

You spot her across a crowded room and you know she's the one. His eyes meet yours, and you melt into each other. Your heart pounds, a thrill rushes through your body, and you know it's that "chemistry" that tells you that the two of you are meant to be together. Books, songs, and movies are replete with such scenarios that fuel hope about that exquisite high, or plunge us deep into despair if it doesn't work out.

Just what is that "chemistry"? Whether true love or just plain lust, physiological reactions can get triggered in attraction. In a heightened state of arousal, the body releases a number of hormones and chemicals. One of these, adrenaline, triggers the "fight-or-flight response" that explains symptoms such as sweaty palms, palpitations, and weak knees—similar to anxiety symptoms triggered by a final exam or the near-miss of a traffic accident. Other chemicals flood into your system, including oxytocin (the "cuddle chemical"), phenylethylamine (the "natural high chemical"), and endorphins (the "pleasure chemicals").

Dating Data

Research indicates that the brain plays a large role in our experience of love. A study of people who underwent surgery for the removal of pituitary tumors found that these individuals had more trouble than other people falling in love. The pituitary gland releases hormones essential to mating behavior and scientists think that blocking crucial pathways (as can happen in surgery) prevents certain hormones related to the feeling of love from reaching their proper receptor sites in the brain.

A cycle between the physiological and psychological aspects of attraction is created: When we are aroused, our bodies release chemicals that stimulate the smooth muscles and sensitize the nerve endings. This makes us even more sensitive to pleasure and more emotionally responsive. As you interpret your body signals to mean you are "in love," your enthusiasm escalates.

The feeling of being magnetically attracted to someone may also have to do with the bioelectric fields that surround our bodies. This is explained by the term I introduced in Chapter 1 as "energetics," where you feel that electricity between you. The term evolved from magnetic therapy, which involves placing magnets on body parts to balance energy within the body. Think of a magnet surrounded by metal pieces. The pieces automatically gravitate toward the magnet, attaching themselves to it. Pull away the magnet, and watch the iron pieces move toward it, attempting to get closer and attach. Relationships can operate in much the same way, where one person draws the other inextricably and uncontrollably into the relationship.

Dr. Judy's Dating Do's

Think about those people you date (or have dated) to whom you seem inextricably attracted. Whether they were "good" or "bad" experiences, each person served as a "lesson." Never have regrets—they were all preparation on your path to love.

Check off these signs that you are experiencing positive energetics:

- ❏ You smile when you see your partner.
- ❏ You feel comfortable in his/her presence.
- ❏ Your body internally feels at peace when you are together.
- ❏ You want to get closer to him/her.
- ❏ You feel like you "know" your partner.
- ❏ Your movements seem to be synchronized and flow without effort.
- ❏ You feel a "pull" toward each other, as if magnetized.

Signs of poor energetics include the opposite of the above:

- ❏ You feel like you're not on the same wavelength.
- ❏ You feel bad vibes between you.
- ❏ You feel uncomfortable in each other's presence.
- ❏ You find that you're always frowning.
- ❏ His/her actions make you want to move away.

Love Scripts

Chemistry and deal points are just part of the reason we choose the people we do. We also use what I call a "love script." This is like a blueprint that tells a story about how we'd like our love life to go. Think of it as a movie of your love life, where you cast a partner for the leading role. Our love scripts come from several sources, including emotional needs, experiences, beliefs, and desires.

Our love scripts often lead us to people who offer us emotional protection. A common example is women who date unavailable men in order to get the love they always wanted but never got from an unavailable father. In another more idiosyncratic example, one man who claimed a "special thing" for women who weighed over 200 pounds, convinced himself that full-figured women would never reject him, so he felt safe. To find out why you are attracted to a particular trait, ask yourself: What meaning does this have for me? How does being with a person like that make me feel (safe, protected, important, powerful)?

Love scripts are affected by our early childhood experiences. It's sometimes obvious, like when you keep picking women to date who look like the girl in grade school you had a crush on but who never noticed you. Sometimes it's helpful to dig deeper. For example, Geoffrey discovered the sources of his attraction to large women, in that his extremely thin mother never hugged him, while his only nurturing came from a very full-figured aunt, making him pleasantly predisposed to other women with a similar body type.

Writing the Movie of Your Dating Life

To make your love script clearer, and to show how you are in control of your love life, do the following exercise I use with people in my workshops and classes. Imagine yourself in the movie of your dating life. What is happening? Who is doing what to whom? Also imagine what movie your date would picture him or herself in. Do the movies have similar themes? Does your date know the role you have cast him in? Realize that you are always writing, directing, producing, and acting in all the roles of your life movie. Is yours a comedy or tragedy, an action adventure or drama, PG- or R-rated? Do your plots overlap? He could be in an action adventure and you could be writing a romance story—if so, your love lives may not be on the same track. Tell him your story and see if he can enjoy playing a role in it.

The Movie of My Dating Life

Title of the film: _____

Main characters: _____

Director: _____

Producer: _____

Summary of the plot, including critical scenes:

_____

_____

If you like the scenes in your movie, you can rehearse them in your mind to make them more likely to come true (as long as you don't get caught up in an unrealistic fantasy). If you don't like what happens, imagine how you *would* like it to go. Talk through an imaginary script of a dating movie with a date, to learn about what you each expect, fear, or desire.

Conditions That Enhance Attraction

In one study, men who had exercised vigorously found a pretty woman even more appealing than those who had exercised for only a short period of time. In another study, men coming off a narrow, swaying footbridge, 230 feet above the rocks, asked a female research assistant out on a date more often than men walking across a low concrete span.

The explanation: Arousal (as from the pounding heart and pumping blood associated with fear) can be interpreted as excitement, making the men more susceptible to attraction. That's why high-intensity dates such as riding a roller coaster together can sharpen Cupid's arrow (as I'll explain in Chapter 4).

Experiencing grief or loss stimulates a desire to reaffirm life, bringing people together in the face of tragedy. Sometimes these relationships flower beautifully. Working intensely on a project together—whether at work or in a play—can also lead to intense attraction (it's no wonder Hollywood actors and actresses

Woo Warning

Beware of forming bonds based on temporary need. After Lance broke his arm, he ended up in physical therapy. Finding solace in the sweet physical therapist who tended him, Lance felt he was falling in love. But once on the mend, Lance called her less and less often, until he finally felt no desire to see her. When his need diminished, the attraction faded.

fall in love with each other). But it doesn't guarantee lasting love, so don't be surprised if the relationship fizzles after the common bond dissipates.

Opposites Attract

You know the old saying, "Opposites attract," and we have all seen this adage in action. This is supported by the psychological theory that "the exotic becomes erotic" meaning that what's new to you is a turn-on. But over time, differences that were once appreciated can become sources of irritation. Renée's boyfriend loves country music and honky-tonk bars. At first she was captivated by this because she's more the alternative music, pierced belly-button type. But the novelty of their differences soon began to wear thin. If Renée and her boyfriend want to keep the relationship going, they both have to learn to accommodate their differences. To help opposites keep attracting, couples need to keep in mind what I call the three A's necessary for a lasting relationship: acceptance, appreciation, and adjustment of their differences.

Common Dating Myths

When you become depressed about dating, it might be because your mind is telling you discouraging thoughts. Many of these are blatantly untrue! Here are some common misconceptions, and the truth about them.

MYTH: There is no one for you.

REALITY: Negative thoughts create negative outcomes; positive thoughts allow positive realities. Remember, the world is full of possibilities. As my mother used to say, "There's a cover for every pot." You always have a chance. In the movie *Dumb and Dumber*, Jim Carrey falls hard for Lauren Holly and asks God what his chances are. "One in a million," is the answer. Carrey then cheers, "I have a chance!" Even if it's true that you have a one in a 7,397,685 chance of winning the lottery, someone has to win it—and it could be you! Be encouraged by Nelly's example: He called my radio show and admitted, "I'm not attractive and I fell for this gorgeous girl. I thought she'd never look at me once, much less twice, but surprisingly I won her heart. We started out as friends and we got to talking. She told me she had been abused when she was younger, and that I made her laugh. Now she says she never felt as comfortable with anyone in her life."

If you do need statistics, be heartened by these, shown in the following chart. The U.S. Bureau of the Census reports show there are more single men for women than you might think (especially for those under 40 years of age).

Number of Men per 100 Women
by Age Group: 2000

Source: U.S. Bureau of the Census (March 2000).

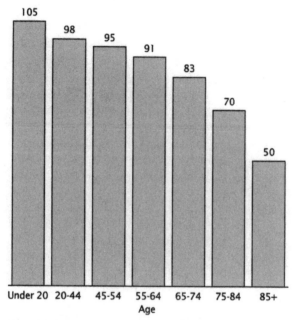

Source: U.S. Census Bureau, Current Population Survey, March 2000.

MYTH: There is only one person right for you.

REALITY: There are many fish in the sea. There is no "one and only" Mr. or Ms. Right, and no "perfect" person—only real people, with real imperfections. It's totally true that finding love means being open to many possibilities and making compromises. The next chapter explores this further.

MYTH: It's impossible to find someone to love.

REALITY: Love can come in unexpected places and times, and in unexpected partners. For example, Jeannette was morose in her search. She told all her friends to be on the lookout, went to all the "right" parties, and joined all kinds of clubs, but seemingly to no avail. Finally, while visiting her sister in another state, she went to a museum exhibit. As she stood in front of a painting, a man with a small child asked her what she thought of the work. As she wandered to the next painting, and then the next, he seemed to follow her. Finally, he asked her to join him for lunch. They've been painting the town together ever since.

MYTH: Finding the right person is simply a matter of "fate"—being in the right place at the right time.

Dr. Judy's Dating Do's

Chronic pessimists may have only themselves to blame! I've found in years of counseling singles that women and men who insist they can't find anyone are often afraid, unwilling, or not ready to commit themselves. Overcome this problem, adjust your too-rigid criteria, or tune your love antennae to whir for the right kind of date.

REALITY: As Jeanette's story shows, fate and timing are important, but you have to be open, receptive, and ready! You may not be able to ensure that any one activity or place will manifest love (in fact, you should not have any expectations), but when you are open to possibilities, feeling good about yourself, and going about your life with joy, more people are bound to be drawn to you.

MYTH: All the "good ones" are taken. There are no good men or women left.

REALITY: Even if many "good ones" are taken, it only takes one. You may even know that good person now and just need to open your eyes.

Naughty or Nice

The lament of the nice guy is a common one that I hear often. Vincent echoes the troubled refrain of many guys: "Why is it that girls stay with guys who treat them poorly, but nice guys get stepped on?" Vincent is right—many women *are* attracted to "bad guys." Billy is similarly befuddled: "I spared no expense romancing this girl for two weeks, opening doors for her, taking her horseback-riding, buying her gifts. But she said I was too nice and left me for some guy who acts tough and treats her rough. What's wrong with me?"

Dating Data

Some nice guys go for the "bad" girls, heartbreakers who party hard and don't return their interest. Just as is the case with women who go for bad boys, these men have to learn to retune their love antennae to women who appreciate them.

What's wrong with guys like Vincent and Billy is that they opened their bank account and heart too fast. Showering someone with gifts does not ensure her approval. But before he jumps to conclusions that being nice isn't worth it, such guys have to examine what they might be doing wrong, such as choosing a woman who is unavailable and unattainable. Their love antennae need retuning.

Although in many surveys I give to groups about attraction, women rate arrogance, dishonesty, and selfishness as undesirable characteristics in men, many still go for the "bad boy." As Christie says, "I like exciting guys. I know they're jerks and I'd like to like another guy I know who's sweet, but I can't help it. The rats just turn me on."

These women, like some men, often find themselves in this trap of being torn between two loves—one nice and one "exciting." What's really going on is that they are addicted to a challenge, and need to prove they are desirable. You can only escape this trap when you feel secure within yourself and find your own life exciting.

So many women still want—and need—the book I wrote, *How to Love a Nice Guy* (see Appendix A), which outlines an excellent 10-step program to help you fall for the partners who are good for you instead of ones who seem appealing on the surface, but make you miserable. (It also works well for guys who fall for the wrong dates!).

Fortunately, as women become more emotionally, financially, and sexually secure and independent, they increasingly choose men who treat them well instead of those who are thrilling, "hot," or who fill some inadequacy in their lives. Someone who loves you is a far more substantive life partner than someone who is chasing a challenge.

One of the steps in my *How to Love a Nice Guy* program, following my "Mirror Law of Attraction," advises that if you're always attracted to unavailable, unattainable dates, look at why you need to have partners who don't appreciate you. It might be to prove that you're okay (because of low self-esteem; if so, value yourself as you are), or because

you need to prove that all people are hard to please (look at your history and see why you resent men or women), or because you are really afraid of commitment (so you pick partners who would never want to settle down either).

Given that there is "energy" that draws people together, sparks will either fly or fizzle. A woman in one of my workshops only got turned on by "take charge" guys, and sure enough in a mingling exercise she was drawn to those participants rather than the more mellow men. Fortunately, the attraction was mutual.

Dr. Judy's Dating Do's

"Nice" used to be the kiss of death, implying doormat, nerd, or wimp. But the new nice (male or female) can be good-looking and exciting. The one thing the nice guy or gal may lack is mystery or elusiveness—in its place is sensitivity, caring, sincerity, and reliability. Which qualities would you rather have over the long term?

Nice people are there for you in an emergency, give even more than they take, and listen when you need to talk. They're your best friends, the ones you call to complain about all the others who treat you poorly. They may not show up like fireworks, but they'll warm your heart by the fire. And they'll probably remember your birthday. I'm often asked, "Where do I go to meet someone nice?" The nice guy or gal often shows up as somebody's good friend. So look right under your nose. Ask friends, relatives, and co-workers to introduce you to their best friends. The nice guy may be the one who lets you out of the elevator first in your office building or the one who offers you a seat on the bus. The nice gal's the one with the smiling face you bump into many mornings at your favorite coffee shop. Once you've determined that "nice" is the one quality you won't compromise on, your "love antennae" will be attuned to that type of person, and he or she will show up in your life.

The Good Friend Test

I always marvel at how people accept things from lovers that they would never accept from a friend. As Zenia says, "My boyfriend cheats on me, he lies, he always forgets to call me … but I still love him." Before you set out to find your ideal date, think about what friendship means to you. After all, you want your lover to be your friend, don't you? List the things that are important in a friend (steadfastness, honesty, reliability), and then consider whether your current or past lovers have these qualities. If anything, you can be a little more lenient with friends, but should compromise less when it comes to a love partner—where you have to invest more and have more to gain or lose. I explain more about qualities to watch out for in Chapters 16 and 19.

Woo Warning

Don't date a person purposefully to change him or her. The challenge will get greater the longer you're together. Accept, appreciate, and adapt to one another.

Compatibility Test

Here's a simple compatibility test that helps you gauge if a relationship is going to work. If you're not seeing someone right now, remember to turn back to this test when you start dating. Compatibility is essential if a relationship is going to work. Ask yourself these questions:

- **Do the two of you have similar values?** Research shows that shared values are crucial in keeping a relationship together.

- **Can you resolve your differences?** Every couple has arguments, but can you resolve them, respecting one another's opinions and needs? If you argue more often than you agree, you're in trouble.

- **Do you have similar needs for closeness or separateness?** If one person wants to be inseparable while the other feels suffocated with too much togetherness, you're in trouble.

- **Do you have similar sex drives and priorities about the importance of sex in your relationship?** Sex doesn't have to be on top of the list for every couple (and keep in mind sex drives can ebb and flow), but in most happy relationships, partners have similar feelings about sex and its relative importance.

- **Do you share similar lifestyles?** Some differences can be worked out (he's an early riser while she comes alive late at night), but others can tear couples apart (she wants children and he doesn't).

A "no" answer to any of these questions could spell trouble. Since each one of these can determine whether your relationship is happy and lasting, concentrate on how you may differ and make efforts to apply those three A's I mentioned earlier: acceptance, appreciation, and adjustment.

Playing the Field or Playing with Fire?

"Playing the field" can be a good way to get an idea of what you're really looking for. Laurie Handlers (whom I mentioned earlier in this chapter) coaches people to date more than one person—in fact, seven—at a time. This way, she says, you give the process time so you don't get swept away by sex or chemistry, and you can compare appealing and distasteful qualities over time, and eliminate some suitors from the running while others look like better prospects.

That's fine if you're unattached, and as long as you make it perfectly clear to those you date that you're also dating others. Some people get fired up by competition. But most singles don't like to know they're in a contest for attention. It brings out that green-eyed monster and all kinds of fears and anxieties. Though fear of losing you can put a fire under a sluggish suitor, be cautious about someone who goes after you *because* somebody else wants you.

The Three-Month Observation Period

Yes, I believe in love at first sight. But before jumping to conclusions about any relationship, make sure you observe your partner over time. Follow my "three-month observation period" guideline—the minimum amount of time necessary to truly assess someone's character (trustworthiness, security, reliability, kindness). Falling too fast leads to trouble, so take things slow. You don't want to cast someone into your love script without really knowing that person.

The Least You Need to Know

◆ Attraction seems a mystery, but can actually be explained—by your experience, physical reactions, and the situation.

◆ We often seek in others what we wish for in ourselves.

◆ It is possible to open yourself up to fall in love with a different "type" of love partner.

◆ Ultimately, the best partner is someone who is secure and who really cares about you. Pick the woman idolizer instead of the womanizer.

◆ Remember, you always have a chance!

Expanding Your Options: Diversity Dating

In This Chapter

- ◆ The variety of potential mates
- ◆ How to expand your options
- ◆ Understanding other cultures, backgrounds, and preferences
- ◆ Ways to bridge your cultural or other divide
- ◆ Dealing with your own and other's attitudes

In the last chapter we began to unravel the mysteries of attraction, and why you choose one candidate for love over another. In this chapter, we'll delve a little deeper into this issue. The goal is to expand your options for dates. As I've said, you might be very surprised about who ends up being "the one"—if you only gave him or her a chance.

Let's say you're still thinking, "There's no one out there for me." The best way to beat any perceived shortage of eligible men or women is to be open to possibilities of who might be good for you. Does he really have to be a certain height and have a particular job? Does she really have to look like your perfect image? Look around. There are many more couples that you might never imagine before would be together. Catherine towers over her new boyfriend Carlos, and while Wong doesn't speak much English, he and Georgia peach Priscilla seem to be communicating very well.

Rather than looking for "the one," be open to possibilities. Make the most of every date, not in terms of success or failure, expectations or desperation, but as an adventure, a way of enjoying and learning about yourself and others.

December–May and May–December

Research shows the ideal relationship was once considered to be the man being three-and-a-half years older than the woman (from an anthropologic point of view, younger, more fertile females were desirable to propagate the species). But the much older man/younger woman pair has become common. And the reverse is also taking hold.

"Men can date women young enough to be their daughter," Priscilla told me, "so why can't a woman do the same?" Today's trend of older women with younger men is increasingly popular, and some surveys have shown these matches can be successful. Some female celebrities are known for this, like Cher, who often dated men 20 years her junior; Joan Collins, who in her 60s married a much younger man; and Demi Moore, who at 40 years old is currently an item with 25-year-old actor Ashton Kutcher. These relationships work because the older woman is often more emotionally, financially, and sexually mature and secure, and because younger men often have grown up respecting independent, mature women and are more comfortable with equality compared to men in older generations who are not used to such independent women.

Dr. Judy's Dating Do's

One of the biggest challenges for singles is finding someone with similar values. Even in a nontraditional pairing, make sure you share similar values about life, to better chances for your relation-

The Princess and the Pauper

While some cultures traditionally have strict class divisions (as in India), white-collar/blue-collar unions are more acceptable and common in other countries. Princess Stephanie of Monaco had two children by her bodyguard before she married him, and Elizabeth Taylor married carpenter Larry Fortensky (even though both marriages ended in divorce). Roseanne divorced her producer-husband Tom Arnold to marry her chauffeur-bodyguard.

As more women become financially independent, they are more willing to marry for love rather than money. A female lawyer from a wealthy family who earns a good salary is more willing to consider romance with a middle-class repairman, chauffeur, or carpenter, not judging him by his portfolio or social class, but welcoming the man's love and support. These "Lady Chatterlys" (referring to the fictional character who had erotic adventures with men "below her station") find good lovers in men who are the "salt of the earth."

In a discussion I ran after a screening of the movie *Crush* about an upper-crust teacher who falls in love with a much younger "common folk" guy, I gave the audience a survey about relationship issues. In rating their feelings about an older woman with a younger man, only about 10 percent disapproved. But twice as many disapproved of a wealthy, educated woman marrying an uneducated man.

The Cultural Divide

While strict cultural customs in countries all over the world reigned in past generations to keep youngsters marrying within their clan, assimilation and globalization in modern times is changing that dramatically. We live in a veritable melting pot, as more people travel internationally, are born to parents who themselves inter-married, and are exposed to potential mates of other cultures in school, work settings, and through the Internet. I'm sure you're well aware of how people are intermingling, and much more diversity is evident in couplings today.

C.J. is black and attracted to a Pakistani Muslim girl. Abe's girlfriend is Lutheran and he's Jewish. Pete is Irish and finds Hispanic men sexy. Janice's girlfriend was born in Mexico but grew up in Germany. It is not uncommon to see a Caucasian guy with an Asian woman on his arm, or a tall blond woman dining with a dark-skinned Middle Eastern suitor. After her painful divorce from Prince Charles, the late Princess Diana supposedly found solace and love with Dodi Al-Fayed, son of a wealthy Arab businessman. Parents may still dismay if children marry outside their faith or ethnicity, but couples are now bonding despite fear of family disapproval.

While love can flower, such couples still need to understand each other's cultural roots and practices. The following sections review some dating traditions from different cultures. Keep in mind that these descriptions are stereotypic, and globalization is changing entire cultures, such that they are becoming far more Westernized, with youth refusing to follow traditional taboos and restrictions.

When my friend Laurie Handlers (whom I mentioned in the previous chapter) was a matchmaker, she always came up against people's obsession with their picture of their ideal mate and resistance to look "outside the box." She literally twisted their arms to go out with people they didn't feel attracted to by their photos, or people of divergent backgrounds or big age differences. The successful marriages that happened were mostly couples she had strongly encouraged to date, despite their objections. Why? Because, as she says, "I really listened to what they said they wanted, but I knew that what they really wanted could be hiding in packages different from what they imagine." Of course, some people insist on the packaging. Laurie didn't; she's a Jewish woman in her 50s in a committed relationship with an African American man in his 30s. His mother, who is Laurie's age, finally calls her "family."

> **Dating Data**
>
> Attitudes toward interracial dating have changed. A survey conducted over 50 years ago showed that 59 percent of Americans thought mixed marriages should be illegal. But mixed-race marriages in the United States are now reported to number 1.5 million and are roughly doubling each decade. Forty percent of Asian Americans and six percent of African Americans married Caucasians in recent years. Another study showed that Asian, Hispanic, and African Americans were significantly more likely to date interracially than European Americans.

Oh La La: Les Français

The French deserve their reputation as lovers. Men are not shy to make eye contact—for extended periods of time. Flirting, touching, and sweet-talking is so *de rigueur* that a woman from another culture may mistake it for great interest in her. People are not afraid to show affection in public, holding hands or even kissing. A typical date would be a good meal and a leisurely glass of wine or café and croissant at an outdoor café, preferably along a busy street or waterway, chatting away. Because of the stereotype, you may have to be on the alert for fidelity and commitment.

Italy

Another romance language population, the Italians probably outrank the French in their reputation as lovers. Public displays of affection are common, and flirting involves lots of eye contact, physical touching, and innuendos. The dating process emphasizes family and food—what could be more pleasurable, than an Italian dinner surrounded by a big happy family! The traditional Italian household revolves around a family gathering after Mass on Sunday to enjoy a big meal of pasta, meatballs, and, of course, Italian wine.

Youth groups facilitate socializing, including a group known as Fieri, Italian for "pride." www.fieri.org is an international organization of students and young professional celebrating Italian culture and catering to 18–39 year olds.

Strict Roman Catholic tenets proscribe premarital sex, contraception, abortion, and divorce, although modernized young people often do not obey these rules. Italian men are raised to "be a man" and support the family while the woman's job is to be a good cook and run the household. Though the stereotypic Italian lover fools around while his wife becomes the Italian "mama," raising the family and gaining weight from her generous and delicious cooking, the concept of family is always honored.

Latin Countries

Outdoing even the romance language Lotharios, Latin lovers have the grandest reputation for uninhibited romancing and living it up in general. Many Latin cultures are still very "macho."

Many countries in South America are predominantly Roman Catholic, with strict codes for male-female relationships and sex. These often include a double standard for men and women, where the latter are meant to remain pure and virginal while the former are supposed to be inaugurated into the ways of love.

The Islands

Vacationers may thrill to life on a beautiful island retreat inhabited by kind native peoples with beautiful smiles. But closed doors can hide some problematic relationships. As Luis recounted upon his return from the Dominican Republic, "I heard a man tell his wife, 'There was a wrinkle in my shirt in the back. You better not do that again. Next time I want my shirt done right.' The women work and are busy all day, but then come home and have to serve their husband like a maid and a slave." A friend from Samoa told me of extensive domestic violence there. While the women are struggling for more liberation, many men are having a hard time adjusting to the changes.

On one remote island in the South Pacific, the average "good girl" has 3–4 boyfriends, starting from age 13. Women are encouraged to have many sexual partners before marriage, but afterwards must remain faithful to their husbands while the men are encouraged to have affairs.

Islamic Countries

Dating in Islamic countries is vastly different from the West. Traditionally, males are raised strictly separate from females, make all decisions, and have the final word. Young people might meet at university or work, but are generally introduced by friends or family members. The male's parents play a major role in initiating contact, judging whether the girl is acceptable according to her family background and their financial status, and then making an offer. If the girl's family is interested, they research the guy's family and accept with a gift. Girls' families do not reach out for a match, or she would be perceived as loose and therefore undesirable. Modesty and conservatism in females is valued. On the first date, the man and his parents come to the girl's parents' house (since going out is not allowed), where she serves them tea as they all sit and chat.

In more modern families, the guy can take the girl out alone, or with her parents, to a coffee shop or ice cream parlor to chat. He might also take her to the movies, a park, or a recreational site. The man always pays and the amount of money he spends measures the amount of his interest. If the man's parents spend a lot of time talking, or ordering more food, that shows they are enjoying the girl's company.

Holding hands is seen as offensive (the police can send a couple to jail for this!). The woman are expected to wear modest clothes. In strict Muslim society, three dates means the couple is ready for marriage. Then the engagement would last two years. For Iranian Jews, the couple would date three months to decide if they want to marry and they exchange gold jewelry (ring and watch). Then the family elders would come to the girl's house for tea where he requests permission and the families discuss what each side brings to the marriage.

Dating Data

There are some dating horror stories in countries like Bangledesh, where a man can throw acid in a woman's face if she refuses a date or his advances. He could even kill her (called an "honor killing"). Civil rights groups are attempting to stop this.

In Iraq, as in other Muslim countries, the importance of family (or "kinship groups") is dominant in transmitting values through the generations. Women have traditionally had no say in whom they marry, and there has been little or no courtship or dating. However, since the war and downfall of Saddam Hussein's dictatorship, the country is moving toward democracy and customs are falling away with more Westernized dating practices slowly creeping into the culture.

Orthodox Judaism

In unique dating customs of the Orthodox Jewish community, males and females are forbidden to touch or kiss until marriage. When walking they must keep enough distance between them to prevent bumping against one another. If still interested after five or six dates, the couple usually starts thinking about marriage.

The Land of the Rising Sun

While women in Japan are making great strides in financial and emotional independence, surveys have shown that less than half of the men are satisfied with this change and would prefer more traditional gender roles. Having spent many years in Japan (my radio show was broadcast there, I wrote many books and magazine columns, lectured at colleges, and ran workshops for companies), it was obvious that the changes in Japan were modeled after those in America about 10 years earlier.

The traditional "perfect" male for a Japanese woman has three "highs": height (taller than she), high education (more highly educated than she), and high finances (wealthier than she). Japanese men work excessive hours. Men and women tend to go out in groups and meet at coffee houses, bars, or discos. And I've noted the Japanese are as innovative in dating means as they are in the electronics they produce. I saw their "telephone clubs"—where singles sit at tables and can ring up a man or woman at another table on the telephone, long before such gimmicks popped up in America.

Intimate relations are restricted by lack of space and privacy since most young men and women live in tiny apartments or with their parents. Love hotels abound, where you can pay for a two-hour stay. When I was there, couples were even meeting and smooching in the most private place they could find—graveyards!

The average age for marriage is 30 for men and 27 for women. While tradition expects a wife to stay home and concentrate on the children (especially on a son's education) and divorce has not been common, modern Japanese women work long hours outside the home, like men, and want to marry later in life in order to pursue their career. In another trend, these young women have been interested in marrying Western men, who accept more liberated women; for some time it was even "cool" to date an African American man. Homosexuality is taboo, but nonetheless, there is a gay population in Japan.

China

In this culture that prizes scholastic achievement (as in Japan), young people are discouraged from dating in order to concentrate on their studies. Men, and especially women, are traditionally shy, and therefore hesitant about dating. But with increasing globalization, social and sexual mores are changing dramatically. Where women were once subservient to men, those especially in larger cities are now career-oriented and exert their independence.

Knowing China as I do, and as you might expect from such a big country, there are many nationalities with their individual cultures and interesting traditions (a wonderful park in Kunming shows these customs). In the Li nationality, for example, the family builds a hut next to their house when a girl turns 13 for her, where young men can come and sing songs to her. Sexually active young girls are not made to feel guilty. In another group, parents who arrange marriages rely a great deal on a fortune-teller.

On New Years for the Tai people, the girls will give chickens to the boys they like, but raise the price of the chickens for boys they do not like.

Dating Data _____

A study in the *Social Science Journal* compared 188 college students from a Midwestern university in the United States and 190 counterparts from a Chinese university in Shanghai. Results indicate that American college students generally entertain a liberal attitude toward dating, tend to date young, date more frequently, and are more likely to develop sexual relationships. In contrast, their Chinese counterparts are less permissive toward dating, start dating at a much later age, and are less likely to have sexual relationships.

There are some wonderful aspects of Chinese tradition that I hope don't change: Family is revered and children are expected to honor and care for their parents throughout life. I have found men and women extend this honoring in their relationship—to me and each other. Further, I experience such amazing appreciation from my Chinese friends. Both men and women are so surprisingly helpful, they even anticipate needs and fulfill them (a magical quality in a relationship!). They say glowing things when you do something nice for them, appreciating your time and attention, and like to return nice gestures. Contrary to what people think, I have found men charming and gracious (some even more so than in America!) in giving compliments, and open about sharing (even more than women, possibly because women have been brought up for so long to be shy). Things are changing fast—women are become more assertive and empowered. I've collaborated with a group of wonderful colleagues at the Shanghai Center for Reproductive Health Technical Instruction, and we've written a book about answers to thousands of questions to a unique hotline. I've found these questions asked about dating and relationships so similar to those I've heard for so many decades in America!

India

Traditional Indian society regards marriage as more of a relationship between families than two people. As a result, youth do not date and the parents get together and arrange their children's partnership. A girl's worth is measured by the amount of money her family can offer as a dowry. The Indian male is supposed to be dominant and the girl very modest, demure, proper, and quiet. Men may touch palms in greeting, but women are supposed to stay at a distance. But Indian youth are becoming quite modernized, meeting their own choice dates at school and other places.

Findings from a study of heterosexual peer networks and partnerships among low-income, unmarried, college-going youth in an Indian metropolitan city (Mumbia) showed three types of peer networks: platonic "bhai-behen" ("brother-sister like"), romantic "true love," and transitory and sexual "time pass" relationships. Boys engaged in multiple type relationships, while girls mainly stayed with their one "true love" type.

The Land Down Under

For a Western country, Australia is quite a free-for-all when it comes to dating and sex. With such freedoms, both women and men are forward in approaching others, asking for a date, and deciding whether to have sex whenever they choose. A typical Australian date starts at a restaurant, and progresses to a pub, parties, and active nightlife. Friendly, relaxed, and expressive by nature, Australian males and females have no hesitation about flirting, showing their interest, or demonstrating it publicly, whether smooching on the beach or dance floor.

Dating starts early in Australia, as cross cultural surveys show that Australian boys tend to become interested in the opposite sex starting at age 11, earlier than in other countries. The age of marriage is rising (29 for females and 31 for males); the marriage rate is decreasing while the divorce rate is on the rise.

Africa

In Guyana, parents arrange for young men and women to meet and the girl's family will take them to the movies (though some sneak off without the parents). They can also meet at school or social clubs where the girls sew and cook and the boys play soccer and do woodworking. They don't go to restaurants, but cook at home with the girl preparing a cake. Men talk at the table, while women listen passively (being aggressive is considered offensive). Flirting consists of handholding and chatting in the yard or under a tree.

Other Countries

In the rural Philippines, a guy brings flowers and serenades a girl beneath her window, then meets—and offers gifts to— her parents before dating her. Women aren't supposed to make eye contact with men. Dating is usually in groups, out for a meal and then dancing. Fathers are strict, but couples can usually sneak a kiss at the end of a date.

In the Micronesian Islands, it's considered disgraceful if a woman does not reject a guy's first request for a date (made through a third party). After she relents, they meet in private.

A popular site for a Korean date (as well as in China) is a karaoke bar.

In some Native American Indian tribes, young men and women engage in elaborate courting ceremonies. For example, the young man approaches the girls' tent carrying a colorful blanket (woven by female members of his family) and offers the girl shelter under his blanket, with the entire tribe as witness. If her parent's deem him suitable, he returns at night to serenade her with a traditional "love flute."

Making It Work No Matter What

Differences in culture, race, and religion can seem insurmountable. Parents and friends may object to such pairings, causing these couples to argue. Yet any difference can be overcome if you truly appreciate each other and work out major lifestyle decisions (about kids, careers, family visits).

Dating Data

Become familiar with your date's special holidays. For example, Ramadan for Islamic people is an extended month (that can vary every year) with restrictions about what you can do and eat (no meat). Three Kings Day is a day of gift-giving in early January in many Latin cultures recalling the legend of three kings who traveled to Bethlehem with gifts for the baby Jesus. Kwanzaa is an African harvest festival from in late December where each day is devoted to observing different principles, like unity and faith. Diwali is a popular five-day "Festival of Lights" in mid-November celebrating the homecoming of India's Prince Rama and his wife, Sita, after 14 years in exile.

To make such relationships work, such couples have to ...

- Teach each other about their background, perspective, culture, religion, ethnicity, and any other factor that influences their life.

- Get past their own and society's prejudices.

- Be prepared for life changes.

- Make agreements about important lifestyle decisions.

- Appreciate the reasons for their attraction. Build the relationship on true connection, intimacy, and desire to be together, not on rebellion, obstinacy, or defiance (of parents, society, or conventionality).

- Listen to others' opinions about their pairing, but make their own decision. You're the one living your life!

- If others' objections get to you too much, realize that they are triggering your *own* hesitations. Examine these doubts within yourself. Are you worried that your attraction is an escape, or a challenge, or proof of your independence?

- Declare a moratorium on the worries and spend time strengthening your relationship so it can withstand objections.

Shared Storytelling

One way to both test—and increase—your compatibility is to find out how well your dating scripts match. I use a unique and fun technique for this, called "shared storytelling." The purpose of this exercise is to get you to weave a story together about the date that you both can enjoy. Throw out a line to start the story. Then your date adds a line. Take turns until you think the story is complete. For example, he says, "We're having breakfast on our hotel terrace on the beach on the Greek island of Mykonos." You say, "I'm feeding you a champagne-dipped strawberry. Your fingers lightly glide up and down my back." He goes next.

Examine the story carefully. What actions did you add? What did your date add? Were your details romantic or sexual? What feelings did you describe? Did you start the story one way, only to have your date shift gears? Does this reflect your relationship, where you feel alone, or you disagree? Or do your ideas spark one another, a good sign that you appreciate and support each other's real-life story?

If you're on different story tracks, start another story and see if you can better agree on where the story goes. Doing this can help you learn to resolve differences and accommodate each other.

All You Need Is Love

People often ask me, "Is it possible that if you love each other, you can overcome anything—different religions, backgrounds, careers?" I can't be unrealistic; these are real challenges that can't be ignored. It won't be easy, especially if other loved ones object. But you can overcome any odds—if both of you really *want* to.

An All-Sex Alert

Keep in mind that whether you are straight, gay, bisexual, or bi-curious (basically attracted to the opposite sex but also intrigued about or have experienced sexual encounters with the same sex), the issues dealt with in this book all apply to you. The feelings, conflicts, and solutions are the same no matter who you are and with whom you get involved. But some questions that arise regarding dating are specifically related to sexual orientation. Many people ask me whether their actions or thoughts mean that they are gay or bisexual.

Our culture has definitely become more accepting of people's varying choices concerning partners and lifestyles. In several dramatic examples of this, homosexuality was removed from the American Psychiatric Association's manual of diagnostic disorders. A talk show host's popularity and ratings nose-dived when she discussed homosexuality as "abnormal." And gay and lesbian rights groups have made significant legal strides for rights in some states. But many would argue there is still a long way to go (for example, our culture seems to be more accepting of bisexuality in women than in men).

Rather than being exclusively attracted to one sex or the other, it is more reasonable to consider sexual behavior and partner choice along a continuum. Some men and women may be attracted to same sex partners from the time they are young, while others either "experiment" or make a choice when they are older and well into midlife, even after marrying and having children. What is most important is to come to terms with where you are, to know about your partner, and to avoid any misunderstandings.

Dating Data

Unique aspects of lesbian dating in a study of 38 young and midlife women showed that friendship was the preferred and most common method of courting (more than sex) and that relationships formed quickly. Few subjects took on traditional gender roles of being either masculine proactive, but those who reported assuming the feminine reactive role rejected the traditional notion that females should limit sexual contact. Reported in the *Journal of Lesbian Studies*, both verbal declarations of interest and nonverbal behaviors were primary means to communicate sexual attraction.

The Least You Need to Know

♦ Keeping an open mind about who is right for you opens up vast options for potential partners.

♦ Cultural traditions about dating vary greatly around the world, but these traditions are fading in the face of globalization and youth rejection of ancient customs.

♦ Couples today are connecting in many nontraditional ways, despite gaps in age, differences in race or ethnic background, or nontraditional sexual preferences.

♦ Couples can bridge differences in age, background, or other characteristics in order to achieve compatibility, but they must understand each other's backgrounds and not judge themselves or others.

Chapter 4

Get Going: Good Ideas on Where to Meet People

In This Chapter

- ◆ The best hunting grounds for singles
- ◆ How to improve your chances of meeting someone
- ◆ Where the single men and women are
- ◆ New ideas on where to meet people that may surprise you

"Where do I go to meet someone?" This is the most common question that single men and women of all ages have asked me over the years.

If there is one lesson about this question that you learn from this book, let it be the following: Don't worry about where you go, just be open! You don't always have to do something special or go out of your way to meet your future mate. In fact, you can meet this morning while waiting for the train, at lunchtime while standing in line for your grilled chicken sandwich, or this evening while riding the elevator. The point is to enjoy your life. Wherever you are, send out vibes that you're happy, open, and available!

Just Go About Your Life

When the energy is right, people will come into your life without any effort. It happened to Janey. One day an electrician came to rewire her apartment—and now he is igniting her passion as well.

Research shows meetings are conducive in places close to home where people feel comfortable and safe enough to talk to friends of friends and even strangers. You become attractive when you are going about your normal activities because you are unselfconscious and just being yourself—which is, after all, what everyone really wants to be loved for! So talk to people at your mailbox, or in the laundry room, and let them know you're available. Shop at the supermarket, go to the cleaners, visit the health club—and keep your love antennae tuned.

Be Proactive

Although it's not necessary to travel far to find a mate, you can improve your chances of meeting someone by being proactive in your search. There are three good strategies:

1. **Do something you enjoy.** This has a number of benefits. First of all, when you are actively engaged in something that interests you, you automatically become excited and emanate sex appeal. Secondly, you'll meet people who have similar interests to yours—one of the best foundations for a relationship. Meeting through a common interest provides both an instant bond and an icebreaker for conversation.

To help you accomplish this, do this exercise. Write down three interests you have and where you would go to pursue them:

Interest Inventory

	Interest	Where to Go
1.		
2.		
3.		

Use the following table to help you with this exercise.

If Your Interest Is:	You Might Meet People Here:
Sports	Health clubs, tennis lessons, pool halls, teams at local schools, YMCAs, sports bars
Dancing	Parties, dancing lessons, clubs, weddings
Intellectual	Courses, lectures, book clubs
Art	Classes, museum exhibits and courses, art supply shops
Music	Classes, concerts, record stores
Health	Health clubs, retreats, health food stores
Spiritual exploration	Yoga classes, holistic health expos, encounter group meetings, weekend getaways, tantra seminars, trips to holy places

2. **Choose places to go and things to do based on your personality style.** For example, if you are a quiet person who loves to spend time reading or listening to music, go to a bookstore where you can discuss your favorite novel or CD over cappuccino. Or attend lectures where authors speak—during a break, you can talk to people who like the book or the author. If you're more adventurous, go where the action is—amusement parks, sporting events, and concerts. Places like these give you the freedom to release your inhibitions.

3. **Go to places where the type of mate you're looking for might be.** Travis wanted to know where he could meet a classy girl. I told him to consider, if he were a classy girl, where would she go—a fancy restaurant, or art history class? A salesperson "targets" potential customers by zeroing in on their specific interest. In the dating equivalent, go to places where the type of person you would like to meet is likely to be. What type person would you find if you test drove a sports car versus a station wagon? Find upscale outdoorsy men at a boating regatta, or volunteer to work with underprivileged children to meet a caring, devoted woman.

Always be ready—you can meet that special someone at the most unexpected times and places. Dawn went on a fishing trip with her friend even though she hates to fish, and met James, an avid fisherman, who hooked her line and sinker!

Make up an activities calendar of places to go and things to do for the week, for fun and singles scouting. Write in hours that suit your schedule.

Do Your Homework!

Remember what it was like to do a term paper? At first, your mind could have been blank. But as soon as you began to research the topic, ideas popped into your head and creative juices started flowing. Meeting someone is similar: At first you may be void of clues of where to go, but once you do some research and brainstorming, you come up with good ideas. For now, use the following sources to get started (and also check Appendix A):

◆ Websites catering to singles, dating services, and events

◆ Yellow pages for clubs and groups

◆ Free publications at bookstores, music stores, newspaper stands, convenience stores, health food stores, doctors' offices, school lobbies, popular nightspots, and libraries

◆ Local or neighborhood newspapers with special sections on activities and events

◆ Magazines for special interests

◆ National newspapers for travel ideas

◆ Friends and other singles (ask waiters and waitresses too, as they usually know about "in" places)

◆ Newspaper gossip columns that cover upcoming events

◆ Chamber of Commerce listings and pamphlets

◆ "Around town" books and pamphlets found in hotel rooms and lobbies that describe where to go and things to do

◆ Attendance lists or mailing lists used by various clubs and party promoters to promote new events

Dating Networks

Think of finding a partner like finding a job. Besides going through the want ads or visiting employment agencies (or going to bars, clubs, or singles parties), networking is important. I'm sure you know people who got a job—or met a neat date—through a friend or other contact. Ask people you know for ideas about how they met dates. You'll hear many interesting stories!

Remember the concept (and play) "Six Degrees of Separation"? It means that everyone is connected by up to six contacts that they may not be aware of: ask six people and you can get to anyone. You're that close.

To develop your dating network, here are some suggestions:

- **Create a Dating Prospecting List.** Remember the infamous "little black book"—those "secret" address/ratings books that men used to keep of women? Keep a record in a notebook or a file in your palm pilot, as a working list of prospects and possibilities (like a sales prospecting list), including people you can call on for dating contacts.

- **Get a little help from friends.** According to numerous surveys, friends are the number-one source for finding a good date. The more dangerous life becomes, the safer people feel being introduced to someone by friends. Friends offer a ready-made character reference, as well as a ready ear for feedback about the date. It's inspiring to hear a story like Sara's. Her roommate fixed her up with her now-boyfriend, and he fixed the roommate up with a friend of his—and now they're happily double-dating.

- **Consider the unexpected fix-up source.** Would you cringe at the thought of your mother wanting you to meet the son of one of her friends? Be willing to try it. What have you got to lose? One young man agreed to be fixed up by a friend of the mother of his ex-girlfriend, who had never met him but heard about him and thought he'd make a good match for a girl she knew. He was curious, since the source seemed so unlikely, and his gamble was well rewarded as he ended up marrying the referred woman!

Dr. Judy's Dating Do's

Risk going on a blind date. It doesn't have to be a total mystery—or surprise—if you talk a lot on the phone beforehand, and get a good description from the person who fixed you up.

- **Don't rule out distant co-workers.** Although love affairs at the office are often too close for comfort, look beyond immediate co-workers. For example, you may find potential mates in other departments of the company or on other shifts.

Classic Good Places to Meet People

Even common places you go can lead to new experiences, when you have a new out-look. Consider these:

- **School's in!** Get more than an education at any age. What better place to meet people with common interests than in school, especially elective courses. Study history, cooking, a new dance style, real estate, or photography, and meet like-minded people, and have ready-made topics for conversation. You might even try a workshop on dating (many people have met at ones I run!)

◆ **Bookstores and libraries.** Browse the aisles of bookstores and ask other shoppers for recommendations or offer advice about a book you've read that's on the shelf. Go to a public library, or school library in your neighborhood (a medical school, law school, or art school); the air of studiousness can provide a perfect backdrop for an intimate conversation about a heady subject.

◆ **Museums and cultural events.** There is an infinite number of museums, art galleries, and dance and theater groups that you can attend or participate in. Jeanette and Larry both lingered over a Degas painting and ended up going through the rest of the art exhibit together. Jackie marveled over Janis Joplin's 1969 painted Porsche in the Rock-and-Roll Hall of Fame, saying, "Can you believe it really only cost $3,500 back then? I'd sure love to own one now," half to the display case, and half to the guy next to her—who ended up offering her a ride home in his Porsche.

◆ **Clubs and hobbies.** Remember the extracurricular activities in high school and college (I belonged to the ski club, journalism club, and drama club) that were great places to bond with friends? These same opportunities exist now—at a book club, wine club, or tennis club. Think of clubs or societies you are eligible for, from your school (call the alumni association), profession (from sanitation to psychologists!), or the armed services. Ask the human resources director at your job. Join a national association and check member procedures for private club meant mostly for dining (like the Kiwanis Club or Friars Club) but that also has busy calendars of events from golf outings to theatre performances.

Dr. Judy's Dating Do's

One of the best classes to enroll in these days is computer training. It's ripe for conversation about which laptop to buy, how a program works, or a website to check out, while checking out each other.

◆ **Bars.** The dating scene is constantly evolving. Bar hopping is "out" for picking someone up for casual sex, but "in" as a fun way to socialize. Even without drinking, you can listen to music, play games, sit in comfortable lounge chairs, or dance (to get energized and drop your inhibitions).

Getting Back to Your Roots

While I've explained in Chapter 2 how the exotic is erotic (we are often attracted to people who are different from us), we also feel comfortable—and therefore can get turned on—to those who remind us of our past and our roots. We can find them at places like religious centers (most churches and synagogues have singles' clubs that sponsor evening social and educational events and trips); community centers (form bonds with neighbors while you lobby for mutually important issues or plan block parties); and reunions (for your high school, college, camp or any other organization, where you can rekindle old friendships and maybe even a first love!).

Food That Feeds Good Company

Because food is already a symbol of love, eating can easily set the stage for romance. Look for places that facilitate mingling, like restaurants with fireplaces and piano bars; theme restaurants for sports, movies (such as Planet Hollywood), and music (such as the Hard Rock Cafe) that feature memorabilia that can be used as ice-breakers to start conversation; and coffee shops that are expanding their business to give people a reason to linger, and where you can discuss what flavor is "hot," and then sit down together to see if you like it—and each other.

Busy Spots

Research has shown that people form relationships more quickly in crowded places. So talk to people at places like …

- **Shopping malls.** Most feature food courts, scattered benches, entertainment, and even art galleries, all of which can facilitate meeting people.

- **Supermarkets.** Ask an interesting stranger, "Do you think this cantaloupe is fresh?" You can observe a person's eating habits by taking quick glances at his or her shopping cart or food basket. Good single shopping hours are between 6 P.M. and closing, particularly in the frozen-food aisle (that could lead to a hot romance)!

- **Festivals, arts and crafts shows, and street fairs in your neighborhood.** Use these events to meet locals as well as tourists. Chat with interesting-looking strangers at booths and in bleachers watching events. Keep your eye on local papers or TV channels for announcements and listings.

- **Public parks.** These have become great places for people to meet while they jog or walk their dogs (talking about—or to—the dog is a great icebreaker). Ask to join a volleyball or Frisbee game.

Dr. Judy's Dating Do's

More singles today find themselves new and alone in town because of job transfers or breakups after following lovers to different cities. Make new friends by talking to neighbors, attending local events, and checking out local newspapers, tourist magazines, and pamphlets that cover what's going on around town.

◆ **Piers, boardwalks, and marketplaces.** Many cities have sections of town, often along waterways, where there are restaurants, museums, or specialty shops. There are bound to be people hanging out, skating, walking their dogs, roller-blading, and looking for distractions. Check city guides.

Dr. Judy's Dating Do's

A good way for single parents to meet other single parents is at their children's after-school activities (dances, sports, classes, and rehearsals), single-parent clubs, meetings, or events (listed in local newspapers and singles newsletters), and local parks where kids can use the jungle gyms. While their kids were watching the puppet show at the Renaissance Fair, Al and Francine started talking about the puppet shows they used to put on when they were kids, and found a common interest in drama—and each other.

Cybercafes

A recent craze in the cafe scene is the "cybercafe." These are restaurants and coffee shops with computer stations (particularly useful when traveling abroad). Even though most people get absorbed at their individual station, you can talk while you wait, and share computer stories.

Personal Growth in More Ways Than One

While learning new skills or getting in touch with yourself, being in an atmosphere where people expect to grow facilitates confidence, communication, and openness. Here are some places to do that.

Business Seminars

Seminars on money management, financial planning, time management, or other skills are good places to meet people climbing up career ladders. Some seminars are expensive (hundreds of dollars), while networking clubs have offerings for under $30, and you might even find free introductions to company services (call brokerage houses and financial institutions).

Conventions

Industry-related conventions draw big crowds, and offer many mingling opportunities at social hours and exhibition halls with many booths with activities where people intend to network and connect. Plan your schedule to stay that extra day for the golf tournament, party, or tour. Billy met Betty Lou at the jalapeño-eating contest at their district advertising convention. And when Candace stopped by Cal's booth at the annual gift show, he offered her free samples—and dinner. Check with the local Chamber of Commerce, concierge at local hotels, and convention halls for their schedules. Sometimes admission is not restricted, and you can just pay to get in (the Nassau Coliseum holds a magic convention open to the public).

Health Courses, Clubs, and Stores

Health is an increasing concern for men and women of all ages these days, so courses, workshops, and retreats about any aspect of health are fertile ground for meeting like-minded people. Shop for food in health food stores and ask advice about soybean milk. While health clubs are not meant to be pick-up joints anymore, meeting others is inevitable. Pumping up your muscles also pumps up your self-esteem, and making conversation is easy with built-in icebreakers about workout routines or advice about nutrition. Offer to "spot" someone who's weight training. Many clubs offer classes in everything from karate to ballroom dancing, and trips for sports and socializing.

Support Groups

Although they're divorced now, Elizabeth Taylor once fell in love with unlikely match Larry Fortensky at a rehab center. The bonding makes sense, since intimacy comes from sharing raw feelings and being accepted when at your lowest point. There are support groups to deal with everything from pet loss and shyness to alcoholism, love addiction, and codependency. While they're not meant as places to meet dates, many people connect at such meetings. Refer to your local hospital or telephone directory for local 12-step self-help programs that offer regular meetings (for example, Sex and Love Addicts Anonymous, Alcoholics Anonymous, or Alanon).

Dating Data

Many organizations hold social events for gays and lesbians. Check local and specialty newspapers that are distributed free in many stores and on college campuses. Also, surf the web and check the phone directory for clubs and organizations listed under "Gay" and "Lesbian."

Self-Improvement Workshops, Retreats, and Expos

Not long ago, I returned to the granddaddy of all "new-age" retreats—Esalen—on the Big Sur. Esalen became famous in the 1960s for self-awareness seminars (and hot tubs) where you could "let it all hang out." As soon as I set foot on the grounds again, I felt myself opening up, relaxing, breathing easier, and smiling to everyone who walked by. Since everybody comes to a self-improvement workshop with the intention of being open, half your work is done, and half your fear erased. Women will be especially glad to meet the sensitive men drawn to these experiences. Courses can last a day, weekend, or longer, with group mealtimes, and classes with built-in exercises designed for inter-active activities, structured to help you get to know other people.

Hundreds of people with similar interests show up at expos advertised in publications and booklets distributed free of charge in various stores and street vending boxes. For example, the New Life Expo is held in cities around the country several times a year, featuring lectures and exhibit booths on everything from clothes and jewelry to "magnet mattresses" (to balance your energy) and powdered health potions. You can get a Reiki massage, get ear wax removed with candles, and find your soul mate.

The latest wonderful way to find like-minded spiritual souls is at a tantra seminar. Tantra is an ancient Eastern art of cycling energy to reach higher states of consciousness and ecstasy. At seminars that I and other experts teach, amazing human beings show up, eager to experience more openness and love for themselves and others. It's magical—many people find new, deeper and richer friendships than ever before, fall in love, and even marry!

My Favorite Arousal Arenas

In Chapter 2, I pointed out that attraction can easily happen in places where excitement level heightens arousal. Here are some of my favorites.

Concerts

If you've ever been to the opera, symphony, a rock concert, or karaoke or piano bar, you know how music brings people together. Also, chemicals flow in the body that physiologically create a feeling of relaxation or excitation, making you more open to falling in love. It's so easy to talk about the concert—or to dance and let your bodies do the talking!

Sporting Events

If you're an active participant—whether in softball or scuba diving—get out there! Sports, especially team sports, easily bring people together. Join a softball game in your local park, or volleyball game on the beach. Take up something new, like ice skating or roller blading. Go to a shooting range, putting green, or batting cage. Some clubs team you up with others (like in golf or tennis), so you don't have to worry about making your own contacts.

Instead of watching games at home, go to sports bars or restaurants that have giant-screen TVs, electronic sports games, and lots of food and drinks, so you can mingle with other fans while watching your favorite sport. Go to sporting events (football, baseball, basketball, even rodeos) and talk to people sitting around you. Attend tournaments (like golf and tennis) where you can wander around instead of staying put in your seat. Stand next to an interesting stranger and talk about a player's great line drive or an incredibly fast serve. Strike up a conversation in the memorabilia shop, or while waiting on the food line.

Dating Data _____

The best cities for singles are ranked every year by *Forbes* magazine (www.Forbes.com) based on nightlife, culture, job market, cost of living, and "coolness." Cities in the top ten have included Austin; Denver; Boston; Washington, D.C.; Atlanta; San Francisco; Los Angeles; New York; Raleigh-Durham; and Dallas. The cold northwestern states of Alaska and Washington have high percentages of single men to women. Nashville is kind, and while New York and Los Angeles may be thought of as rude, as big urban centers they offer a wide variety of people to meet.

Entertainment Arcades and Amusement Parks

As the electronic age intensifies, video arcades are evolving into elaborate entertainment centers. Ask someone who just stepped out of a virtual reality game what it was like to play that virtual golf course, or race that car. When fun and fear mix, they create arousal and open the door to falling in love. Based on "Theme Park Therapy" that I developed at Universal Studios Florida related to research on the scary Jaws exhibit, and amusement parks throughout England, it's easy to meet someone special or spice up your love life at an amusement park, theme park, state fair, carnival, or festival (like Albuquerque's Hot Air Balloon festival or Milwaukee's Harley Davidson festival), because of the magical mixture of four F's:

- ◆ **Feelings** (allowing yourself free expression)
- ◆ **Fear** (getting "scared" on rides, while knowing you're safe)
- ◆ **Fantasy** (suspending reality in imaginative settings and rides)
- ◆ **Fun** (experiencing uninhibited glee reminiscent of childhood)

Chemicals flow in the body as you get excited on a theme park ride, causing a physiological high. In addition, the joy of returning to childhood creates psychological benefits that put you in a positive and open mental state to fall in love.

Going to a theme park is also a good way for single parents to meet someone and at the same time entertain their kids. Or you can take a date and allow your child to get to know the new person in your life in a fun and nonthreatening way.

Comedy Clubs

Since I mentioned to you that humor is a top attractive quality in both men and women these days, comedy clubs are a great place to meet people, or take a date. Laughing brings out the best in you, reduces inhibitions about approaching someone, and helps you be yourself.

Dancing Clubs and Classes

Dancing is not only fun and arousing, it's "in" these days. More people are interested in learning how to do specialty or ethnic dances from different cultures. In some tango classes, there is the added advantage that people are required to change partners, making it easier to meet others.

Helping Others and Yourself

People are drawn to others who give of themselves. And giving makes you feel good about yourself. This win-win combination can happen at …

- ◆ **Openings.** There are innumerable public events in every town, from free openings of museums, community centers, and health organizations to invitation-only galas and expensive fundraisers. Make sure you make it to the cocktail party where the real mingling takes place. Call the organizer beforehand to arrange to be seated at a table with interesting people. Sit where you can see the other people and scan the crowd for interesting-looking people.

◆ **Marathons.** At events such as Walk-a-Thons and Dance-a-Thons many singles come to have fun while raising money for various charities. Because you don't have to be an expert in any of these activities, you'll meet all kinds of people with shared spirits, "do-gooder" attitudes, and interests in being active.

◆ **Fundraisers.** These can be an expensive ticket, so consider getting a job or volunteering for a public relations company that works on them. Or organize one yourself, like Heather Mills did. The then-30-something woman with a prosthetic leg met Beatle Paul McCartney, over 20 years her senior, whom she invited to the event, and later married.

◆ **Political campaigns.** Politics can make not-so-strange bedfellows, since competition can spark an attraction between opponents. (A good example is the marriage of Republican television commentator Mary Matlin and Democratic Party leader James Carville). Also, when two people team up against a common enemy, they protect and value each other—a good reason why political volunteering is a good hunting ground. Being informed and committed offers you an even better chance to get into an impassioned conversation with someone.

Dr. Judy's Dating Do's

Single parents can bring their children to clubs, marathons, and other events listed in this chapter (kids can be company and great conversation starters). But make it obvious that you're a single parent.

The Party Scene

Meeting people at parties is easier for confident and adventurous souls, but even shy people can grow from the challenge of a party situation, from small friendly gatherings and special events, to big singles mixers. Some singles parties have icebreaker techniques; for example, write on a card what your main interest is and find someone in the room with the same interest. Throw a theme-related party, and ask each guest to bring two new friends. Here are a few strategies to adopt when at a party:

◆ Place yourself where you can be seen, or "cruise" the room to get comfortable with your environment. Adopt an inviting "look."

◆ Have a positive attitude. Instead of feeling embarrassed or ashamed ("I'm a loser"), or thinking of past failures ("I was always a wallflower in high school"), think positive thoughts ("I'm having a good time"). Distract yourself from negative thoughts by observing the color of the room or how the food is displayed.

Dr. Judy's Dating Do's _____

It's easier to approach someone who's alone rather than in a pack. In roping a steer, a cowboy isn't supposed to throw his lasso into the herd, but coax one selected animal aside. When Patty goes skiing with her girlfriends, she always gets on the singles line for the ski lift so she can pair up with another single for the ride up the mountain.

♦ Amuse yourself. "People watch" or focus on someone who interests you. Enjoy playing mental games, imagining what that person is like. Watch what makes your love antennae whir and what makes it wilt.

Vacations

If you've got the time, money, and interest, traveling to some exotic spot—for a weekend getaway or longer journey—can be the perfect setting for possible romance. Just as places that are close to home facilitate comfort for meeting strangers, the escape from daily life and excitement in a new adventure allows freedom from stress or old patterns, and sex appeal for romance.

Dr. Judy's Dating Do's _____

Stay at or visit a 5-star resort to meet some fancy folks. But lodging at budget places and even youth hostels (no matter your age) can also be great for meeting people, as others are usually more open to strangers, and eager to share travel experiences. Americans often seek out each other when traveling abroad, but should purposefully make new friends from other countries.

Most people feel safer having a companion along on a trip, but going alone can make you befriend others, talk to strangers, change plans easily, or spend time with someone you might meet. Don't be afraid to go alone. I'll never forget the year I had an unexpected week off from work and because no one could take off the same time, I simply called United Airlines and told them to book me a ticket to the farthest place they fly. I ended up in Australia where I made lots of new friends—whom I probably would never have met had I not gone alone. Here are some tips for making the most of these trips:

♦ Pick a destination known for drawing singles or that has activities for singles (clubs and shows) and interesting tours. Do research on airlines and travel organizations that book vacations, tours, camps, cruises, and trips for singles to resorts, sports outings, and exotic destinations.

- Consider all-inclusive packages such as those offered by Club Med, where you don't have to worry about what to do and where to eat, since the set-up provides instant playmates and meal companions.

- Be clear about your intentions. Do you want to loll around the beach all day by yourself, or be active (horseback riding or scuba diving)? Many organized out-door singles trips feature special interests, like hiking, biking, rafting, safaris, archeology, and more.

- Consider spiritual trips to sacred destinations where you are ensured that even if you don't meet your soul mate, you can get more in touch with your own soul. Outward Bound–type trips have become popular in the past decade; while em-barking on a journey for survival, you discover yourself and bond with others. Recapture the fun and camaraderie of camp at adult camps, like Club Getaway.

- Sharing in a summerhouse is a popular way to cut costs for a vacation and in-crease your social contacts. Everyone chips in for food, so dinners can be par-ties, and there are always new people dropping by to visit friends.

Woo Warning

A consideration about meeting potential dates while traveling is that they most likely live in a distant place. Be prepared for a long-distance rela-tionship!

Unexpected Places

Anywhere can be a place to meet someone. You can be on a bus, waiting in a line, buying something, stopped at a stoplight. All it takes is being open, having the guts to make a move, or responding to someone else's approach to show your interest.

Your flight's delayed and you're stuck at the airport for two hours. You're about to settle a case in small claims court. You notice an unusual building down the street. At first sight, these events and situations don't seem like a means to finding a date. Well, look again ….

A Tourist in Your Own Town

You don't always have to travel far to meet interesting people. Be a tourist for a day in your own town. Check sightseeing opportunities from listings in the back of your local city magazine, or free tourist flyers from hotel lobbies and your own city cul-tural or convention center or visitors' bureau.

Despite the fact that you can expect more couples and families on these tours, as well as tourists (risking a long-distance relationship if you do meet someone!), a like-minded local might show up. Stacy met John on a Rock-and-Roll bus tour of New York City, while Pam fell for Larry on a behind-the-scenes tour of Madison Square Garden.

In any case, the experience can help acquaint you with sights that you may have never discovered on your own (like museums and entertainment centers), where you can return, and that could lead to meeting people closer to home.

Hotels

Hotel lobbies—even in your own town—can be a potentially great place to meet people. Yes, travelers may be tired and preoccupied, but they also could be lonely and receptive to you extending a warm welcome. Hotels are designed to be attractive to out-of-towners in need of entertainment and relaxation, but many hotel bars and restaurants are also popular among locals. Wander into the lobby and check it out. You could find cozy corners where you can sink into comfortable couches and leisurely sip a cappuccino, or perhaps you could find a piano bar. Some hotels allow guests to use facilities (pools, hot tubs, exercise equipment) for the day (for a fee), where you might meet someone.

> **Woo Warning**
>
> Some dating destinations can end up being a bad bet. Shannon and Billy both loved making the two-hour drive to Atlantic City even for a day. But over time, this became their only date destination, and they had to realize that they had a gambling addiction. They needed to find other exciting ways to be together.

Airports and Airplanes

Everyone is more mobile in this new age. Consider airports like the grocery store. With check-in lines, vendors, coffee stands, and even delays or waiting time between flights, there are endless opportunities to meet people and strike up a conversation. It's easy to ask "Where are you traveling to?" and transition into finding out if she lives to travel, or where he would most like to go. The woman sitting next to you on your flight, or the guy who helps you lift your luggage into the overhead compartment, could be a fascinating new friend.

Courts

Let's face it: The law is "in." You cannot turn on TV without *Judge Judy*, *Law and Order*, or some other courtroom drama popping up on the screen. There's even a whole cable channel, Court TV (that I often appear on, discussing psychological explanations for various criminal acts of the defendants on trial). Chances are, you'll find yourself in court for one reason or another—maybe just to renew your license or perform jury duty. Rest assured that your visit will involve long waits and long lines, So use the opportunity to talk to others around you.

The Least You Need to Know

- ◆ You can meet that special someone simply during the course of your daily life.

- ◆ To increase your chances of finding someone to love, get involved in an activity you enjoy doing.

- ◆ Think of where your ideal person might be, and then go there.

- ◆ Go where lots of men (sporting events, conventions) or women (dance lessons, self-improvement classes) are.

- ◆ Keep a "dating networking list" of contacts and possibilities.

- ◆ Be open to—and ready for—all possibilities.

Chapter 5

Services to Help You Search and Make a Match

In This Chapter

- ♦ What to know about dating services
- ♦ The variety of matchmaking services available
- ♦ The best policy: honesty and creativity
- ♦ Checking out a service
- ♦ Speed dating and other trends
- ♦ Dating services in other parts of the world

Ah, you may think there is no one out there for you, but the truth is there are so many options, so little time. The dating scene is definitely a world of its own with so many people to meet—in every shape, size, and style. So where do you start? If there were only a magical way you could "order" your soul mate and have the "package" sent to you overnight. Then again, you'd miss the fun of dating, and appreciation of the gain—after all your effort!

In ancient days, marriages were arranged to ensure fiefdoms, conquer countries, and obtain dowries. In modern times, matchmaking became nobler and less opportunistic, with good-natured relatives and friends pitching in to bring two people together. In more recent years, matchmaking has become big business, with dating services charging big bucks for the promise of love. The newest way to meet people in this new era is through the Internet, which I'll address in the next chapter.

In this chapter, I'll go over various services to help you in your own search. The good news is that dating has become such a hot topic these days that there are many new services and opportunities to help you meet your match. Each service has benefits and limitations. Don't be afraid to give them a try, but also be realistic about the outcome. Check Appendix A for more information about such services.

Dating Services: Essentials to Know

These services run the gamut, with some offering parties, socials, and other singles events, and others sticking to simple introductions based on answers to a question-naire and photographs. Some are open to anyone while others specialize in fixing up specialty clients (religious groups, successful professionals, and so on).

Save money and aggravation! When you sign up for a dating service, you are putting your heart into it as well as your money. To avoid rip-off or fly-by-night dating services, investigate what you're buying. Call or e-mail for detailed information (how long they've been in business, who owns it, number of clients). Follow these tips to decide what's right for you:

♦ Make sure the service offers what you are looking for. Do you want dates or a serious relationship—or even a family right away? Are you into "e-paling" (my new word for the old concept of pen pals who send e-mails instead of letters)?

♦ Call the service if there is a phone number given, and see if you like the "energy" of the people! I've called some places and really didn't like the people—if they were nasty or not forthcoming to me on the phone, how would they really help my love life? If they were nice, then I'd feel good about them handling such an important part of my life.

♦ Make sure they respect your privacy. They should not disclose your phone num-ber, address, or other personal information without your permission.

♦ Be clear about fees and services offered. Read all the agreements and contracts about your obligations and what you get for your money, including how many dates you're entitled to and over what period of time, and whether you can can-cel or sell your contract if you no longer need or want the service. (The Better Business Bureau at www.bbb.org can tell you if any complaints are filed.)

- ◆ Know your contact person. If it's a big company, get a member-services coordinator and call often with questions or to ask advice.

- ◆ Ask for success rates and feedback from customers. Don't feel obligated or pressured.

Oldies but Goodies

Personal ads, video dating, call lines, and plain old matchmaking may seem "passé," but they are still worthwhile options. In fact, since they've been around for a while, some of these services have expanded, like onto the Internet (read on to the next chapter for more details on cyberdating).

Such dating services have also become more socially acceptable; people are not as embarrassed or afraid to use them. As a result, a wider group of people is participating, giving you a better chance of meeting someone "right" for you. So go ahead and try them out. As long as you exercise the usual precautions, you don't have much to lose. In fact, the cost of many of these services can be so reasonable that you're bound to find one suited to your budget.

Woo Warning

Keep in mind that repeated efforts are usually necessary in order to get your message out in advertising or public relations. So don't be discouraged if, similarly, your first attempts at dating services do not lead to a big or successful response.

Personal Ads

One of the least expensive matchmaking services, personal ads are now carried in almost every type of publication. Before placing an ad, think carefully about the type of person you are trying to reach. Study the contents of the publication and assess the readership so that you get responses from the type of person you are looking for. For example, someone advertising in a sex magazine would probably not have the same intentions as someone placing an ad in a local daily "family" newspaper. Signing on to a service that requires a fee might net a higher quality date than one that was free (some dating services online are free for women, but men must pay—hardly fair, but true).

Remember, when you submit a personal ad, you are an advertiser selling yourself. As such, you want to "break out of the clutter" (one of my favorite phrases from the advertising world), meaning stand out from the crowd. You also want to attract the desired "customer" to your "product"—you. Remember, the goal is not the quantity of responses, but the quality.

In writing your ad, be honest, creative, and descriptive about what you offer and what you want. Make sure your personality shines through. For example, a funny person might say, "Why can't Miss Piggy count to 70? For the answer, call me." Or a spontaneous person might say, "Want to fly off to Bali tomorrow?" Or a romantic might say, "Come sit by my fire and share dreams …" (I'll give you more details about how to write your ad in the next chapter.)

Success stories are always encouraging. I'm sure you know some as well as I do. My cousin placed an ad in which she described her love of cats, the poet Baudelaire, and sonatas by Bach. Her passionate descriptions drew her now-husband to her ad and the altar. Another friend met his wife through the personals by describing himself this way: "36-year-old dancing psychiatrist likes ballet and sports, prefers nonsmoker 25–35. Hopes for lasting relationship and family."

Dating Data

In a study reported in the *Journal of Communication*, older dating advertisers (50 years and above) tended to express restrained, modest, and nonsexual relationship goals, and restricted references to age, giving less emphasis on physical appearance, than ads written by younger people.

If you have trouble describing yourself, ask a friend to help. Also, have a friend help you go over responses to your ad to get an objective perspective.

Personals do have a downside. It takes time to get responses, and you can count on some people being less than truthful in their advertising.

Answering Ads

In answering an ad, the same rules apply as in submitting one: Be honest, creative, and descriptive. Use the guidelines for good communication and listening described in Chapter 16. Besides telling about yourself, respond to the specific points the person wrote about, with comments or questions (just as you would in a good conversation).

Get as much information about the person as possible, just as you would a job prospect. Go on Internet services like www.google.com and www.anywho.com. Ask to call him or her at work, and try to speak to friends he or she talks about during your conversations.

Ask for a photo—not just to see if the person is your type, but to get a "sense" of the person. "Read" it: Is his posture open or closed (arms crossed, hands hidden)? Is she stern or smiling? What's the setting: a stark background or warm surroundings? Kathie sends a picture of herself hugging her puppy, and not surprisingly she wants a guy to snuggle with. Since Paul is perched on his motorcycle, you might wonder if he has a wild streak.

Be cautious about getting together. Be sure that you speak several times on the phone before you meet for a date. Interview the person and ask direct questions. Do "due diligence" (a legal term for doing your investigative homework)! Meet during the day, in a public place, preferably with a friend.

If the date doesn't work out, or if there is no spark, don't waste time dragging it out. Simply say, "It was nice meeting you" or "Not everybody is a match made in heaven."

Finally, keep your expectations in check by remembering an analogy to sales. When you send out a "mass mailing" (which is essentially what happens when you post a personal ad), you cast a wide net to a large audience, and a 1 or 2 percent response rate is considered acceptable.

Dr. Judy's Dating Do's

Many personal ads have voice mail as an added feature—helpful since voices are revealing. Write out your voice-mail message before you record it. Be creative. Instead of saying "Call me" and leaving your number, respond as if you were giving your personal ad by adding intriguing details (interests,

Video Dating

The more senses you can use to get an impression of a stranger, the easier it is to determine whether you are simpatico. Seeing a person and watching how he or she talks and moves gives you much more information than a written personal ad, and saves time and energy in helping you make a decision faster. But you won't save money—video ads are more expensive than personal ads.

Video dating involves joining a private club, filling out a computerized personal profile, and making a videotape. Your profile, photo, and tape become part of the club's library, available to other members. You, in turn, can look at the library offerings and, if you see someone on video you would like to meet, submit a meeting request. If the person is interested, he or she can screen your video. If both are in agreement, phone numbers can then be swapped.

Video dating boomed a while ago and like all other means of matchmaking, became overshadowed by computer dating services. But increasingly, these services are all merging so everything is available on the Internet.

Dating Call Lines

Telephone party lines were popular in the early 1990s, when ads for these services flooded late-night cable TV. Some still exist (like one Temptation call line). The premise is simple: By dialing a certain number, you gain access to a public phone line with a group of other callers who want to talk or make dates. These lines tend to cater to young people. These can be costly—you are charged per minute, and when you are chatting on the phone it's easy to lose track of time. Be wary!

Professional Matchmakers: Fix Me Up!

Like Yentl of *Fiddler on the Roof* fame (a perfect example of a kindly soul who loves to fix people up), matchmaking has a long tradition, especially among certain ethnic groups. Matchmakers are fixtures in a given community, and spend considerable time getting to know the singles. They do things the "old fashioned way"—based on intuition and experience rather than on answers to a prescribed set of questions.

Some people like the personal touch that matchmakers provide, compared to Internet dating. Some matchmaking services are as difficult to get into as some of our nation's finest schools. Others take you under their wing, offering makeovers. One matchmaker I spoke with puts a whole team of professionals on your case, including a handwriting analyst, private investigator, psychologist (for a battery of tests), and an image consultant (for fashion and make-up advice, as well as for advice on weight reduction and plastic surgery). Costs can range from the reasonable hundreds ($250) to the stratospheric thousands ($5,000). Some people get so confident after going out on the fix-ups that they meet someone on their own.

I have been very impressed with the kindness and caring personalities of some matchmakers I interviewed for this book. They were so much nicer than big companies I cold-called for information. (See Appendix A for details about the services I mention here.)

"I try to make people happy," says Joseph Fields of the family-run Fields Exclusive Dating Service, a fourth-generation "old-fashioned marriage broker." The Fields get to know you personally, go through massive files of about 100,000 clientele, and make some matches, and then recommend that "the gentleman calls the lady" (notice the terminology). The Fields maintain that such hands-on personal service is far better than Internet dating where you never know what the other person may be hiding, or you commonly never see them again, or the e-mailer is lying, or worse yet, married. "You have to *see* people," says Fields. He advises, "Don't talk too much the first time on the phone because something might not go right; if you talk in person, you give each other a better chance."

A conversation with Judith Quinn, owner of Visual Preference, also showed her dedication. Quinn says she has been getting more calls from men because of Viagra, giving them more confidence sexually! She also has more older men clients calling, because of late-life divorce. Says Quinn (whose service is localized in the northeast), "Men come to me who have been married 33 years and their wife says, 'I don't want to cook for you anymore'." Her oldest client is 72 years old, but she says, "He looks better than some guys in their 40s!" Based on her 30 years of experience, Quinn gives the following advice:

- "Women should be hopeful. More men are marriage-minded these days."

- "Be patient. Some people expect fast results, like women whose biological clock is ticking. A 35-year-old woman didn't talk about the match, just about wanting a child."

- "Don't blame the matchmaker. Some people are so sick of dating, they just need someone to complain to, or about. They meet for five or six dates and change their criteria, or say no one's right for them, and that it's my fault."

- "Women can be more difficult to fix up than men. Since men are visual, they'll see a photo and say, "not interested," and that's the end of it. But women are very picky and have so many complaints after the date, like getting upset over a word he said, or a Polo shirt he wore that she didn't like."

- "Be realistic. If a guy looks like Humpty Dumpty and wants a Marilyn Monroe, it's not likely!"

- "Don't be cheap. Some men don't even want to buy a soda. One woman complained about a guy who took her on four dates but only bought coffee and she was hungry. He called it a 'light meal'."

- "Women expect a man to pay. A woman shouldn't have to ask, 'Are we going Dutch?' She can reciprocate another time."

- "Some men complain that women quiz them as if they were on a job interview."

- "Men want women to work, but they also want a woman to be soft. Feminists wouldn't like this, but women can be too independent and should concede to men and act helpless sometimes, so the man feels needed and useful. Ask him to open the jar for you. The man is King and woman is Queen; treat him like a King and he'll treat you like a Queen."

Dr. Judy's Dating Do's

Some restaurants and clubs sponsor events, such as wine-tastings or movie screenings, designed to bring singles together. These events can provide a comfortable meeting atmosphere, reducing pressures and expectations. The "Single Gourmet" is a good example of such a club, at whose events I've spoken and done book singings, and that is now franchised around the world (see Appendix A). The clubs offer dinners as well as day, weekend, or week-long trips. Most of the members have an interest in food and wine, and also travel.

The Latest Crazes

The current heated-up search for love has both created and been able to take advantage of new ideas and technologies. Here are some trends.

Speed Dating

Research shows people decide if they are attracted to someone in less than a minute. I recommend you give someone a chance—at least through the date! But a craze in the search for "the one" gives you just eight minutes to state your case and make an impression.

Speed dating started in Los Angeles in 1998, the brainchild of a Jewish educational network called Aish HaTorah. Now there are many offshoots and variations, all adding up to big business, like "8minuteDating," "FastDater" and "Hurry Date." Even *Today Show* host Katie Couric tried it and liked it.

Events are run in cities from coast to coast and around the world, mostly for upscale 20- and 30-somethings, but also for groups targeted by age, race, religion, interests, or sexual preference. Singles gather to munch on nachos and sandwiches, sip cocktails, and participate in a new round-robin musical chairs matchmaking game. About 40 men and women (it has to be equal numbers) pay up to $38.88 (note the "8"s) or less for early birds. At the evening's event at a bar or restaurant, they sign in and get a card with a number and random assignments to other numbered hopefuls for 8-minute rounds of chat. They sit down at a table for their first chat with a stranger, and when a bell rings after each 8 minutes, each person moves on to his or her next assigned matched number. In an intermission, singles get to mingle freely.

Dating Data

Sociologists at Columbia University have studied Speed Daters to see what qualities cause instant attraction.

If you're interested in seeing someone again, you note it on your card. Afterward, you log on to the website and if two people entered each other's information, the organizers will tell you there's an "interested match," and you can use a blind e-mail system to get in touch (or give out your real e-mail address if you want).

The night I gave an opening talk and book signing about dating and relationships to kick off an 8-minute dating evening run by my friend Darcy at a trendy New York bar, the participants all looked attractive and involved enough. But some, like Lisa, found the pressure of having to talk fast in such a short time a bit much. George told me he solved the problem of "performance anxiety" by practicing at home. The organizers say hopefuls like Lisa and George have an up to 70 percent chance something will come out of the evening.

How fast can you get an idea of whether you are interested in someone? How long does it take for you to put your best foot forward? Try it in three minutes—as much as you get in some speed dating events. Of course, some shy people balk, but most who try it like it. And of course, the companies boast of couples who connect, and even a few who supposedly commit.

Rotate at Dinner

Ever felt stuck at a dinner party, not being interested in who's sitting to your right or left? Enterprising singles solve this problem by hosting switch-seat dinners where roundtables of singles rotate during the courses of the meal to give them a better chance to enjoy their tablemates.

There was even a report that enterprising subway-riding singles in New York tried to set aside certain cars for meeting and mating while on their commuter ride.

TV Dating Shows

Given the range of shows on TV and expanding cable channels, TV dating competitions will likely continue in some form. You can try to get on one. You have to fit some producer's profile, but that doesn't mean you have to be perfect. On one show, the 20 male contestants who competed for one woman's hand were clearly typecast, by looks (one balding guy), by job (one student, one millionaire, and one unemployed guy), and even by race (one Hispanic, one Black, one redhead). Check local TV listings and read the media columns to find out about the shows. Log on to their websites to find out the procedure.

Cyberdating

Connecting on the Internet has become the next generation of personals and dating services. All you need is a way to access the Internet (through your computer or any number of other advancing technologies). There's much more about this in the next chapter.

What's Happening in Other Parts of the World

Some countries have unique dating services to serve singles in ways that may surprise you. Some examples I've encountered through my various travels are explained in the following sections.

Business Lends a Hand

Hats off to the innovative Japanese for coming up with this unique dating service: on-site matchmaking at major corporations! These "matrimonial" companies act as commercial nakodo (go-betweens) for omiai (marriage interviews), introducing prospective brides and bridegrooms. Some boast about a 50 percent success rate. Granted, the need is there: Japanese workers spend most of their waking hours on the job. By contrast, American companies discourage office romances.

The Government Gets in on the Act

Here's a real surprise: the government of Singapore, famous for its social engineering, is probably the leading dating service provider in that city (which is also a country). The social development unit (SDU) has been matchmaking since 1984 when the government got worried about smaller families and larger numbers of single professionals who didn't have time or skills to find partners. The agency sponsors dating clubs, an Internet site, and innumerable activities and events, all to facilitate people falling in love, marrying citizens of the country (instead of foreigners), and make babies to prop up a sagging population. There are dining, exercise, and travel opportunities, as well as events like "Zodiac Dates" (where singles with compatible horoscopes meet over tea), "Blind Dates," and "Speed Dating" (with a reported high success rate: three out of four singles leave with at least one promising match). Recently, the SDU promoted a month-long "Romancing Singapore" campaign to coincide with Valentine's Day.

Tips in the dating guide the SDU published, "When Boy Meets Girl! The Chemistry Guide," sound like the good advice in this book: "Smiling is a great way to break the ice, but don't grin like a Cheshire cat the whole time. A date is very similar to a job interview. You have to sell yourself. People are drawn to good listeners. But don't just sit there passively; engage whomever you are with."

The Least You Need to Know

- There are endless options for finding a date, from the low-tech to the high-tech.

- Whatever your method of contact, always be honest about yourself.

- Keep your expectations in check and be on the lookout for stories that sound too good or too wild to be true.

- Dating services are going global, and some governments even offer unique opportunities for singles to meet.

Chapter **6**

Ineedadate.com

In This Chapter

♦ Using technology to find love

♦ The vast new world of Internet dating services

♦ Cyberdating pros and cons

♦ Do's and don'ts of flirting online

♦ How to post a winning profile and write an e-mail that gets noticed

♦ Turning cyberinterest into a real-life date

It's still great to meet through friends and other ways mentioned in the previous chapters, but the computer age has produced the next generation of personals and dating services: cyberdating. Finding love online is now possible through e-mail, chat rooms, and online dating services. You now have access to instant intimacy with complete strangers on your block or anywhere in the world. And you can connect 24–7 (meaning *all* the time) in the comfort of your home—despite bad weather, having nothing to wear, being shy, or suffering from just a plain old bad hair day!

I'm asked so many questions about this method of looking for love, like "Can you find true love on the Internet?" "If we meet in real life, will it ruin a good online relationship?" and "Can you trust someone you meet talking online?" I'll address these questions and more in this chapter.

Keywords: Date Me!

The number of websites catering to singles and offering dating services, with new ones popping up all the time, is enough to make your head spin. Knowing where to go to meet someone can be as daunting a task in cyberspace as in real life. There are well-known sites like match.com, matchmaker.com, personals.yahoo.com, and nerve.com ("trendy" according a favorite student of mine, Ben, who likes questions they ask users, like "If I could be anywhere at the moment …" and "Five items I can't live without"). Think of any words that imply matching and mating, dating and hooking up, and chances are you can find a site (like iMatchup, FriendSearch, PeopleMeet, Udate, crushclub, and so on). There are sites connected to the speed dating craze and even all those TV dating shows. Some have a "hook," like one that banks on the concept that you'd feel more comfortable going out with a guy that your girlfriend reccommends as a great boyfriend. Some sites such as www.nyone.com cater to locals, while others such as blinddaterworld.com and www.worlddatingservice.com have affiliates all over the world, as their names imply. Check their websites for different locations.

Options abound for making contact. You can post an ad publicly or share it selectively. You can add photos, voice, and video greetings. You can send anonymous e-mails or instant messages. With all kinds of wireless gadgetry, you can have constant access to dating opportunities wherever you go. You can even "see" each other on web cams (cameras attached to the computer that show real-time streaming video) to get transported right into people's living room—or bedroom! Be prepared to enter the Matrix!

Here are some popular ways to make e-contact:

- **Chat rooms.** Chat rooms exist for almost every hobby, television show, and news headline, making it possible to meet people with similar interests. Some target specific age groups, geographical locations, nationalities, and just about any dating criteria you have. Locate ones that interest you through specific web servers, or surf the Net, exploring.

- **Bulletin boards.** Also built around specific interests, as with chat rooms, hundreds of bulletin board services advertise new websites, upcoming web events, and chat rooms.

- **Online communities.** An online community links people of similar interests like joining a club, sorority, or fraternity. For example, fans of musical artists form these types of online versions of a fan club.

- **Home pages.** These days, anyone can create a website or home page economically. Post your photo, hobbies, and favorite jokes, giving a window into your life.

E-Mail

The electronic form of leaving a phone message, e-mailing is a fast way to fire off a quick note to someone you just met, ask how his or her day is going, or suggest getting together. All you need is an e-mail address, and some servers will give to you one for free.

Woo Warning

One woman gave a guy she met online her personal e-mail address and he wouldn't stop instant messaging her. Use the same discretion when giving out your e-mail address that you would with your telephone number. Create a different e-mail address for people you meet online who you want to keep at more distance (like having an unlisted and listed phone number) so you can cancel a screen name if you get into trouble.

Online Dating Services

Internet dating is big business. The choices are becoming more and more endless! In fact, practically every service for singles is tied to a website, with content, product, and dating opportunities.

Some services are targeted to certain special interest groups, like age, race, ethnicity, or sexual preference. Lavalife's "manline" is for men who want to meet men and "womanline" for women who want to meet women; www.fieri.com caters to Italian pride; and www.JDate.com was started for Jewish singles. A "Hip and Single" site for Chinese couples once interviewed me about dating—and the article showed up on a Russian dating service site. There's even a site for dog-loving singles!

You can also choose whether you're interested in friendship, dating, a more serious relationship, love, or intimate (read "sexy") encounters. The sites invite you to chat, flirt, search, and e-mail.

Some services are free for "introductory membership" (usually new sites aiming to build their member base), or free when you post an ad, but responding costs money. Others have stages of membership, where you pay for added features. Or you pay a fee per month, say $19.95, but then you pay per person you want to contact. Always check the Terms of Use to see what rules and costs apply, as well as termination procedures and confidentiality.

Many online services are expanding their businesses (making money on all ends) to include offline, live events (just like other in-person services are going online!). One major company expanded to offer their clients salsa-dancing parties, walking tours, cooking classes, evenings at the symphony, and expensive vacation trips.

Can You Find Love on the Web?

The possibility of finding true love on the Internet is one of the most popular new questions I'm asked about online dating. The answer is "yes." Of course there are no promises or guarantees. But the more exposure you get to different people and the wider you cast your net, the more circles you form, the greater the likelihood of meeting someone who interests you.

I'm sure you've heard of successful online matches. Carla, a 32-year-old divorced mother of two from Long Island, took part in a poetry chat room and met a woman from New Mexico who not only shared her same interest in Elizabeth Barrett Browning's works, but was also newly divorced with a son. Soon they began e-mailing about the mutual problems of single parenthood. Months later, the woman and her children moved to Carla's town and into her house to live together.

My former radio show engineer, a single guy who worked nights and lived far from the studio, barely had time to go out to meet people, but being a computer geek, he often surfed the Net and checked out people's home pages. In one random search, he came upon a young woman's home page, with photos of her with her two young boys. As he read her statements about how she loves her children, his heart went aflutter. He sent her an e-mail, she responded, and they exchanged computer messages and later phone calls. Months later, he flew to her hometown in Rochester to meet her, and they fell in love. Sometime thereafter, tragedy struck, as she developed breast cancer and needed treatment. Yet Scott was by her side, and soon they were planning their wedding.

Dating Data

In a survey of 190 men aged 17–53, reported in an AIDS Care journal, a majority actually met in person, and 30 percent of those who admitted engaging in sex reported inconsistent safe sexual behavior. The results suggest that Internet chatters should be a target group for

Upsides to Cyberdating

There are many advantages to connecting on the Internet, including …

 ◆ **The immediacy.** Opportunities are just a click away. You can be writing a document or surfing the Net, and switch over immediately to e-mail, or send an instant message.

◆ **Cost.** Computer contact can be less costly than phone calls, and certainly less costly than a date. Compare service provider plans for the best deals.

◆ **Access.** Whether wireless or through a phone line, hook-ups are easily available.

◆ **Control.** You're in total control of when, where, and with whom you connect, so the pressure is off. Imagine going into a large room, having innumerable choices, feeling free to approach anyone without fear, only responding if you're in the mood, or moving on entirely if you feel like it—that's what's happening in cyberspace.

◆ **Practicing social skills.** You can make mistakes without severe consequences, because you never have to "see" that person again. Knowing that no one will ever have to know about strikeouts gives you more courage to try new approaches.

◆ **Learning verbal expression.** When you type your profile or messages, you practice expressing yourself the way you want to, and when the other person also types, you get a sense of how articulate and expressive the person is (and if he or she's too busy to spellcheck!).

◆ **Developing relationships.** Computer contact can help foster the friendship that is the basis for a long-lasting love by allowing the time and safety for a relationship to grow. If you hold off visual contact (though photos and web cams are increasingly common), you can start out relating to someone whose physical characteristics are a mystery— so the connection is based on more substantial qualities. Anticipation can build for meeting in person (one woman claimed that chat was the best beginning to hot talk on the phone and an even hotter in-person meeting).

◆ **Accessibility.** Those who live in small towns, isolated places, or who can't easily get out because of physical limitations, illness, or other conditions can still be in close touch.

Dating Data

The electronic age has boosted the odds for females who have feared a lack of men to go around. The typical ratio of male to female users ranks well over five to one. Some services report 75 percent male users.

Dating Data

For those on the go, computer access lines are increasingly available in public places. Ask information booths or store owners about their availability, and look for banks of telephones that are being outfitted. (Outfit your equipment accordingly.) Business centers of hotels are sometimes open to nonguests.

Downsides to Cyberdating

For all the convenience and advantages of online dating, there are also downsides and dangers. These include …

- **Dishonesty of others.** Since anybody can be anything on the Net, you have to be extremely wary of liars and con artists. Don't immediately believe everything you read. Take precautions before meeting in person. If you do meet, pick a busy public place in the daytime and bring a friend along.

- **Your own dishonesty.** As with personals in other formats, you can also hide behind the anonymity of words and make up stories about who you really are or what you really look like. But it's best to be honest about yourself, especially if you really want to meet someone in person. If you get to that point, you'll have a lot of explaining to do if you haven't been completely above board.

- **Escaping real relationships.** Cyberlove junkies can escape real-life person-to-person relationships without realizing it. Online minutes easily become online hours, without everyday dating problems. In-person love and sex can be replaced by eroticism from a distance. Don't just get off on netsex, but get an offline life and a lover you can see and feel!

- **Lack of personal touch.** Some "good, old-fashioned" matchmakers have major criticisms about Internet dating, like disappointment, deception (10-year old photos, married users looking for affairs), and danger (one divorcee even met a pedophile who was more interested in her children than in her). "There's no human touch by just typing a profile," one matchmaker said. Another maintains that nothing beats being treated like a real person from the start, with someone who really *cares*, whom you can call and talk to about your date, feelings, and needs.

- **Fears of revealing personal information on the Internet.** While there are some measures you can take, privacy is still not fully ensured when it comes to logging on the Net (even I have been the victim of an identity theft that involved the perpetrator using the Internet).

Woo Warning

As the saying goes, "If you cast your net too wide, you're bound to snag a few bad fish." Some married people take advantage of the Internet to have "virtual affairs" online, to escape marital blahs or have what they think is consequence-free seductions. But this betrays the spouse, and misleads singles, leading to disappointment and even divorce if the spouse finds out. There are ways to find out what's in your computer even if you think it's deleted.

New Cyranos: Changing Men in Positive Ways

This is one of my favorite points: Cyberdating can be credited for producing more passionate male lovers. Why? Because men are learning to express themselves in words (the very complaint women have always had), and though they feel more comfortable doing so computer-to-computer rather than in person, at least they're "talking."

A man can become Cyrano, winning the heart of his lady love with charming prose, like the fictional ugly poet who recited romantic soliloquies out of sight under the lady's balcony to stand in for a handsome but inexpressive Communicating through the Internet—without visuals—can force men to focus on something other than a woman's looks. This gives women not in the Julia Roberts–Cindy Crawford categories (which is nearly 100 percent of us) a far better fighting chance! Men benefit too, since cerebral lovemaking gives those Cyranos a fair chance to win the lady of their dreams over a more traditionally handsome—but less articulate—Prince Charming.

Online Dating Etiquette: Do's and Don'ts

Just as there is etiquette in dating (see Chapter 10 on flirting), there are guidelines if you want to use the Internet to meet people—and if you want cyberlove to cross over into real life. Here are some codes of etiquette to follow when communicating online whether in profiles, e-mails, or chat:

- ◆ DO be honest about yourself. If you ever get to meet in person, it's a rude awakening if you've said you're a 105-pound blonde and you're really not.

- ◆ DO respect the other person's privacy, without demanding too much.

- ◆ DO be wary of life stories that are too fantastic, glamorous, or dramatic to be believable. This person could be lying and a loser, or successful and bored, or any combination thereof.

- ◆ DO carefully pick your e-mail address and username. "Kitten girl" or "lovelonging" can lure a trickster or prowler, and "Loverboy" can imply that you're a player or a womanizer. Try out different names and see what responses you get.

- ◆ DO find out what information is available about you in cyberspace. Type your name into a search engine (such as www.google.com) and see what comes up (do this repeatedly because new information gets inputted). Find out what your server makes publicly available.

- ◆ DO have realistic expectations. You really can't judge compatibility, or a person's true personality, until you get to know someone face-to-face.

◆ DO be patient. Internet dating can be frustrating and it may take time to meet someone you really like.

◆ DO understand that cyberdating is subject to the same breakups as real-life dating (ceasing to respond, wiping out their online contact address, or e-mailing that it's over). In case of "cyberdumps," see Chapter 26 for tips on handling rejection.

◆ DO block a member who offends you or report them to the webmaster.

◆ DO have your antennae up for people putting you on. Trust your intuition. Notice if someone sounds too slick, stilted, is inconsistent, reluctant to reveal, or unreliable in connecting again.

◆ DO use a person's screen name as you would their real name in person.

◆ DO be courteous and pleasant with other members.

◆ DO make your e-mail response stand out (say what you found appealing about the other person's profile and how it relates to you, offer interesting tidbits about yourself, and let your sense of humor shine through).

◆ DO realize that online connecting may not be as easy as it seems. You can test out various approaches, but developing real skills takes time, energy, and commitment.

◆ DO be clear if you are not interested, instead of leading someone on. A simple "thanks, but I'm otherwise engaged" is gracious without being hurtful. You'd want to be let down easy too.

◆ DO keep a positive attitude!

◆ DO be wary of people using the service to advertise, create spam, and send slogans, hyperlinks, website addresses/URLs, or bulk mail.

◆ DO watch how the conversation in chat rooms is going before jumping in. Ask a question of the room in general or of a specific person, or pitch in an opinion. Use good communication tips from this book, just as you would in face-to-face encounters.

◆ DO be wary of "lurkers"—people who read along during a discussion without contributing.

◆ DON'T reveal too much about yourself initially (your real name, phone number, or other identifying information) until you know you can trust the person.

◆ DON'T be insensitive to how others react to you. If someone seems disinterested, back off.

◆ DON'T be ambiguous or confusing in what you say.

- DON'T jump too quickly into "talk-ing" about sex, just as you wouldn't in a real-life encounter.

- DON'T purge your resentment or anger from other bad experiences onto Internet contacts.

- DON'T use profanity or sexually abu-sive language.

Dr. Judy's Dating Do's

Attraction happens on several sensory levels (sight, sound, touch), so the more ways you con-nect (including the phone), the better you know each other and the stronger a foundation for a trusting relationship.

Evaluate the Service

You should be protected! Only join a service that protects its members, which is why I emphasize that you should read the rules and procedures. Make sure the service …

Woo Warning

The dangers of potential perverts prowling the web targeting children have become more known. Prevent problems by keeping computer equipment in a family room, set-ting specific times for use, and discussing safety.

- provides a friendly, warm environment, judged by how you "feel" using it. Make sure you feel as good as you would with a live person.

- reacts if you notify them that someone is using unpleasant communication. They should terminate that person's membership.

- respects your privacy—does not disclose your identity, phone number, or personal e-mail address without your permission.

- has detailed membership profiles to shorten your search.

- does not rope you into buying other products or services.

Posting Your Profile

Online dating services have preset profile forms, with stock questions like age, education, where you live, occupation, athletic interests, religious preferences, interests (art, music, dance, theater, sports, and so on), and smoking preferences. In my opinion, answers to open-ended questions tell you the most about a person.

Posting a good essay is key to drawing attention—or getting passed over! Remember, it's an ad. You have to think like any advertising executive designing an ad campaign for a product, where here, you're the product. What can you say about yourself that would make the person you want to attract take note, and want to "order" your product (you!)?

This isn't always easy, especially for people who are shy or modest. Turning it into a joke out of embarrassment ends up self-defeating. Roberto went on singles sites with his friends one night for fun. They decided to register him on a service and cooked up outlandish statements for his profile, clicking on entries they thought were funny in the questionnaire, but weren't really true about him (he never tasted Vietnamese food but they entered it anyway). What a waste of his and other people's time.

Here are some tips in putting together your profile or personal statement:

- Let your personality shine through. What are the most wonderful things about you?

- Be specific about what you are looking for in a date.

- Be honest. The truth will come out in the end—if you get any further.

- Ask friends to help you compose what you want to say (as long as they're honest, too). Practice aloud with them.

- Avoid negativity, self-deprecation and describing your *worst* qualities, although you might want to include some honest peccadilloes (you're so busy that you forget to water your plants, you pull all-nighters, so early birds should be forewarned).

- Include your best picture, but make sure it accurately shows you and is not some shot that's computer altered or from years ago. You may be hesitant to submit your photo, but photo ads get more responses.

- Keep it short and sweet. Save going on and on and free-associating for your therapist … or for later contacts.

- Review and edit what you wrote, making sure it's grammatically correct and free of typos (use the spellcheck feature on your computer).

- Be descriptive. Make your expressions come alive by giving a real example or lively adjective. Instead of saying "I'm smart," say "I got all A's in college." Describe your eyes as "emerald" instead of "green."

- Be creative. Look at the following samples to help stimulate your own creative juices.

Write Your Sample Profile Essay

The purpose of this exercise is to write a personal essay for your profile to get clear about how you would describe yourself and to clarify what you're looking for in a date. Write about yourself. Then describe the person you are looking for.

My personal profile: _____

_____

_____

What I'm looking for: _____

_____

_____

Examples of Profile Phrases

Here are some phrases that people have used in their personal ads (that come from a contest I hosted for *Details* magazine). I picked these samples because they represent some particularly vivid, honest, or humorous descriptions:

◆ "Always gets spring fever, into Sunday brunch and a good tennis game for a love match."

◆ "Priceless '60s mint condition, presently garaged, looking for experienced driver to step on my accelerator."

◆ "Looking for well-built muscle man—not too kinky, but into body worship."

◆ "Fifth Baldwin brother seeks Barbie with brains."

◆ "I admit I'll soon have to join Hair Club for Men."

◆ "By day I'm a mild-mannered businessman who does origami; by night I'm a winged creature who battles the forces of evil. If you're my damsel in distress, let me be your superhero."

◆ "Jane Fonda look-alike seeks rich, well-heeled, TV exec."

Turning Virtual Love into Real-Life Love

Many people ask whether they should meet a cyber-interest for a live date. The story usually goes that they have been e-mailing with someone for a while and now want to meet. However, what if you finally meet your love interest and that person doesn't live up to your expectations? Will the magic be gone when you meet face to face?

This is possible. The person's physical characteristics may not be to your liking: He may have less hair, she may be more full-figured. However, the advantage of meeting someone in person after you've developed some kind of contact or rapport online is just that—an advantage. You may be able to put aside the fact that the person doesn't fit your "type." You may have already developed a close, caring online relationship before physical attributes got in the way. You could be in for a happy surprise!

A Final Word on Cyberdating

As the Internet becomes more popular as a means to get dates, some singles are finding that cyberdating is too impersonal, that users are not completely honest when it comes to revealing personal information, or that in-person meetings never unfold. It is obvious to me, especially from my experience being on the radio, that people love to talk and make human contact, a need that will only increase as the mechanization of life, work, and relationships also increases. The more people sit in front of a monitor all day long, the more they will need real human contact.

Movie companies worried that easy accessibility of home videos would drive people away from the cinemas. But people still go to the movies because, among other things, they want to get out of the house. The same will be true of Internet dating. Though people will sit home and connect, they will still have the desire to reach out and touch someone.

The Least You Need to Know

- Used wisely, the Internet can be a valuable tool in meeting new people with whom you would likely never cross paths otherwise.

- Despite many advantages to online dating, there are also disadvantages; but on the whole, it's worth a try.

- Check out lots of services and ask friends for referrals before you pay to join. Check all the pages on the site, especially About Us and Terms of Use.

- Always be honest in your communications on the web, as in person.

- Meeting online can lead to real-life love, as long as you're honest and play it safe. Exercise caution when meeting any stranger in person.

Part 2

Preparing Yourself So You—and Others— Love You

Let me let you in on a big secret in dating: Sex appeal comes from self-appeal. You are most likely to meet someone when you are feeling your most attractive. Let's face it. Would you rather date someone who is insecure and down, or someone who's vibrant, energetic, and fun to be with? Look in the mirror. What do you see? Would you look forward to having an evening with you? Do you consider yourself a catch? I hope so—because then others will want to be with you, too!

Do you remember the old saying: "Smile and the whole world will smile back at you"? This is absolutely true! Self-confidence is contagious. If you feel good about yourself, you'll make others feel good about being around you … and ultimately about themselves. It becomes a positive cycle, upward. Read this section to find out great tips and exercises to boost your self-esteem and your social self. Remember, if you enjoy your own company, others will want you, too.

Chapter 7

Putting the Best *You* Forward

In This Chapter

- Become a master of attraction
- The steps to building self-esteem
- Exercises to discover the real you
- How to develop body confidence
- Talk yourself into self-love
- Get over the need for approval

> *"Girls don't seem to like me."*
>
> *"I can never get a date."*
>
> *"I'm not ugly, but I'm not great-looking either. How will I ever find somebody?"*

Do you indulge in negative thinking? Are you constantly dumping on yourself and imagining the bleakest future possible? In this chapter, I'll go over ways to boost your self-esteem. It's true that if you love yourself, others will be naturally drawn to you.

Give Yourself Permission to Like Yourself

What will you gain as you gain self-confidence? Sex appeal! People are drawn to self-confidence. I'm not saying you should be an egotistical, selfish narcissist, but neither should you be so humble or self-effacing that you fade into the background or put yourself last. Love yourself enough to be self-confident; this will draw others to you and give you a solid foundation from which to appreciate and love others.

Love yourself with the same unconditional love that a mother (ideally) gives a child. That means love yourself regardless of your IQ, your wardrobe, your job, or your looks.

Believe that you are your own best date and most entertaining companion. Too many people seek dates or mates because they are bored with themselves. If you bore yourself, there is little reason to think that someone else will be thrilled with your company. Give yourself all the love and attention you would like from the best partner.

Feel Deserving

Trevor told me: "I've been dating a woman who lately has been treating me like crap. She criticizes me constantly about everything from my clothes to the way I hold my fork. But I can't bear to think of my life without her." If you find yourself with people who don't appreciate you or who are overly critical, walk away. You deserve more. Learn to train your love antennae to pick up on positive signals and people who treat you with the respect and love that you deserve.

Embrace Your Individuality

One night I stood at a club watching a really cool female punk band, the Lunachicks. The kid to my right told me that he was wild for the guitarist, and that he'd even hung out with her and kissed her once. A few minutes later, the guy to my left said, "I can't stand that short girl playing the guitar," and described how he had met her also and been really turned off by her antics. Same girl, two guys, two opinions. Should she change so that guy number two changes his opinion of her? Should she punish herself because some guy finds her undesirable? Heck, no.

One person's poison is another's aphrodisiac. The very characteristic or behavior that turns one person off may turn another person on. There's the ultimate proof of this point in the story of Rudolph the Red-Nosed Reindeer, whose nose, you'll remember, made him the butt of the other reindeers' jokes, but was beloved by Santa, who gave him a prime spot at the front of the sleigh. So if you think your nose is too big, your chest too hairy, or your breasts too small, love yourself anyway. Someone will appreciate you for those qualities!

You in Your World

In classes I teach, I have people explain "Who Am I" by describing an object that is dear to them. Talking about the object eliminates self-consciousness and makes it easier to say things that are revealing about how you feel about yourself. For example, one of my students brought in a stamp, and talked about how stamping the date on everything helps her keep track of things. Saying that made her realize how organized and reliable she likes to be. Another student brought a saber like one from Star Wars that made him realize how he often feels vulnerable in life and wants to feel more powerful against people who challenge him.

Discover the Real You

True self-esteem means finding out who you really are. According to a certain psychological theory, the self is made up of different components: the real self (the inner you), the ideal self (what you'd like to be), and the social self (how others perceive you based on the face you show to the world). Think about all those components, and how they operate in the dating world.

Another exercise I use in my workshops and classes helps you gain insight into these three selves: what you think of as the "real you," as opposed to how you would like to be or what others think you are. This exercise offers clues about things that you would like to change about yourself. It also offers insight into the image you present to the world—which may or may not be the one you want to project. Finally, the exercise can help you integrate your three selves.

Describe yourself in the following table. Use as many adjectives or phrases that come to you. Write these down spontaneously without editing them.

Me as I See Myself (Real Self)	Me as I'd Like to Be (Ideal Self)	Me as Others See Me (Social Self)
I am:	I'd like to be:	Others see me as:
_____	_____	_____
_____	_____	_____
_____	_____	_____
_____	_____	_____

Interpreting Your Descriptions

Look closely at the adjectives you used in each column and compare the ways in which they differ. Connect any adjectives by drawing a line between them with a pen. The more similar the adjectives, the more comfortable and fulfilled you feel—your real and ideal images are in synch.

Review the adjectives in each column and put an "x" through the qualities you do not want to have. Imagine those no longer being a part of you. Now highlight with a highlighter pen or put a star next to the ones you like. Close your eyes and imagine yourself being this way—this makes it more likely that you will be.

Create Your Ideal

Imagine yourself the way you would like to be. The brain doesn't know the difference between a real image and one you fashion, so it will operate on whatever you picture. Visualize relating to someone in a charming, energetic way. Since your brain doesn't know if the image is true or false, your muscles will behave accordingly—your face will look as if you feel charming and energized.

Athletes have long understood this process of imagery, and will imagine a goal or an action before performing it. You can do the same thing with your love life. Visualize how you want to look, how you want to come across, and how you want your love life to be. Now try to experience how you would feel if all of these things were true.

I also recommend the "repeat performance" technique. Remember a time when you were at your best, most successful, or most seductive. Picture how you looked, sounded, and acted. Anchor this picture in your muscles and visceral body system by doing something physical (such as pressing two fingers together or snapping your fingers). Eventually, the physical act alone will trigger your nervous system to "remember" the outcome, and fire the appropriate mental and physical state associated with it, making it more likely that you will repeat this similarly successful behavior and positive mental state in the present.

Exercises to Help Build Self-Esteem

Building self-esteem is like having an exercise program to keep your body fit. You have to focus on certain activities and repeat them in order to change your bad habits, improve your outlook, and maintain the benefits. The following exercises will help.

Morning Wake-Up Call

Be your own perfect parent. Think of how you would wake up a child in the morning, with a smile and a cheerful, "Good morning, honey!" Instead of starting the morning with a sneer, slamming the alarm, cursing your reflection in the mirror, and dreading the day, use a mental channel changer to change the program in your brain and in your behavior. Say instead, "I've got something to make you happy today." This may seem unnatural at first, but if you do it, it can become a good habit.

Smile!

When you look in the mirror, whether you're shaving, brushing your hair, or checking your reflection in your car's rearview mirror, don't frown and point out your various flaws. Change the program in your brain and smile instead.

Be Your Own Cheering Section

Like sports players need a coach and cheering squad, you need ongoing pep talks to spark up your energy to do your best. When you feel your security waning and your shyness escalating, picture an angel on your shoulder cheering you on: "You can do it!"

Dating Data

As soon as you smile, your facial muscles alter your brain state to a calmer frequency, lifting your mood. Remember throughout the day to turn your lips into a smile even if you don't feel much like smiling. The physical "set" of your muscles will actually

Self-Pump (Instead of Self-Dump)

Whenever you feel down or afraid to approach someone for a date, remind yourself of all your wonderful qualities. If you tend to focus on the negative ("I'm too short and chunky," "My nose is too big," "I stutter when I'm nervous"), refocus your energy on the positive.

What happens when you constantly criticize yourself? People will eventually believe you. After all, who knows you better than you? Often we say negative things about ourselves as a kind of protection, to minimize other people's expectations, or to deflect their jealousy. Avoid this trap. Instead, tell others all the terrific things about yourself, what you do, what you know, and what you can do for them.

Do this exercise. Quickly think of three good things about yourself and list them in the first column of the following table (I'll get to the other two columns in a moment).

	Self-Description	Up the Ante 1x	Up the Ante 2x
I am:	_____	_____	_____
	_____	_____	_____
	_____	_____	_____

By writing down your assets, you fix them more firmly in your mind. Next, get a tape recorder and record the same information. Before you go to sleep at night, play the tape—the semi-hypnotic pre-sleep state makes thoughts stick more in your mind.

Do a visualization exercise where you picture your biggest fan making a speech about how great you are. Save complimentary notes from friends and colleagues, and take them out when you need a lift. I have to smile when I re-read my mother's birthday cards where, being a master of superlative adjectives, she describes me as "the most wonderful, beautiful, gracious, creative, thoughtful, independent, energetic, stimulating, loving daughter"—I pause on each adjective and drink in how it feels to be that way.

If you have similar cards or letters, put the messages on a small card and keep them in your wallet. Refer to the card while you're on hold, in an elevator, on the subway—whenever you have spare time. Or put these words of praise on tape and carry the tape with you to play in your portable tape player. As you hear the words over and over, they'll become part of your self-concept. Don't feel embarrassed or silly doing this. Take these in as honest truths about yourself. Revel in your triumphs enthusiastically and extensively. Enjoy your successes.

Now you're ready for the exercise I call "Pump It Up." I use it at many college lectures and other workshops. Go back to your asset list and get ready to fill in columns two and three. "Up the ante" on each asset—the next highest level of that quality, and then the next level after that. Do you feel good? Say you feel good … now better … now *great!*

For example, if you wrote "funny" in column 1, write "hysterical" in the second column. Up the ante again in the third column, writing "side-splitting." If you wrote "smart" in the first column, write "very intelligent" in the second column, and then "brilliant" in the third. Now, say "I am" and call yourself aloud the qualities in the third column.

Dating Data

Treat yourself like a modern day love goddess or god, advises interfaith minister Laurie Sue Brockway, author of *A Goddess Is a Girl's Best Friend: A Divine Guide To Finding Love, Success and Happiness*. That means, "honor yourself and the men/women in your life … desire partnership based on soulful and sacred loving … recognize a connection to the divine, or the creative power of our universe, even if they do not call it Goddess or God … Most importantly, be true to your own heart and, where dating and relationships are concerned, be guided by intuition and the call of the soul."

Self-Talk

All of us have a running monologue going on in our heads, as we comment on situations, feelings, and moments in our day. Sometimes the monologue is filled with negative messages ("How could you be so stupid? He really hates you now. You'll never find someone.") Negative thoughts deplete self-esteem and create self-sabotaging actions. We turn people away by the "vibes" we send out.

Get rid of negative thoughts in two ways. First, picture a street sign in your brain that reads "No dumping allowed." Next, go into the computer program in your brain, print out the negative program (the one that says, "You're a jerk, you blew that, no one loves you"), then press the delete button and type in a new program, one that says "I'm a neat person," "I am a lot of fun to be around," "I have so many interesting things to do and say in my life," "Lots of people want to be around me because I am stimulating, warm, and fun."

Dr. Judy's Dating Do's

Be your own public relations agent! Think about what a public relations agent does to promote a product. That person pinpoints all of the attractive features so that others will be interested. Do the same for your best product—you!

Affirmations

Affirmations are a form of positive self-talk. The rule on affirmations is to start your self-affirming statement with "I am" (not "Other people say I am …"). Don't start with a negative, such as "I am not fat, sloppy, or boring." When the word "not" is

Woo Warning

Avoid saying negative things about yourself in the hope that the other person will say it's not true to bolster your self-esteem. The other person may not bite, leaving you in a lurch.

attached to a statement, the mind conjures up the negative images (of fat, sloppy, and boring) anyway. It's like being told, "Don't think about a pink elephant." What's the first thing that comes to mind? A pink elephant, of course. Resist putting thoughts in your head that you don't want your mind to latch on to. Instead, put only those thoughts in your head you want your mind to remember.

Express Yourself

Do this self-expression exercise. Look into a mirror and think of an encounter with someone. Speak your mind—do this without any fear of judgment, criticism, or disapproval. Watch your face and your expressions, and picture being another person looking into your face. Adjust your face to please you, and practice different looks that make you appear commanding or sexy.

Center Yourself

Dr. Judy's Dating Do's

Meditation is a good way to relax and achieve inner peace and higher states of consciousness. Research proves it works. Get a copy of my book, *The Complete Idiot's Guide to Tantric Sex* (see Appendix A) to learn all about breathing techniques and other intriguing practices to bring you to these higher states.

A lot of self-consciousness, nervousness, and fear comes from a feeling of being "outside" yourself, as you worry about being judged, rejected, or acting foolish. Do the following technique to regain your "center." Take a deep breath and follow your breath into your body, down into your solar plexus (a network of nerves below your rib cage and behind your stomach). Press there, from the front, with your hand to help guide the breath. Focus on your feet, and feel their connection to the floor. Then press on your "third eye" (the spot on your forehead right between your eyes), concentrating your mind and breath toward that point to focus on your spiritual energy, giving you strength.

Ghost-Bust Your Past

Past rejections and bad dating experiences over the years may still haunt you. I call those "ghosts of the past." Do some ghost-busting. That is, separate yourself from past hurts and prevent them from interfering with the present. You are not a slave to the past. Whatever happened then does not have to repeat now. You can redesign your life by making new love choices, and acting in new ways that will lead to happier outcomes.

Dr. Judy's Dating Do's

Growing up on military posts (my father was a dentist in the Army), I fully appreciate the Army slogan, "Be all that you can be." Realize your potential by remembering this. Dress and act your best at all times. Instead of saving your best clothes for special occasions, take them out and wear them! When you look good, you'll feel good, too.

Be Thankful for What You Have

Appreciate what you are, what you have, and what you do. In Japanese Naikan therapy, you say "Thank you" to all the objects and people in your life. Say "Thank you" to your toothbrush every morning for keeping your teeth clean, "Thank you" to the movie seat for supporting you while you are being entertained, and "Thank you" to your mother for all the times she calls to ask how you are. Showing such appreciation makes you realize how many people and things support you in your life.

Forgive Yourself

Emily says, "When I was younger, I constantly went out with guys who cheated on me and treated me badly. Now I try to date men who care about me, but I feel bad and embarrassed about my past, and don't want to share the details with anyone."

Progress and change take time. You may find yourself taking two steps forward and one step back. Appreciate your forward motion. Talk to yourself and accept that you did what you did for a reason. Keep up your affirmations: "I am worthy of love." Acknowledge your progress.

Make Yourself Over

Magazines are full of make-overs. Treat yourself to one. Try new things and take risks. It's fun! Do those things that you always said you'd do if you had the guts, time, or opportunity. This can be as simple as trying a new hairstyle, a new style of clothing, or a new tone of voice. You'll feel empowered by being assertive.

Body Boosting

It's hard to relax on a date if you've got the "What-if-she-doesn't-like-my-body" blues. These exercises will help you learn to love yourself—so that other people will!

Developing Body Confidence

Most of us have at least one body part we obsess about, a part of us that makes us feel unattractive. The irony is that other people may hardly notice the part that we're so focused on! It can be unnerving to think about someone seeing you in a bathing suit or naked for the first time, with no slimming black dress or dazzling fuchsia sweater to distract their eye. Fears that you won't measure up can put a real damper on dating.

Body Talk Exercise

Here's another exercise I use in my workshops. This one shows how body confidence is the key to self-confidence. It's based on a popular technique in Gestalt therapy that involves treating each body part as if it were a separate being communicating to you about how it feels. In this exercise, you "speak" to the body part as if it were a person. In this way, you find out what it has to tell you about its own condition.

For example, say you have frequent backaches. Sit quietly on a chair and close your eyes and put your consciousness into that body part—in this case, your back. Ask, "Back, what are you telling me?" Now imagine being your back and have a conversation with yourself. For example, your back might say, "I am tired of holding you up all day." Press for your back to talk on a deeper, more revealing level, like "I am hurting because I feel like you put a burden on me. I am buckling under the strain of all that anger you are holding in." This exercise can give you clues about what you are really feeling.

Look in a full-length mirror at your body. Rate how positive or negative you feel about your various body parts (with 0 being very negative and 10 being very positive). Write the numbers on the picture if you're using one. If any part gets a rating below 5, have a "body conversation." Imagine what that body part would say to you and what you would reply in order to feel more positive about it. For example, describe what your arms/breast/penis/hips are saying to you. If you write, "I'm fat, please love me, I can't take the pressure," you might consider responding, "I love you anyway, don't feel bad, it'll be fine."

Everyone has a body part they hate. What's yours? Bobby hates his big nose. Joni gets disgusted with her narrow eyes. Learn to love what you hate. If that part of your body could talk, what would it say? Love me. Ultimately, you can find someone who will love you if not for it, in spite of it. Consider how supermodel Cindy Crawford turned her mole into a million-dollar trademark, or how Jay Leno's square jaw is part of his distinctive look.

Dr. Judy's Dating Do's

Build sexual self-confidence by appreciating your private parts. I'm always surprised by how many women (in comparison to men) haven't looked at their genitalia, or don't love what they see. After a bath, examine those parts and love them.

Posture

There is scientific evidence that posture affects mood—slouching produces a down mood, while standing tall lifts your mood. Try it. Here's another exercise I use in my workshops. Take a deep breath and stand tall. Imagine a root running from your feet into the floor (grounding you, making you feel secure). Now imagine a string running from the top of your head into the ceiling, lifting you up. Picture your spinal column giving you a solid base, where no rejection can blow you over.

Woo Warning

Most of us have mild dissatisfaction with our bodies ("My nose is too wide" or "My shoulders are too narrow"). But if you experience severe body disgust, what therapists call body dysmorphia, please seek therapy.

The Moving Body Exercise

Our physical actions both reflect and affect our inner being. For example, a frown reflects the body's inner sense of sadness and also "freezes" the emotional state into that state of sadness. Merely by taking another body position, the physical state can be changed. For example, research in neuro-linguistic programming (NLP) has shown that looking upward lifts the mood. The upward look of the eyes connects, or triggers, the brain to lift the spirits or emotions.

Overcome Your Dependence on Others

So many women, to this day, still try to wrap themselves around men, as if their life has no meaning without this attachment. When they do this to unavailable, unattainable men, it's like trying to squeeze blood from a stone. What these women really need to do is focus on themselves—be their own tree, with solid roots, rather than clinging vines.

For example, Josie was going out with a charismatic TV reporter. Every time they were out together, people listened with rapt attention to his stories and opinions. He was constantly being invited places, and Josie loved living in his glow. When he dumped her, she was devastated. She had been living her life through him. Josie wasn't able to achieve true satisfaction, so she sought it through other people. When she lost her boyfriend, she felt as if she'd lost herself.

If you feel that you are overly dependent, follow this bit of advice: Become the person you're looking to marry. Don't look for a partner to fulfill your dreams. You won't become rich, great-looking, fun, or fulfilled by clinging to someone who is. Rather than seeking a mate to fulfill all your needs, become whole yourself.

Making Dreams Come True

We all have dreams of how we would like our life to be. Realizing your dream brings you closer to realizing your potential and increasing your self-esteem. Here are ways to do that:

◆ Make a list of everything you desire in life, and imagine that you are achieving it now in the present. For example, say, "My body is looking more like the way I like" instead of "I want to lose weight."

◆ Be positive. Negatives only reinforce that negative behavior.

◆ Be specific. Think "I will sing more and enjoy free time to take long walks" instead of "I want to be happier."

◆ Make an action plan that you put in your daily planner or calendar. Translate "I want a rich guy" into "I want to be rich" And then design a plan of action on how you can make money, by asking for a raise or getting a new job.

As Nike advertises, "Just do it." Japanese Morita therapy advises the same: Stop obsessing over feelings and just "do what has to be done."

Free Yourself from the Desperate Need for Approval

Almost everyone has mild fears of rejection and a need for approval, whether about dating ("What if he doesn't like me?"), shopping ("If I return this, what will the salesperson think of me?"), or work ("If I speak up at this meeting, will they think I'm foolish?"). The desire to please others can be charming and promise to enhance your self-esteem, but the need for approval becomes a serious problem when you lose your sense of self, your self-respect, and your self-control.

Barbara was so desperate for Kent's approval that she couldn't get dressed for a date without trying on everything in her closet. She would then ask him over and over if he liked her outfit—turning him off with her insecurity. Larry was so afraid he'd say the wrong thing to a date that he'd barely speak at all—and women found him either dull or snotty. Ironically, people who desperately need approval sabotage themselves, suffocating others with demands or driving them away.

Here are some ways to break free from seeking approval:

◆ Deliberately change thoughts or beliefs that you need someone else's approval to get by.

◆ Realize that the worst that can happen is temporary or tolerable.

◆ Change your behavior to do what pleases you first.

◆ Get to the root of your insecurity (for example, did your father constantly tell you that you were worthless?).

◆ Rehearse behaviors that risk disapproval; for example, practice saying no and disagreeing with a date.

◆ Decide what you need and either fulfill the need yourself or ask someone else for help. This can be a simple request ("Could you please get me a glass of water?"), or a more emotional request ("I'd like a hug").

Take Yourself Out on a Date

I am very serious when I say you need to take yourself out on a date. Go out to dinner, a play, or the movies. Treat yourself to the very best. It will raise your self-esteem and give you untold independence. You will never again be devastated if you're alone on a Saturday night, or if someone turns you down (despite the great tickets you got especially for the evening).

Think of something you'd really love to do. Ask yourself out to do it. Make plans, just as if you were trying to impress the most exciting date. Imagine yourself saying yes and getting excited. Mark the date on your calendar. When the day comes, get dressed up as you would for someone special.

You should imagine another "you" going with you. Have an imaginary conversation about what fun you're having and how great it is to be with you. Say all the things to yourself that you would want to hear from a special date.

This should be a fun and satisfying exercise—one that will shore up your confidence and give you an excuse to spend a little time and money doing what you'd like to do but never had a partner to do it with. Think of it as an inoculation against rejection, a character builder, a self-esteem booster. You'll also gain independence that will serve you through any date.

Getting Feedback

As you must know by now, I am very much in favor of open communication. If you wonder what someone's thinking, or why he or she behaved a certain way, ask. If you can't figure out what your date meant by that remark, ask. Don't waste time wondering. A date is like a research project—giving you an opportunity to learn about your own (and others') motivations, fears, and needs. And just like any other research project or experiment, you must collect data to make progress.

Do your dating research. If someone seems interested in you, ask for feedback. If they say they want to stop seeing you, ask for an explanation (reassure them that you're not trying to control or change them, but just want to learn something for next time). Ask questions like "What did you mean when you said …?" or "How did you feel when I …?"

Be prepared that some people may be unwilling (or incapable) of responding honestly. They may be afraid, inexperienced, or insecure. If you like open talk, it's best to associate with people who also like open talk, or you may wind up frustrated and unfulfilled.

Don't Put Up with Crap

Yes, "crap" is a nasty word but it's a word that people use to describe how they feel when they experience bad treatment and downright disrespect. Take Gloria, who gets swept off her feet but suddenly left out in the cold. Or Tony, who spends big bucks on fancy dining for his dates but never gets return phone calls. It's easy to end up feeling depressed and discouraged, and decide that dating is, well, not worth it.

Dr. Judy's Dating Do's

Measure how much attention, respect, and love you receive from a date by comparing the treatment to a loaf of bread: Are you getting crumbs, a few slices, or the whole loaf? Trust your instincts. If you feel bad about an interaction, stay away.

You don't have to put up with disrespect. Never blame yourself for being abused. But do take some responsibility. According to my "Mirror Law of Attraction" described in Chapter 2, we bring to ourselves relationships that reflect what our own needs and insecurities are, giving us the opportunity to see exactly who we are in the reflection of the person we are with. If you put up with bad treatment, consider whether you feel you really don't deserve to be treated better—and decide that you do!

Beware of Suitors with Unsuited Confidence

Gravitate toward people who make you feel good and stay away from those who drag you down. Watch out for these types of people:

- **Braggarts.** Bob loves to wine and dine women, but can't figure out why he never gets a second date. When I asked how he acts on his dates, he explained, "I told them they'd never find a guy who would treat them better. I have a fancy car, know all the best wines, and have been places they have only dreamed about." Bob's excessive self-promotion portrays a desperate need to impress and reveals his deep-seated insecurity that ultimately drives people away.

◆ **Apologizers.** Pointing out your weaknesses can be just as off-putting as excessive bragging. Sally admitted to me that she thinks she's pretty, but if a man compliments her, she quickly tells him how homely she was as a child, or that it's only makeup, or just the outfit she's wearing. Her secret hope is that the man will heap on more compliments to counter her self-criticisms. Instead, men tend to take her at her word and back away. This is self-sabotage at its saddest.

◆ **Manipulators.** Peter's girlfriends are always jealous and possessive. At first, he's flattered by their behavior, but always ends up cheating on them. Deep down, Peter is projecting his own jealousy and possessiveness onto the girls he dates as a way of denying his own insecurities. Their behavior acts as a mirror of his own, and when he senses this (unconsciously), he gets angry and punishes them for it by pushing them away.

◆ **Abusers.** Statistics of the number of women and men mistreated in relationships is shocking. But awareness makes singles more determined not to put up with these negative experiences. Check out Chapter 18 on dating disasters, which covers how to know if you're in an abusive relationship, why you might stay, and how to get out.

Alcohol and Drugs: False Self-Esteem Boosters

These two stories have a common theme:

◆ "I went to an office party where I had too much to drink. My co-worker told me that I really came on to my boss. I don't remember a thing."

◆ "My boyfriend wanted me to have sex with one of my girlfriends. I was shy about it, but after a couple of drinks I did it anyway. Now I can't even look at the girl when I see her, and I'm afraid that she's after my boyfriend."

Research has shown that alcohol does lower inhibitions. One drink over dinner, in a responsible dating situation, can give you the necessary boost to feel more relaxed and comfortable. But beware, because excess alcohol leads to impaired judgment, which can get you into trouble. Everyone has a different tolerance level, but the danger level appears to be roughly three drinks. Overindulging leaves you prey to anyone else's desires, and you are apt to do things you wouldn't consider if you weren't drunk. I hear too many sad stories about unwanted pregnancies, betrayals, and contracted diseases because someone drank too much and then claimed that "it just happened."

The Loser Magnet

Janice complained, "I constantly fall for losers, guys who can't hold a job, or who are always down on their luck. Why do I do this?" She does it because it boosts her own shaky self-esteem and gives her a false sense of power. Janice was finally able to see what she was doing: "If I can help them, I feel better about myself, but maybe the only real way to feel better about myself is to do it for me, not for them." Right on, Janice.

The Least You Need to Know

- A healthy self-esteem is the ultimate sex appeal.
- What you visualize is what most likely will happen, so visualize dating success.
- Consider yourself your own best date.
- Remember, you deserve the best life and love has to offer you; don't put up with crumbs.
- Replace self-dumping with self-pumping.
- Enjoy your own company and you'll naturally attract the company of others.

Chapter **8**

From Shy to Social Butterfly

In This Chapter

- ◆ What makes people shy?
- ◆ Tips for overcoming shyness
- ◆ Listen to how you talk
- ◆ Ten steps to overcoming love panic
- ◆ Beyond shyness: symptoms of social phobia

> *"I just can't go up to talk to any girl. I get so tongue-tied and end up going home alone."*
> —Mike, sound engineer at a rock music club

Nearly everyone has experienced shyness at some point in their lives. Even politicians, seemingly extroverted comics, and celebrities admit to it. Men feel it as much as women do. But to win in the dating world, it's helpful to be comfortable stepping out of that shell when you want to.

What is shyness? At best, it's being reserved; at the most painful, it's feeling so insecure or fearful of being judged that you don't act like yourself or you withdraw completely. Shyness can be caused by a history of rejection, by rules and behavioral patterns instilled in us as children, and even by chemical imbalances in our brains. No matter what the source, shyness is not something you have to suffer from.

In this chapter, I encourage you to redefine your idea of shyness. Don't see it as a negative trait. Shy people can be charming and endearing. For every shy person there can be a wonderful partner, shy or not, who adores you the way you are. Just know that you can be less shy if you choose, and here I offer help on how to do that.

Why Am I So Shy?

Shyness may be a result of past experiences of not being accepted or loved. Shy people may have been bullied or criticized by their peers or by adults when they were children. They may also be copying their parents' own shyness. Or they may have been taught to be cautious, being told "Don't try that" or "Don't speak until you're spoken to."

Shyness can also be inherited. For instance, 10 percent of the population is born with "stranger anxiety," which is partly caused by the balance of certain chemicals (monomaine oxidase, serotonin, and cortisol) in the brain. Researchers at Harvard University also found that shyness may be governed by the amygdala, an almond-shaped "switching center" in the brain responsible for stimulating reactions like fear and withdrawal. But even if the genes fit, you don't have to wear them. You can change by increasing your confidence.

These explanations aren't meant to put the blame elsewhere or let you off the hook— you are responsible for how you are.

Disinterest or Shyness?

I've often been asked the question: "Why do some men and women act like they're not interested, when you're almost 100 percent sure that they are?"

Some people are too shy, inexperienced, or socially scared to be up front about their interest. They don't know what to say or what to do if you respond. Or they're afraid their friends will tease them! I'm reminded of the classic scenario of the boy who pulls the girl's pigtails in class, making her think he hates her, when really he likes her. His actions are his awkward way of showing her attention. The lesson: consider being more direct if you like someone instead of playing games or acting indifferent to cover up your feelings.

Dating Data

Dating is like the stock market. Consider if you are a bull, a risk-taker who is not afraid to put himself "out there", or a bear, someone who takes things slow and is more cautious about what's going on.

As I mentioned, shyness can be charming, disarming (making others less fearful or threatened), and engaging (inspiring others to make you more relaxed and comfortable). But it can also give the wrong impression, and intimidate or frighten others away.

Sadly, shy people often risk being thought of as boring. Kelly complained, "Men always break up with me because they say I'm too nice," when she is really just easygoing and laid-back. Whenever someone asks, "Where do you want to go?" or "What do you want to do?" she says, "Whatever." Her ambiguity leaves others with the burden of being in control, and also leaves them feeling confused about who she really is and how they should behave. Kelly should instead speak up and be clear about her preferences: "I'd like to eat Italian food" or "I'm in the mood for a funny movie."

Overcoming Shyness

Overcoming shyness may seem overwhelming or impossible. Not so! It takes effort, just like changing any behavior, but it is very possible—and well worth the effort. Remember, your fears are inevitably much worse than the reality of a situation. Here are some helpful tips on how overcome shyness:

◆ Work on improving your self-confidence, as I discussed in the previous chapter.

◆ Understand why you are shy. What are you afraid of? Judd was afraid girls would think he's a loser. "I'm losing my hair and I'm shaped like a pear," he bemoaned. Judd is his own worst critic. People don't focus on our flaws as we do (and if someone does, do you really want to be with that person anyway?).

◆ Play-act. In the privacy of your home, act out the way you would like to be— taken to the extreme. For instance, walk around the room puffing out your chest and raising your voice. By going to the extreme, you slough off hidden anxieties, embarrassment, and shame, and come back to your center refreshed and reenergized.

Dating Data

Studies have shown that men often suffer more from shyness than women because they are expected to be more assertive in dating, careers, and life in general.

◆ Mimic someone you admire who is not shy. Imitation is a key to learning. Other people's actions can be a guide on how to act the way you would like.

◆ Do something that makes you feel good about yourself. Start a project, clean out clutter, or master a musical instrument. Becoming a success is a potent aphrodisiac to turning you—and others—on.

◆ Be prepared to be seen or discovered whenever, wherever. Many people don't bother to look their best some days, either out of laziness or thinking that it won't matter. I'll always remember one hairdresser who chastised me for letting my hair get uneven and unruly. When I offered excuses—that I was too busy and had other priorities—he threw his hands up dramatically, proclaiming, "Oh my dear, but every day is show time!"

◆ Forget the "I'm not worthy" routine. Keep your mind on a power track with affirmations. Repeat to yourself, "I am a worthwhile person." No matter what happens, you are worthy. You deserve to have and be what you want.

◆ Redefine shyness (not as fear, but as enjoying observing situations).

◆ Combat your fear of rejection. Expect and accept that everyone at one time or another gets rejected. Rather than taking rejection personally, decide that you and that person just don't "fit" or the timing is off, and move on to something or someone else to distract and engage you.

◆ Take risks. Nothing ventured, nothing gained. As one woman, Marianna, told me, "Everything in life has an end, so take risks, because you have nothing to lose." Or, as another friend says, "If you don't *take* a chance, you don't *have* a chance."

◆ Use self-disclosure. Confess to people that you're shy, so they won't misread you. The confession in itself can be endearing and an icebreaker to a conversation. If it scares someone away, that person isn't right for you anyway.

◆ "Practice" dating. Nothing feeds success like success. As you gain more pleasurable dating experiences, you can feel more confident and your anxieties ease.

Feeling good about yourself is a key to overcoming shyness. One way to do this is to look your best. You must believe that you are attractive and worth getting to know better. Don't underestimate the possibility of overcoming any limitations you have in the looks department by making up for it with your energy, excitement, interests, and personality. But do make the most of your looks. Play up your good features (with a hairstyle that accentuates your pretty eyes, or form-fitting shirts that show off your muscular build) and hide less desirable features. Good grooming always pays off, so pay attention to cleanliness and good style.

Also consider dressing up once in awhile; you don't always have to wait for special occasions. Are you one of those people who buys nice clothes and saves them for special days—then rarely ends up wearing them? Put away raggedy old things—unless you can make them stylish, you'd do better to give them up.

Do the "closet-clean-out." Organizing experts say a good rule of thumb is "When in doubt, throw it out." They recommend getting rid of clothes clutter by clearing out whatever you haven't worn in a year (although you might want to save meaningful things). This makes room for new things. Also, keep your best outfits in good shape, ready to go.

Let's Talk

How you talk and what you talk about can say a lot about your personality—whether you're timid and shy or outgoing and spontaneous. Learn to speak up and say what's on your mind. Also, listen to your figures of speech. Do you repeat phrases such as "like" (which, by the way, drives me crazy), and "uh"? I once knew a woman who ended every sentence with "that is." Valley girls are made fun of because they make every sentence into a question. If your voice inflection goes up at the end of every sentence, concentrate on deliberately dropping your voice at the end of a thought.

Practice your most inviting and soothing voice. Like a sweet smell, a voice can emanate sex appeal. Speak deliberately, at a medium pace and volume. Then ask the other person, "What's the most interesting thing you did today?"

Broaden your vocabulary. My father taught me the value of a broad vocabulary (he'd open the dictionary and test me), so now my favorite book is the thesaurus, as I enjoy hours of looking up synonyms for words I'm using even right now for this book, to get the exact right one. Do this and you'll get more enjoyment out of talking with people. Purchase study guides for the GREs (Graduate Record Exams) that are available in university bookstores, and contain lists of vocabulary words students need to be familiar with in order to do well on the test. Or jot down a few words from the dictionary, and study them while on the train or in your car. My radio producer, Scott Hodges, admitted on the air that he keeps a dictionary in his bathroom, and studies a new page for interesting words every time he is on the toilet.

Use these new words in conversations or e-mails to people. Also, practice describing things in interesting ways, with vivid imagery. In radio—called "theater of the mind"—you learn to paint pictures with words. Instead of simply saying she has pretty eyes, say her eyes were "glowing" or "piercing."

Read good books to expand your vocabulary and give you ideas about how to describe things in interesting ways (as well as to give you something to talk about with others).

Dr. Judy's Dating Do's

Like everything else, learning to speak up and speak well takes practice. Make it a point to speak to three new people each day, whether at the supermarket, in a movie line, or in an elevator. Be prepared for different responses; some people may be less than enthusiastic about your approaches.

Love Panic

Francine stood in front of Rick's door, ready to knock, when suddenly she was flooded with a rush throughout her body. The hallway felt warm, but her hands were cold.

Her heart started pounding, and her knees went so weak she feared she would collapse. Adam explained, "I want to ask this woman out, but every time I look at her I end up sweating like a pig." And when Jocelyn was out with Tom, a guy she felt was "perfect" for her, she couldn't stop shivering.

Francine's flushes, Adam's sweats, and Jocelyn's shivers are symptoms of love jitters—frightened feelings you experience when faced with someone you're attracted to. It's like the alarm you'd feel if you were standing on the edge of a 30-story building with no handrail, or if a car was coming at you head-on at 65 miles an hour. People experience these things in situations ranging from giving a speech to having sex.

But what's the difference between love panic and just having a case of the jitters? We all experience dating jitters sometimes, but intense fear can stop you dead in your tracks. Jitters can be helpful—to prepare you to deal with a stressful situation or motivate you to solve a problem—but love panic can flood you with so much anxiety that it interferes with your ability to do what you want and to be your charming self.

Woo Warning

Symptoms of love panic are intense terror, trembling, sweating, chest pain, heart palpitations, shortness of breath, choking or smothering sensations, hot flashes or chills, nausea, faintness, numbness, and feelings of unreality.

You're having a serious bout of love panic if your symptoms prevent you from taking your desired action(s), are persistent and frequent, or make you send out the wrong signals. For instance, Francine would have a real problem if she vowed never to return to Rick's house again for fear she would pass out at his door.

So how do you handle love panic? Both drug and non-drug therapies have been developed in the past decade to treat panic attacks. What works best depends on the person, but often a combination of therapy and medication is effective. If you think you've crossed the line from simple jitters to panic and extreme anxiety, please seek professional help (start by checking the resources in Appendix A).

Here are 10 tips that are designed to help change self-defeating thinking and actions:

1. Understand the experience. Examine your symptoms, whether you're experiencing a racing heartbeat or weak knees. Why do you think your body is acting the way it is? For instance, Jocelyn realized that although she thought Tom was perfect, she also knew she wasn't ready to have sex with him like he wanted. As a result, her body was reflecting her emotions.

2. Instead of interpreting your racing heartbeat as an impending heart attack, your breathlessness as a sign of suffocation, and your crazy thoughts that you're going mad, label your feelings as signs of fear. Reassure yourself that you feel

cold or shaky because you're nervous, and that it's okay to feel nervous. Try one of my favorite techniques: paradoxical intention. Here you reframe the experience as the opposite of how you would normally see it. For example, instead of identifying nervousness as being a negative, purposefully see it as a good sign—that you are excited for action.

3. Instead of trying to get rid of your feelings, become mobilized by them; embrace them to propel you into action. My famous rule to follow is: Turn anxiety into action. Purposefully slow yourself down by breathing more evenly and letting your energy pour out (energy sparks excitement). The former will make you more sensual and the latter more exciting. Instead of Francine holding back her hand from knocking on the door, she should knock more vigorously.

4. Admit nervousness instead of hiding it. Pretending to be calm and collected often escalates fear and self-consciousness. Instead, confidently announce that you are excited, not scared. When Rick opens the door, Francine should admit: "I'd love to appear calm and collected, but my heart is actually beating a mile a minute, from rushing here and from being excited."

5. Brainwash yourself with positive affirmations. Instead of worrying, "Do I look okay? Does he like me?" fill your mind with self-loving thoughts: "I'm a great person and I'm fun to be with."

6. Rationalize your responses. Instead of worrying about how you responded, reassure yourself that you can always have another chance at another time (to explain your reactions to the person or to behave differently).

7. Distract yourself from your nervousness by focusing on something else. Think about the food you're eating or the music you're listening to, since the brain can only think one thought at a time. These thoughts will replace your anxious thoughts about how you're coming across, how you look, and whether your date likes you.

8. Breathe to calm down. Anxiety causes your throat and chest muscles to tighten, which constricts your breathing—all of which make it difficult to talk. Inhale deeply through the nose and exhale through the mouth. Repeat this three times before you speak.

9. Give yourself an "out"—one that is actual or imaginary—from the anxiety-provoking situation. If you're at a get-together and you see a woman you'd like to speak to but realize that you're becoming noticeably nervous, make a graceful retreat if you have to, and go to the restroom or another spot for an "emotional break."

10. Move around or do some activity. Even making gestures can help you to relax and clear your mind. Physical activity burns off nervous energy and increases blood flow to the brain, which makes you more relaxed.

Social Phobia

When shyness and love panic become extreme, it is called *social phobia*. You are suffering from social phobia if …

◆ You avoid people altogether. You won't eat, write, or speak in front of people, won't use public bathrooms, and won't answer the phone. You may even refuse to leave the house.

◆ You experience an unprovoked episode of at least four of the above symptoms within a month, or one attack followed by the fear of having another.

Besides medication, types of therapy used to treat people with social phobia include behavioral therapy, exposure therapy, and panic control treatment.

Behavioral therapies involve breathing and relaxing exercises to help you become less sensitive to a situation by reintroducing you in small steps to the source of your fear while you're feeling calm. In exposure therapy, a therapist accompanies you while you face your fears in the real world. In panic control treatment, physical sensations of fear are aroused in the safety of the therapist's office (this may make you queasy, but if you feel dizzy when dating, you might be spun around in a chair until you are dizzy enough to make the point that dizziness is survivable—and does not cause heart attacks or death).

Woo Warning _____

If you think you're experiencing social phobia, seek professional help. Check the contacts in Appendix A for more information.

More probing therapy includes examining sources of deep emotional conflict that may stem from childhood. During this kind of therapy, some questions I ask my patients are:

◆ What important person in your life have you lost? Losing a parent, close friend, or love—through death, divorce, or other circumstances—can make you afraid of investing emotions in anyone else because the pain of loss is too great.

◆ Were you ever afraid to leave home? Dating fears can sometimes be traced to early separation anxiety, when you were scared to go to school for fear your mother would not come back to pick you up, or be there for you when you came home.

- What are you afraid of losing if you win the date you want? I know this sounds crazy at first, but some people have a "fear of success" because they feel unworthy of success. Or they get a pay-off for suffering (called "secondary gains"). For example, you may complain about being lonely, but secretly enjoy benefits from complaining, such as self-pity, sympathy from others, or avoiding fear of dating.

- Who are you really saving yourself for? Some people hold back from dating because they feel attached to someone already—a past partner (who may have rejected them or died) or even a parent.

It's reassuring to know that even the most extreme forms of shyness can be overcome. You absolutely deserve the joy of feeling confident in expressing the real you

The Least You Need to Know

- Shyness can come from past experiences, behavior copied from or taught by parents, inborn traits or predispositions, or certain chemical balances in the brain.

- You can overcome shyness by many methods, including relaxation, positive affirmations, and increasing your self-confidence.

- An extreme form of shyness is social phobia, in which you avoid people or situations. But this can be overcome with professional help.

- Believe that whatever you do and whoever you are is worthwhile and desirable.

Part  3

Making the Approach Work

So you've raised your self-esteem in the last few chapters, and gone to some of those interesting places and found some pretty good prospects, from the earlier part of this book. Now, how do you get to first base—and then further? How do you get the date? There's good advice in here about how to do that.

You're discovering that my best advice is to be spontaneous—and be yourself—but everyone could use some suggestions about how to break the ice, and how to keep the conversation going. Here's how to make a good impression and how to flirt so it works in these modern times, and how to be irresistible so you get a "yes" to your propositions. You'll learn how to make that first evening a date to remember (so it isn't the last!), from where to go to what to say, and how to handle sensitive money matters. And when that *second* date rolls around, you'll find advice on how to make that happen, and decide whether to keep it going.

Incorrect   Correct   Too much

Chapter **9**

Breaking the Ice: Openers to Get the Gab Going

In This Chapter

- ◆ How to break the ice when you first meet
- ◆ Starting up a conversation
- ◆ Smile!
- ◆ How to keep the energy between you going

Hot on the heels of "Where do I go to meet people?" is the next, related question: "How do I let him or her know I'm interested?" Many people who've asked me where to go to find that special someone have later admitted not knowing how to approach someone or what to say after they've said hello.

My best advice—that has stood the test of time—is: Be yourself. You can put on an act for a short run, but if you really want something worthwhile to work, you have to be accepted and appreciated for who you are. Everyone is in the same boat as you, with the same fears and needs and looking to be loved. So approach life and love with a positive attitude and expect the best. Take the risk and say what comes to your mind.

Don't worry about having a prepared line to deliver. Trust your instincts, be spontaneous and "in the moment." That way you come across as "real" and not, as one of my students said, "as some cheeseball who ripped a few lines off some website." But for fun, here are some ways to pique interest and keep it going.

A Quiz to See Which Openers Work

While being yourself, keep in mind that people react differently based on their personalities, tastes, and experiences. Many guys approach my attractive assistant, Alissa, using different openers. On the basis of their approach, how do you think she rated the following three men?

Dr. Judy's Dating Do's

Remember, anything you say has to "fit" your personality. However, feel free to experiment because meeting people is an opportunity for you to enjoy, express, and expand yourself.

Dr. Judy's Dating Do's

Think of dating as being like baseball. Even the best baseball players strike out more than they get hits; a batting average of .300 is spectacular in the game. For a long time, the great Babe Ruth held the record for the most home runs—and also for the most strikeouts.

GUY #1: "Uh, what's your name?"

GUY #2: "Those are great dangling earrings. I wouldn't mind being that close to you."

GUY #3: "Your smile lit up the room here, so I had to come over."

Alissa thought Guy #1's approach was typical, but a little too simple. She thought he'd be too shy and not much fun. Although Guy #2's remark was creative, it was a little too contrived and forward for her. Although she might consider going out with him, she would proceed with caution in case he turned out to be a player. She rated Guy #3 as the best possibility. Though others might find his opener cheesy, she decided, "He seems like a nice guy with a sense of humor—certainly worth a smile, and probably a date."

Of course, everyone has his or her own comfort level regarding different approaches. Just "hello" or "what's your name?" might be too dull for one person but to the point for another. Don't jump to conclusions. Everyone deserves more of a chance than just an opening line. Unfortunately, we judge people all too quickly, so think about how what you say reflects who you are, and affects how others react.

You Know What to Say!

Although the idea of approaching someone for the first time may seem terrifying, it's really not as difficult as you might think. You don't have to be a poet or a writer to intrigue and attract someone. Simply say what's on your mind or in your heart. The basic point that I want you to remember from this book is that it's important to be yourself. There is no perfect pick-up line. The best opener is whatever is real for you at the moment. Remember these points:

- ◆ Charm and sex appeal come from genuineness—being open, honest, and yourself. Whatever is in your mind and heart will come out naturally and sincerely, and that's going to be far more appealing than some contrived statement.

- ◆ Be the real you. If you pretend to be someone other than yourself and the other person ends up liking you, the relationship will be built on lies. If you slip up and reveal the real you (and you will) and your partner finds out that he or she really doesn't like you after all, you've both wasted time. If you play games successfully and then get dumped anyway, you'll never know what *could* have happened if you were the real you.

- ◆ Share what you feel (excitement, shyness). If you're self-conscious, admit it; hiding makes you come across clumsy. For example, Dave is 22 years old, but he looks younger. "Women avoid me because they think I'm too young," he complained. I advised him to say, "I know I look young, but you might like that when I'm 80, and anyway, I'm really older than I look and quite mature."

- ◆ Don't worry about being rejected. Thinking about the outcome only makes you self-conscious, which can make you clumsy and awkward.

- ◆ Use the person's name. That makes others feel noticed, acknowledged, special, and compelled to pay attention to you. To remember the name, say it several times during the course of a conversation. Repeat your own name, too, and anything else you want the other person to remember.

Dating Data

In coaching over 2,000 gay men, New York–based Jim Sullivan has discovered that single gay men are unprepared for dating because of confusion through teenage years, shame, and a lack of support and role models. They need to know what a date is (a specific time and place with the possibility of future romantic involvement) and how to start a conversation. Sullivan advises admitting shyness (since men, like women, love vulnerable men); say "I'm a shy guy but I find you attractive and

Bold or Subtle?

Should you get right to the point and say something like, "I like you. Would you like to go to the movies tomorrow?" Or should you throw out bait and see if the person bites: "I hear you love movies. Did you see …? I'd like to see it. Maybe we could go one evening or some weekend, maybe this Saturday afternoon if you're free? What are you up to?"

The key to a successful approach is to go with your instincts (you'll hear me repeat this advice at different stages, because it's so important). There are no rules. The direct pitch may be music to one person's ears but static to another. A lot rests on both of your personalities and the mood at the moment. Take Curtis for instance. He approached a woman with the line, "What's up, baby. You look sooo good. What's your number?" Curtis claimed this worked for him. I wouldn't recommend this as a general rule, but obviously he was able to pull it off.

Be Creative

You'll notice that one of my favorite pieces of advice is to be creative. After sensuous eye-locking, switch the mood by saying something off the wall like: "If a UFO landed now, what would the aliens say about this party?" or "Wouldn't it be great to rent motorbikes along the beach in Bali? Short of that, I guess we could go roller-blading in the park. Do you feel like it?" or "I missed being at the Superbowl—let's go throw some footballs Saturday afternoon." I love what a man at one of my workshops reported doing: He goes up to women and gives them a recipe for chicken nachos. Now there's a sure way to either engage an equally fun-loving mate, or turn away someone who wouldn't be compatible anyway.

Some people's minds make unique and unusual connections that others might not initially "get." If you are like that (astrological air signs often are), and encounter someone who appreciates it, you could be off on a really fun, way-out conversation. But if you encounter someone who is more realistic and practical (likely an earth sign), they might look at you like you're crazy. Go for it! Don't be afraid to come out of left field. Try these approaches:

   ◆ Quote an interesting phrase. "Some are born great, some achieve greatness, and some have greatness thrust upon them." I saw that on a billboard advertising Shakespeare's *Twelfth Night.*

   ◆ Ask an unusual opinion about something they would likely know nothing about. For example, ask, "Do you like my hair the color it is or would you dye it red if you were me?"

◆ Pretend you know the person. Say, "I love it when you scrunch up your nose like that. It looks so cute."

◆ Tune in on another wavelength—not to the words, but the feelings behind the words—use your intuition. Say something like, "You sound like your grandmother …"

◆ Be provocative. Ask, "Do you remember that drowning scene in the movie *Titanic*? I didn't get it. I thought she should have given him her life jacket or hoisted him on the wood she was floating on, instead of watching him sink."

◆ Offer help. Say, "I am guessing that you need an electrician to fix your antique lamp and I'm just the person to do it, for free. When can I come over?"

◆ Use the "situation" to your advantage. If it's cold outside, offer her your jacket. If you're taking a class, remark at how you didn't understand the last problem posed and ask him to explain it to you.

◆ Be far-out. Since the occult is really "in," suggest that you'd love to be abducted by aliens. A female comic I caught on Lifetime's *Ladies Night Out* had a funny routine about how "Everyone I know has been abducted by aliens on a date. I want to be abducted on a date. But I want those aliens with feelers …"

◆ Show something outrageous you can do. Paul can roll his stomach. Vera can wiggle her ears. You might stick your tongue out and display your piercing.

◆ Be funny. Humor can be one of the most attractive qualities in a person. You don't have to be Jerry Seinfeld or Conan O'Brien; just be clever. Think of a funny story you heard or talk about something amusing that happened to you.

Dating Data

People become sexier as they talk excitedly about something. You may have had the experience of sitting at a table across from someone you didn't think was particularly good-looking until that person started talking about something interesting, and suddenly you find that person attractive.

My Favorite Pick-Up Line Story

Another key to success is to first capture the other person's interest while making sure he or she feels safe and secure about who you are and how free he or she is to react or turn away. Women these days have to be particularly wary about weirdos or strangers being dangerous, so you have to reassure her that she's safe.

One night, I was eating a sizzling steak alone in a booth in a trendy restaurant when a good-looking guy leaned over my shoulder, ostensibly looking at my plate, and crooned, "It looks good, it smells good, and I bet it tastes good." His provocative glance suggested he meant more than the sirloin. I had to compliment him for how bold and clever he was—even though I wasn't into company and didn't invite him to join me.

While eating my sirloin, I overheard a pick-up line in the next booth. The guy was telling a woman, "My name is Tom. I live in the neighborhood and come in here often." (Good, I thought, knowing where he lives should make her feel safer.) "I also do my laundry across the street," he offered. (Possible good sense of humor she might appreciate, I registered.) "What's your all-time favorite food?" he asked. (Good next step, I thought, he's engaging her to talk, especially about what she likes.) The guy won; he was soon sitting beside her, and I noticed they left together.

The moral of this story is to be yourself, take a risk, get over your shyness, and let your best self shine through, while knowing that not everyone is going to "take" to exactly where you're coming from at that moment. Be sensitive to what others might need to know to respond to you; and be engaging, but non-threatening.

Woo Warning

Years ago, when times were more innocent and fears (about strangers and sex) less rampant, pick-ups were easier. In these days of caution, people are wisely more wary about strangers, so you have to work harder to win others over, revealing more of yourself to show you can be trusted.

Sample Openers

Okay, I know I said you shouldn't worry about using pick-up lines. And you shouldn't. It's important to say what's on your mind and not obsess about the outcome: It either flies or dies. You can always laugh it off. However, I want you to take a look at the sample openers that follow for three reasons: to give you an idea of how many kinds of openers you can use, to show you that an opening should suit your own personality, and to get your creative juices flowing about how to break the ice.

Years ago, I was a regular on a live TV show called *Good Morning New York*, and one of the segments I did was on flirting. ABC-TV weatherman at the time, Spencer Christian, was the host and I'll never forget the cute line he offered as an opener: "Before I came to talk to you, only God and I knew what I was going to say. But now that I'm standing in front of you, only He knows!"

Since then, I've done many shows about meeting people on radio, TV, and the Internet. The following are other suggestions people have shared, used, or just brought up for fun.

Charming Romantic Openers

Being charming and romantic is an alluring, attractive quality. The effort to please and enchant is almost guaranteed to work. Admittedly, some of the following one-liners border on being corny and are hard to take seriously, but you can have fun with them. Say them with a glint in your eye, acknowledging that it's a "line." You're bound to at least amuse someone—remember, a sense of humor is the quality that most attracts men and women today! Although men are known to use these lines, women with a sense of humor can turn the tables and throw one out, too:

> "I'd buy you a drink, but I'd be jealous of the glass."

> "Do you believe in love at first sight, or should I walk by again?"

> "Can I check your shirt label to see if you were made in heaven?"

Self-Disclosure Openers

A totally different technique—but also a useful option—is to reveal something about yourself to ease your stress and give the other person insight about you. Here are examples:

> "This is the first time I've been here. Do you know anything about this place or who comes here?" (Inviting help engages compassionate souls.)

> "I always feel more comfortable in small groups or one-on-one. I never really liked crowds. Do you?"

> "I'm normally uncomfortable going up to someone I don't know, but somehow I felt you'd be friendly." (This disarms the other person and makes him or her less inclined to act rudely.)

Conversation Openers

On a more serious and sophisticated note, here are some ideas for openers. Talk about ...

- ◆ **Current events.** Watch TV news or read *USA Today* to see how stories are told quickly, succinctly, and compellingly. Learn "all you need to know about everything that matters" from the weekly publication "The Week" (www. theweekmagazine.com) that reports the latest news and interesting events (in every subject from politics to sports and entertainment) in short articles that are easy to digest—and repeat.

◆ **Interesting or odd stories** from newspapers or magazines or make computer files from articles you read online or e-mails you get. My stepfather used to clip all kinds of interesting and odd stories that I could use on my radio shows—like the one about the government being criticized for wasting money on studies about the mating behavior of African fruit flies.

◆ **The weather.** This is no longer considered a silly topic due to innumerable natural disasters, as well as the advent of the Weather Channel.

◆ **Health.** People are very interested in the latest vitamin regimens, health foods, or physical fitness workouts (like "yogaboxing" at www.yogaboxing.com), and increasingly open to talking about psychological health as well (handling emotions, going to therapy, and taking medication).

◆ **Common interests.** Research shows that "like" attracts "like," at least in initial attraction. Discover something you are both interested in (old movies, animals, music). Whether it's a big issue (whom to vote for) or a gripe (late trains or too-small print on menus), everybody likes to know others share feelings or experiences.

◆ **Your background or lifestyle.** Did you grow up somewhere exotic? Have you had an intriguing experience? Read a great book?

◆ **A pet passion or pet peeve.** Positives are always better than negatives, but passion supersedes all. Remember: The person who is passionate, attracts. What's your dream: to save the rain forest, travel on the Concorde, write a book? Talking about something you are passionate about immediately communicates sex appeal because you are at your most attractive when you are involved in what you are saying.

Woo Warning

Regardless of how good a storyteller you are, know when to *stop* talking; don't bore your date. My friend, ABC-TV reporter John Stossel, told me that you should be able to tell a story within three minutes (the length of a typical TV feature), starting out with an attention-grabbing opener.

The Power of a Smile

One time in a club, I watched a guy smile broadly at girls until they smiled back. When he approached me, he boldly put his fingers on my mouth to form a smile, and said, "There, that's better." Though I was understandably put off at first by his touching me, after I smiled, I agreed with him—it *was* better! A safer but similar tactic one guy used: Put a smiley face on a napkin and hand it to her!

The old saying is true: Smile and the whole world smiles back at you. Research shows that babies smile more in response to their mothers' smiles. The same response is with us all our lives.

You'd be amazed at how powerful a smile can be in the dating game. Smiling makes you look your most attractive (despite the pouty expressions popular on models) and shows that you're friendly, warm, and open. In my workshops I usually ask people to turn to the person next to them and smile. Notice that it's almost impossible not to smile back. Find a smile you like. Look in the mirror and make different mugs until you find one you think looks inviting and feels good. Purposefully make a smirk and turn up the corners of your mouth into a smile (the actress Meg Ryan has this kind of smile). You'll feel your face, and your mood, lift!

Laughter works even better. My radio show producer Badger once told of how he uses a gimmick when he meets women. The line he uses is the following: "If I called you Shirley, would you laugh?" Usually, the female laughs, and gives him her real name—and the ice is broken. Telling a spontaneous (or a well-thought-out) joke allows the person you're interested in to warm up to you.

Dating Data

Science has proven that smiling improves your immune system by reducing stress, and can make you happy, even if you're not. The muscles used to make a smile trigger mood impulses that are located in the pleasure centers of the brain.

Dating Data

In one survey, women were asked to rate physical characteristics—physique, eyes, smile—in order of importance. They rated smiling first. A smile can even suggest you're richer than you are: In one study, people who made $50,000 a year were found to smile more often than those who made $15,000. Smile, and you're bound to get a smile in return. I'm always surprised when people say to me, "Why aren't you smiling?" As soon as I crack a smile, it changes my mood.

Using Your Voice

Voices are very important to those of us who work on the radio. A voice that is full of energy is likely to get more attention. My radio co-host Chris Jagger was infamous for hanging up on people whose first two words sound faint or too hesitant. Brutal as this may sound, people do this all the time in real life. So make the most of your first impression by using a powerful voice.

Here's an exercise I do in my seminars that you can do. Say this sentence aloud: "What a pleasure to meet you." Notice where your voice is coming from—probably your throat. Now take a deep breath and repeat the same phrase, but this time make your voice come from your chest. Repeat the phrase again, feeling your voice come from your stomach and then from your groin.

Full-bodied voices are sexy. Cheryl asked me, "My boyfriend says he loves how the sound of my voice is so much deeper and sexier after we make love. Why is that and how can I make it like that more often?" A huskier and more resonant voice after experiencing pleasurable lovemaking or an orgasm (called the "postcoital voice") is caused by physiological changes in the body at the culmination of the sexual response cycle (relaxation of muscle groups in the body including ones involved in speaking, like vocal cords, throat, and diaphragm). Confidence from a satisfying sexual encounter also leads to firm and direct communication during—and after—sex, that further enriches the voice quality.

In the book, *Fine Art of Erotic Talk*, Bonnie Gabriel recommends the following exercises to develop a sexier voice:

- Relax your vocal cords by opening the mouth and back of the throat as if yawning, and speak from that position.

- Open the back of the throat and yawn, then keep the lips together, exhale, smile, and push the air out as if silently laughing, and then begin speaking.

- Open your mouth wide as if starting to yawn, then count aloud from 81 to 89, punctuating each count with a breath of air.

Breath-enriched sound makes the voice sound more erotic, with the added payoff that heavy breathing intensifies sexual arousal. Experiment with different sounds, but keep in mind that the most appealing voice comes naturally when you are relaxed, confident, and secure in expressing what you want to an accepting, loving partner.

Making a Good First Impression

Make the most of your first minute! Nine out of ten people in the Arm and Hammer First Impression survey said making a good first impression is extremely important on a date. Other surveys show that people size you up quickly, and can make judgments about you within even the first 15 seconds. Then, they make their overall assessment of whether they like you in a minute and a half.

Putting It All Together

So far you've learned about a number of different ways you can approach someone. You also discovered the importance of smiling and speaking in a confident and powerful tone. Now how do you put everything together? For starters, you should smile first and make a comment about your common surroundings. Then you could ask a simple question (not personal, but on a neutral topic) and add something about yourself. This technique accomplishes several goals. It lets the other person get a sense of who you are, makes her feel safe, and helps her decide if she likes you. It also gives her something to respond to—taking the pressure off having to think about what to talk about.

For example, imagine you are in a music club. Smile and say something like: "This seems like a fun club" (a neutral statement about a common environment). "I've never been here before" (self-disclosure). "Do you know when the band starts?" (neutral question). "I usually like hard-rock music, but I hear this group has a country sound, and I've been to several clubs in Texas that I like" (leaving a few openings: she can respond to different music styles or to traveling, or turn away!).

Show the qualities similar to those of a good therapist: warmth, caring and understanding. Listen carefully to what the other person says.

Dr. Judy's Dating Do's

When you approach someone, keep in mind that what you say communicates only about a third of your message. The other two thirds is communicated by your body language—how you stand, move, and react.

Keeping the Gab Going

Now that you've learned everything you need to know about starting a conversation, how do you keep the rapport going and not run out of things to say? Here are some hints:

♦ Practice self-disclosure. Share interesting things about yourself. You emanate sex appeal when you passionately talk about something that interests you. Even if the person is not interested in what you are saying, he or she can still be captivated by the way you are talking about it. Say how you feel about the circumstances, setting, or anything else.

Dating Data

Surveys show that the biggest complaint women still have about men is that they don't talk enough about feelings.

◆ Read a person's "tell" (what they really care about, or as used by card sharks, their vulnerability). Look for clues in actions or facial and verbal expressions. Addressing what he or she cares about will make you more attractive.

◆ Repeat what the person said to show that you were listening carefully. If you need clarification, ask questions.

◆ Ask provocative questions. Barbara Walters once got flack for asking Katherine Hepburn, "If you were a tree, what kind of tree would you be?" Follow up such a question by asking "why," in order to reveal more characteristics of the person. Here's a question and two hypothetical answers that each tell you something about the person:

"If you were a piece of furniture, which one would you be and why?"

"A chair, because people would sit on it and I like to support others. I'm always the person people lean on."

"A rug, because people are always stepping all over me and taking advantage of me."

◆ Be positive. Avoid judgments, criticisms, saying "no," and changing the subject when the other person is talking.

◆ Keep in mind you don't have to keep talking and fill all the empty spaces. Sometimes silence speaks louder than words. Slow down and stop talking and watch how you communicate.

Now that you have suggestions about what to say, practice! Overcome any shyness. Nothing beats "just doing it" and then doing it again, to improve your dating skills.

The Least You Need to Know

◆ The first thing you say will make you stand out or fade away; you may get a second chance, but make the most of your first impression.

◆ Don't play games; be yourself.

◆ Smile and it's more likely that the world will smile back at you. Remember, smiling makes you feel good!

◆ Take note of interesting stories and practice telling them to become a good conversationalist.

◆ Reveal things about yourself, but also ask open-ended questions to learn about the other person.

Come Here Often?
The Art of Flirting

In This Chapter

- The six rules of flirting

- How to show you're interested and read the reaction

- The benefits of flirting—and what gives it a bad name

- How to use (and read) body language

- A 12-step plan to overcome "flirter's block"

What approach do you use when trying to meet someone? Do you engage others in interesting conversation, or sit back and wait to be courted? Do you "come on" strong or more subtly "flirt"? Flirting became uncool for a while, being seen as trite and trickery, but it's enjoying a resurgence of respect as a fun way to make innocent but interested connections.

Some people have a knack for flirting; for others it takes effort. Of course, there are cultural norms to consider; what's okay in one country may be too forward in another. But certain rules of flirting can be useful for all.

The Six Rules of Flirting

Besides just being fun, flirting can be an effective way to get to know someone. To help you get the most out of flirting, just remember the word FLIRTS:

F is for Flattery. The fastest way to a person's heart is to find something you truly appreciate about how he or she looks or acts. However, make sure your compliments are sincere (there's no sense saying "You have beautiful eyes" when they're obviously not).

L is for Listen. Get him to talk about what he really cares about and listen attentively. The most powerful aphrodisiac is your undivided attention.

I is for Interest. Find a common interest. Remember, similar tastes and interests are the best foundations for a good relationship.

R is for being Responsible. Be truthful, careful, and clear about your interests and intentions. Don't hurt or lead anyone on or choose inappropriate flirting partners, such as your friend's boyfriend or girlfriend.

T is for Trusting yourself and for being trustworthy, someone who can be counted on.

S is for a winning Smile—a sure way to make you feel good, and make anyone feel relaxed in your company.

Benefits of Flirting

There are many benefits of flirting. It can …

- Help eliminate loneliness by enabling you to meet people.

- Exercise and expand your technique for meeting people.

- Heighten your appreciation for what you're doing and where you are right now and in your life in general.

- Boost your ego.

- Give you feedback about how you relate to others and come across.

- Help you make new friends.

- Activate your adrenaline and nervous system. When this body system is switched on, your blood flow increases, and that in turn makes you more alert and aroused, more able to concentrate and take action, and more sensitive to touch. It also stimulates the limbic center of the brain, which creates pleasurable feelings.

- Be fun!

The Flirting Hall of Shame

Flirting gets a bad name when people get too forward or too sexually aggressive. The following shameful flirts perpetuate this bad reputation:

◆ **Blatant flirts** come on too strong, too fast, and overdo it—making the other person feel extremely uncomfortable ("Ooh baby, you're sooo hot …").

◆ **Confusing flirts** give one message, but mean another: "Yes I might like you, but no, I'm not interested in going out." Or they say one thing and do another.

◆ **Egotistic flirts** are the Don Juans and Don Juanettes who always check themselves out in the mirror and need to make everyone in the room drool over them. They can make you feel like a million bucks, but only to flatter their own ego.

◆ **Controlling flirts** tease the other person (misleading you into thinking they're interested when they're really not). They may make others squirm or manipulate people into doing things that they wouldn't ordinarily do.

Woo Warning

Be careful that you don't lead someone on by your flirting. Others may think you're interested in them romantically when you may just be having fun or being playful.

Show That You're Interested

Remember everyone is sensitive to rejection. So if you are receptive to someone's advances, don't hesitate to show it. One key ingredient to effective flirting is to show interest in your potential mate. Let's face it—everyone loves attention and being noticed. Two ways you can show interest are by giving compliments and by asking thought-provoking questions.

Be Interesting

I'm sure you've heard people use the greeting, "What's up?" Answer that question with something interesting that you have done. One of my interns at my radio show, Emily, used this technique successfully. She grew up in a small town, "so you couldn't make up anything, turn on the charm, or make small talk, because everybody already knew you." But when she moved to the big city, she could meet people "with a clean slate." This made for some exciting (though admittedly also fearful) experiences, where she could dazzle people with things she had done "without them going ho-hum, we already knew that." Talking about her most outrageous experiences, including a thrilling time sky diving, worked great in breaking the ice with strangers.

Deliver the Compliment

Paying someone a compliment is not as easy as it sounds. Simply saying, "That's a nice shirt" is not enough to spark an engaging conversation. To deliver a compliment successfully to open the door for a promising conversation, follow these steps:

1. **Take note of details.** Pick out something she's wearing, like a piece of clothing or jewelry, or a hairstyle. Notice something about him—his smile, eyes, or physique. Pay attention to what he's carrying ("That's a beautiful leather case").

2. **Pay attention to what he is doing.** "You play a great game of pool" or "I notice that you're careful about what you buy."

3. **Follow up with a question.** "Where did you find such an interesting piece of jewelry?"

Dr. Judy's Dating Do's

When asking a question, listen attentively to the answer instead of worrying about what your next question will be.

Because I have a habit of dressing unusually and wearing funky clothes, many people notice what I wear. When people compliment me on my fluorescent orange boots with the glow-in-the-dark soles by saying "Those are really cool boots, where did you get them?" they can engage me in a conversation about the store I shopped in (which leads to talking about how everyone hangs out in malls these days, how my conservative mother hates them, how they glow in dark clubs, what clubs I go to, and so on).

Ask Intriguing Questions

What is most people's favorite topic? Themselves. So, ask them to talk about themselves. You've got five W's to consider:

- **Who.** Who's your favorite actor/relative/friend?
- **What.** What's your favorite thing to do?
- **Where.** Where is your favorite place to go?
- **When.** When was the last time you treated yourself?
- **Why.** Why did you come here?

Avoid answering a question negatively. When the brain hears a negative answer—no matter what it's about—it creates physiological responses in the body and mind of a defensive, protective, and shut-down nature. "Yes" boosts deeper and easier breathing, more even blood pressure, and calmer heartbeats that make for better health and a more positive frame of mind.

Let's look at an example. Chaz asked Elena if she goes to the movies often. She replied, "No, I don't," and the conversation came to a dead end. Instead, Elena could have answered, "I prefer to hang out at my friends' houses, so we rent videos instead," giving him the chance to ask about her friends, which videos they rent, and so on.

> **Woo Warning**
>
> Some people feel put on the spot when asked questions. You'll sense this if the person gives you one-word answers, smirks, or simply turns away. To prevent turning them off entirely, tell them something interesting about yourself.

The Flirting Flamenco

Dating is like a dance—a matter of synchronizing your rhythms (but not backing someone into a corner). Sometimes you can't tell if a person is totally disinterested or just shy or reserved. Make your approach using what I call the "Flirting Flamenco." It has three steps:

1. **The approach.** Make your boldest move to gain the other person's attention. This should last a few minutes.

2. **The retreat.** Back off (sip your soda, dig in your pocketbook) to take the focus off the flirtation and to give the person a chance to assess you.

3. **The re-approach.** Test the waters. If your target responds, fine. But if not, definitely move on after three tries.

Body Talk

Researchers have estimated that more than half of communication comes from body language—gestures and movements that we make that reveal what we think or feel. So let your posture, facial expressions, and eyes do the talking for you. One cue is often not enough, so to send or interpret a message, combine several cues.

Eye Contact

The eyes are the window to the soul. When you look at someone, you are saying that you are willing to see and connect with them, and you are willing to be seen yourself. You have only to watch new lovers in a restaurant gazing across the table into each other's eyes to know how powerful eye contact can be.

But how much eye contact is too much/too little/the right amount? Of course, there are cultural norms here, too. Research shows that a constant stare makes people uncomfortable. However, a short gaze may mean that the person is shy, insecure, or insincere. The most effective eye contact is where you glance, linger, look away, then reconnect—holding each other's gaze for at least 60 percent of the total time you are together.

Dr. Judy's Dating Do's

A playful wink is always a good flirting tool.

Once you've made eye contact, longer looks usually work. Use what I term the "Driver's Eyes." You look straight at the person (like you're watching the road), while occasionally glancing right and left (like you're looking at the side-view mirrors) for relief.

Touch

Touch is comforting and also stimulating. There are many sensitive nerve endings in the skin's surface. When they are touched, they set off impulses to the brain that trigger chemical releases and signal pleasurable feelings. Flirt by touching yourself lightly in a nonsexual, safe way, to be suggestive. Primp or preen yourself, smoothing your hair or stroking your own hand, neck, face, or leg. Use an interesting trick based on the psychological principle of modeling—touch yourself wherever you would like to focus attention or where you imagine the other person touching you.

Dating Data

Women have a head start in touch flirting and can be more forward because men are generally less threatened by being touched.

Once you've become comfortable with each other, you can straighten his tie or her necklace, or brush a speck off the shoulder of his jacket. Advance to touching a body part: first covered parts, like the back or shoulder, then hair, and then exposed skin on "safe" areas like on the arm, hand, or cheek. Back off if the person winces or withdraws.

Body Positioning

Research on kinesiology (the study of moving bodies) shows that posture and movement communicate messages. Read and interpret caution or unwelcome signs if the body and head are turned away. Crossed arms could mean he's nervous or closed off. Uncross those arms and see how much more open—and vulnerable—it feels! Better to do that if you want to give the message you're more approachable! Lean in, extend a hand, nod (to signal approval), or puff out your chest or tilt your hips (to show interest). Legs crossed with the top leg nearer the other person signals that you are creating a barrier between you.

Vigorous leg-shaking is a sign of nervousness (a turn-off), while slight movements are stimulating (and a come-on). Mannerisms such as hair-flicking or tie-tugging can be distracting and a sign of discomfort. Also, if someone's hands or mouth are hidden (hands in pocket, or covering mouth), he may be hiding something.

Mirroring or Getting in Sync

When people are in tune with one another, they copy each other's body movements, so one's posture or movements seem like a mirror reflection of the other. Watch how this works—you'll be amused! Observe a couple who seems "into" each other, and notice that if he leans on one elbow, she'll likely do the same thing. If she rubs her lips, he'll reach for his, too. Without even realizing it, people in the seduction mode copy each other.

Dr. Judy's Dating Do's

Purposefully copy the posture or movement of the person you're flirting with, to give the subliminal message that you're interested and on the same wavelength. If she rests her chin in her hand, do the same. If he puts his hand on his hip, you do that, too.

Body Boundaries

How far away do you stand? Respect each person's "SPD"—safe personal distance—measured by an arm's length, usually about two to three feet. Then test the waters: Wait to see if she gives you clues to come closer (body touches, smiles, open body position). Also give clues yourself. Then do the "distance duet": Move in closer to show you're interested and then withdraw to give her "space" to advance and to show return interest.

Make sure your touches are welcome by "reading" the person's receptivity. Make a gesture first and see if the person resists (moves away) or moves closer or smiles invitingly.

Nonverbal Ways to Show You're Interested

You can also show that you're interested in someone and sense if a person is interested in you without using any words. Nonverbal cues of interest consist of what I call the four P's:

- **Presenting.** Present yourself in a sexy and alluring manner. For example, lick your lips, trace the outline of a scoop-neck top, or run your hand down your leg.

- **Preening.** Show that you know you're appealing. Straighten a tie, smooth or toss your hair.

- **Parading.** Stay close and show that you're checking him or her out (think of an animal circling around its prey). For example, Barry had his eye on Jessica at a party. She was being pursued by so many men that she was unlikely to notice him, so Barry made sure he always reappeared in her line of vision, until the end of the night when he offered her a ride home—which she took!

- **Posturing.** Nibble at food or play with the rim or stem of a glass suggestively. How you stand, sit, and walk says a lot about you. Tilting the head implies vulnerability, extending an arm is inviting, cocking a hip is seductive.

Reading Mixed Signals

Lots of people are confused about whether someone's really interested. As Tara said: "I go to bars a lot and I've had lots of guys come on to me, but when push comes to shove, they walk away. What's wrong with me and what am I doing wrong?"

Do reflect about what signals you may be giving that you are not really available, or interested. Or maybe you're picking people who wouldn't be interested in your "type." Don't beat yourself up. Instead of deciding you're not attractive enough, decide that there are other explanations for their not following through. Consider other ways you can behave or other messages you can send out.

Woo Warning

You can turn people off by being too self-consciousness and anxious to please, which comes across as insecurity.

To read other's reactions and be good at seduction, you have to get good at tuning in to what others do, think, and feel. Some people are good at it intuitively, and others need more practice. You're better at it the less you're consumed with fears ("Do I look good?" "Am I saying too much or too little?" "Is what I'm saying okay?" "Does he like me?"). When you focus on yourself too much, you can't possibly read the other person.

Overcoming Flirter's Block

Many singles tell me that they often see someone they'd love to meet but are too afraid to approach. Why? They're afraid of being rejected and feeling like a loser or a fool. Overcome these feelings. Remember: "Nothing ventured, nothing gained." Risk being the first to say hello; the other person is probably just as nervous as you. If you have trouble flirting with someone, don't despair! You can overcome your shyness and inhibitions. Just follow these 12 suggestions for overcoming flirter's block:

1. **Identify and express your resistance.** Realizing that you have flirter's block has won you half the battle.

2. **Review your past patterns with flirting and rejection and reframe your experience.** See what you can do differently this time. For example, think, "The last time I tried talking to a girl, she sneered and walked away. If this happens again with another girl, I'll assume that she's in a bad mood rather than that I'm a dud."

3. **Forget your past.** Don't relive each rejection you ever had. Come to each new experience with a fresh attitude. Clear your slate.

4. **Stop making overgeneralizations.** For example, don't say, "Every time I try to meet someone, it doesn't work out," or "None of the pretty girls/good-looking guys like me."

5. **Identify your faulty or self-defeating negative thoughts.** Don't say things like "I can't meet someone I like," or "The way I look, I'll never find someone." Expecting negative outcomes predisposes them to really happen, like self-fulfilling prophecies.

6. **Think positive thoughts.** Make more enjoyable predictions. Tell yourself, "I will enjoy this encounter," or, if rejected, "It's his loss, not mine."

7. **Eliminate expectations.** Change your intention about flirting from "scoring" (a date, job, or marriage) to simply being an innocent social interaction to establish a friendship. This reduces anxiety (about failure) and disappointment over an outcome.

8. **See things from the other person's point of view.** Someone's nonresponse may have nothing to do with you. She or he may have low self-esteem, be distracted about losing a job, or be involved with someone else. I remember the time I met a top executive and felt hurt that he didn't talk to me. Imagine my relief when my friend told me that he told her, "I can't talk to Dr. Judy now, I just ate garlic and my breath smells terrible!" Here I had wasted my time feeling slighted, and he was worried about being slighted himself!

9. **Reassure yourself.** "I am a (good/interesting/fun) person." Positive self-talk and affirmations boost your self-esteem and chances for success.

10. **Identify the emotional charge on your resistance.** Instead of concluding, "I feel like a failure," "I am a loser," simply state what happened without the emotion ("I approached her, and she wasn't responsive").

11. **Identify the true meaning of the fear—that will often reveal its insubstantiality.** For example, shame is a feeling that you have done something wrong or foolish and that others will think less of you. Decide instead that there is nothing foolish about your actions, and that others either aren't that focused on what you've done, or that their opinion doesn't matter.

Dr. Judy's Dating Do's

It's important to stay positive, but at the same time, don't be afraid of being rejected. Everyone goes through it. If someone turns you down, it just means there's someone else out there better suited for you!

12. **Mentally practice flirting so that when the opportunity arises, your actions will flow.** Imagine how you would like the encounter to go and rehearse it as if you're watching a movie in your head. The more you practice, the more likely you'll behave that way in real life.

The Least You Need to Know

- Besides being fun, flirting can be an effective way of getting to know a person.

- One key ingredient to effective flirting is to show interest in the other person.

- More than half of communication comes from body language.

- To become successful at reading people, practice tuning in to others' actions, thoughts, and feelings.

- To overcome flirter's block, forget past failures, reassure yourself, and anticipate having a good time. Remember, the other person is probably just as nervous as you.

Chapter 11

Scoring the Date

In This Chapter

- ◆ How to increase your chances of getting a "yes"
- ◆ Tips on how to ask for a date
- ◆ How to say "yes" or "no"
- ◆ What to do when you get no response (or a "no" response)

So you've spotted someone who strikes your fancy. Now it's time to take the next step: Make the connection. If you're stymied about what to do, you're certainly not alone. "How do I ask her out?" is a question I get asked all the time. It seems so simple at first—just ask, right? Yet why do you feel so nervous and anxious?

In this chapter, throw out the old rules you thought you had to follow, and learn what's cool and what's not when it comes to popping the question (not *that* question—we're working on the first stages here!).

What's New About Asking for the Date

Give up old ways of asking for the date—even thinking of it as a "date!" Here are the old—and new—ways, that will give you a fresh—and more successful—approach.

Passé:	Now:
It's about "dating."	It's about an "invitation" to spend time together and get to know each other.
There is a right way to ask for a date.	Be yourself. Ask in a way that feels natural (see specific suggestions later in this chapter).
Make the invite "formal" ("I'd like to ask you out" or "Do you want to go out on a date?")	Keep it casual, thinking of it as time to hang out and have fun.
Ask far in advance in case the person is busy.	Ask when something comes up or the time feels right (you can always explain why it's last minute).
Ask if he or she is "free."	Assume he or she wants to go, then find out if the time is good. If he or she's busy, you'll find out soon enough.
Don't call when you said you would.	*Always* call or e-mail when you say you will, or shortly after meeting to keep the contact going.

Dr. Judy's Dating Do's

Use a friend as an icebreaker. Abby had her eyes on Charlie, but she was too shy to approach him directly. Instead, she waited until he was with a friend she knew. After small talk with the both of them, she directed her attention toward Charlie. Shortly thereafter, she had a date to have breakfast with him.

Before asking someone out, brief yourself on the following dating tips to increase your chance of getting a "yes":

◆ Be yourself. That means be free of pressure about what you're supposed to do, or what the outcome will be. Follow your instincts about what feels right. If you're going to be liked, you'll get a positive response no matter what you do.

◆ Your invitation should not build anxiety for either of you. Wait for a moment when you feel relaxed.

◆ Consider what you enjoy doing. Participating in something you're good at, or comfortable with, increases your overall confidence. If you like basketball, take her to a game.

◆ Think of a date not as getting, but giving. Ask yourself, "What's in it for my date?" Just as President John F. Kennedy said, "Ask not what your country can do for you; ask what you can do for your country," offer something before expecting that something be done for you. Point out the advantages ("Come to this party, there'll be people there you'll enjoy." "Even though you don't play golf, come with me and you'll be outdoors getting sunshine and exercise.") What does she like to do? How will the date benefit him? For example, if he is thinking of buying a new car, suggest an afternoon visiting car showrooms.

♦ Face your fears about ghosts of the past. Sammy saw his kindergarten heartthrob at a reunion but was too scared to ask her out, remembering the days when he felt fat and awkward as a youngster. With my encouragement, he called her—and was successful!

Tips on Asking for the Date

When I pose the question about the best ways to ask for a date, many men respond that they use the direct approach. As Mario said, "I just come right out and ask, 'How'd you like to go out?'" Sean agreed: "I just be myself. I say, 'How'd you like to go out?'"

Being direct is fine, but in a more subtle approach, you'd go with the flow when asking, making it a natural outgrowth of the interaction. Popping the question shouldn't come out of nowhere. Ideally, you have just finished discussing something you're both interested in and would like to do. Then you can say, "Let's do that together."

A great technique is my three-step Flirting Flamenco, described in the previous chapter, where you test the waters, each time building to a more definitive invitation. Mention what you'd like to do, change the subject, then come back to it again. Do this three times, so the other person gets a chance to digest your invitation and decide what to answer. Keep the conversation moving, instead of enduring dead silence while waiting for a response.

Be creative! Let's say you want to ask her to go to an Italian restaurant. Talk about how you'd love to visit Italy, and then say you'd fly her to Italy if you had an extra day off, but you'd settle for going to the local Italian restaurant.

Another great tip: Start the conversation by entertaining the other person (offering interesting information or telling a good story) rather than expecting them to carry the ball and entertain you (like asking, "What's up?"). If the other person is the type who likes to entertain, you'll find out soon enough. But if he or she isn't, you've risked turning him or her off by asking questions before you've contributed to the conversation first. Personally, I am more receptive to strangers when they approach me with an interesting tidbit about a great new movie or tell me why hurricanes happen, than if they put me on the spot by saying, "Tell me what you do," right off the bat.

To come up with ideas, allow yourself to "free associate" (a psychological technique) where one topic leads into one another by some (even odd) connection in your brain. You might be talking about baseball that makes you think of amazing players who broke world records (Mark McGwire beat Roger Maris's 1961 record of 61 home runs), that leads you to ask what record in any field of life that she would like to break. Here's how to put these tips together with my three-step Flirting Flamenco. Suggest breaking records, like the number of hours dancing without stopping, and then segue into the suggestion that the two of you ought to go dancing sometime. Then swing into talking about how you heard the tango is a new craze, and that someday you'd like to visit Argentina. Then you can come back to the date—because now she's had a chance to let it sink in—saying how you love to dance and asking if she does. Move into another subject, picking up on the travel theme by talking about your last trip, and then come back to the invitation again. This time you're a little more definitive about whether you will get together and you can say something like, "It'd be great to go out dancing next Friday."

Dr. Judy's Dating Do's

After you ask for the date, don't make that the last thing you talk about. Swing into another topic to complete the conversation on another interesting note. Have a topic up your sleeve that you can talk about,

Who Makes the First Move?

Give both people a chance to call each other. Exchange numbers and e-mail addresses rather than leaving it up to one person to make the first move. But either person can step up to the plate, regardless of gender. Forget about leaving it all up to the man. Most men don't want this pressure anymore. Of course some guys can be intimidated by a woman who takes control, but generally they welcome a woman who can take the initiative. As Ray says, "A woman who's assertive and confident is hot."

Woo Warning

Men who are threatened by a woman's assertiveness may resist her suggestions throughout the relationship in order to prove their own superiority or control.

Hillary Clinton is proud to admit that she made the first move on Bill. She spied him in the Yale Law library, went up to him, and said, "If you're going to keep looking at me and I'm going to keep looking at you, we at least ought to know each other. I'm Hillary Rodham, and what's your name?" (Bill was stunned and couldn't remember his name.)

When and How?

Once you've decided to make your move, when's the right time? Here again, trust your instincts. Tune into your own comfort level, and that of your date. Then strike when the iron is hot (when you feel motivated and empowered) and when your intuition tells you the other person would be receptive. Intuition about when and how to ask for a date (what I call "psychic dating" or tuning in to "energy" between you) may take some trial and error, and some time to develop, but it will come. (Read all about "energy" in *The Complete Idiot's Guide to Tantric Sex;* see Appendix A). No matter what happens, let enthusiasm carry you through the moment.

Let's talk about the "how." The guiding rule here is to get as much feedback as possible. Sending e-mail or a text message can be safe—and a good tool if you're shy. An unanswered e-mail is most likely a sign of disinterest, but you could still be left waiting and wondering. When you e-mail, a lot rides on how you express yourself in writing, and there isn't as immediate a way to gauge the person's response or to get cues about their real interest as there is when you talk on the phone. Try getting the person live on the phone, instead of leaving a message (what if the cat stepped on the Erase Messages button?).

Get over phone fears by taking a deep breath, identifying yourself with some information that connects the two of you ("Remember when we met at Bob's party?"). Talk a short time, and always end with warmth and a compliment: "It was great talking to you" or "Looking forward to seeing you."

Woo Warning

Beep a date only when it's important and you need an immediate reply (you have a last-minute invitation or tickets). Be prepared for a curt or chilly response if you've reached the person at a busy or inconvenient time.

Here are some other tips to keep in mind when asking for the date:

- Pose an invitation as if you're already going, and ask if the other person would like to join you. This makes you sound less desperate, and takes the pressure off you both, especially if he or she wants to say no. A good approach, "I'm thinking about going to see (that movie) sometime this weekend. Maybe you want to see it, too—what do you think?"

- Be casual. Don't jump into water that's too deep before you've tested it.

- Be flexible. Offer alternate times. If all suggestions are declined, drop it altogether.

- Point out all the benefits of the deal, as I mentioned earlier in this chapter.

Closing the Deal

Asking someone on a date is like making a sale—only you're selling yourself. When making the proposition, follow the "Rule of Three Yes's": Ask three questions that will all lead to favorable responses. You never want to ask a question that will lead to a "no." That stops the conversation and injects negativity.

Another trick in closing the deal, like in selling a car, is to say something like, "Which color do you want?" and then, "How do you want to pay for it? In a three-year or four-year plan?" The first question assumes your interest and pushes you deeper into the deal because the dealer acts like its already happening. The second question further clinches the deal because it continues to promote the hypothetical as reality, by making you focus on the choices that surround the "yes" rather than on saying "no."

Dr. Judy's Dating Do's

To test someone's interest, disappear for a while (into the bathroom, or over to talk to a friend). He's interested if he says, "Where'd you go?" and holds on to you tighter, goes looking for you, or seems happy upon your return. It's not a good sign if he's actively engaged talking to some other woman upon your return, and acts disinterested in you.

Apply these methods to dating. Ask which day both of you should meet rather than *if* you should meet at all. Or ask, "Would you prefer going to the movies, eating out, or both?"

Consider this scenario: Doug wants to ask Kate out. He does a little research first and discovers that she likes horror movies. His conversation opener, therefore, can be something like this: "I heard you like horror movies." He then does more fact-finding by asking open-ended questions like, "What's the latest horror movie you've seen?" or "What's your favorite horror movie?"

Or, after a conversation about something else, Doug can close the deal on his date by asking Kate the following three "yes" questions:

1. "So you really like going to the movies?"

2. "And you really like horror movies. Isn't that true?"

3. "Would you like to see … that's playing, or … that's playing at …?"

In case of a lukewarm reception, use another rule in selling: Always leave the door open. You can say, "Okay, I'll check back another time and maybe we can go then," or put it in his/her hands, "Let me know when you'd like to go." This keeps your ego from being totally deflated.

How Persistent Should You Be?

A lot of people ask me how to tell whether someone is interested. Of course, you'd love an enthusiastic "Yes," but my general rule is similar to baseball: three strikes and you're out. That means make three attempts to show your interest, and if you strike out those three times, back off. Someone can turn you down two times for a legitimate reason. Maybe she's really busy. Or maybe he was a little ambivalent. Cut them a little slack. But after three approaches, it's time for you to take your time and energy elsewhere.

The only exception to the three-strikes-you're-out rule would be if the person really gives you encouragement and the excuses ring true. Her mother could be sick. He could be studying for the bar exam and unable to spare the distraction. She could be breaking up with her boyfriend. But don't sit around and wait breathlessly. Move on to other things—or other people—and when the time is right and the excuses are sincere, you'll go out eventually.

Getting the Number

How do you get the phone number or e-mail address? Some people are comfortable not beating around the bush. Some guys like Josh, for instance, simply go up to a woman they fancy and say, "I'd like to have coffee with you sometime. What's your phone number?" He claims this has about a 60 percent success rate.

If you prefer a more subtle approach, slide asking for the number into the conversation. While discussing something interesting, say something like, "Well, we should talk more about that" and add, "How do we get in touch? I should give you my card/e-mail/number. And you should give me yours." "Let's swap numbers/e-mails" tests mutual interest.

Dr. Judy's Dating Do's _____

When finalizing a date, consider giving out your business card. I learned the advantages of exchanging business cards from spending a lot of time in Japan, where it's *de rigueur* to exchange name cards when you first meet someone. That way you don't have to worry about forgetting the person's name, what she does for a living, or how to contact her. Get business cards printed at a local Kinko's, through a catalogue, on your own computer or downloaded free on websites.

Keeping Your Emotions in Check

I've mentioned how important it is to eliminate expectations in dating. Enjoy the journey and not the destination, or you'll be headed for disappointment. The best actions come from the heart, have good intentions, and are not caught up with the outcome. Have fun flirting without worrying whether it'll lead to a ride home, a date, a roll in the hay, or a marriage proposal. Expectations make a date feel obligated, guilty, and resistant. People need to feel free to say "yes" or "no" instead of giving in out of guilt or any fears of hurting you or retaliation.

Accepting the Date

Just as with old and new ways of asking for the date, as described above, there are old and new ways to accept the date.

Passé:	Now:
Refuse dates to prove that you are desirable, or not desperate.	Be honest, and go if you want to go.
If called last minute, be insulted, play games, and pretend to be too busy.	If you're free, accept and have a good time. Appreciate that he or she was inspired to see you now.
Refuse if the date is not fancy or special enough, or if the person just suggests "getting together" or "hanging out."	Understand he or she may be strapped for money or just want to spend unstructured time together. Give it a chance (unless *all* offers are last-minute or disorganized).
Cancel a date if someone better comes along.	Keep agreements to be a reliable, trustworthy person, regardless of what comes up that seems more exciting.

Just Say No Gently

Some men and women feel guilty about saying "no" to an invitation. Like Heather, who said, "I can get stuck talking to some creep at a party, and just can't get away. My evening ends up ruined."

I'm really impressed when someone asks me how to let a casual encounter down easy. It shows that they care about other people's feelings. One rule to remember: always be kind. It could just as easily happen to you, and what goes around comes around.

So I was pleased when Billy said, "I'm a pretty good-looking guy, and lots of girls ask me out. I don't want to blow them off because I've been hurt myself and I know what it feels like. What can I do?"

Kudos to Billy for being considerate. If you've ever been rejected (who hasn't?), you know what it feels like and can be more sensitive to not hurting someone else. Similar rules apply to exiting casual encounters as to ending a relationship (as described in Chapter 25). Let someone down easy by reassuring them that they're nice, and by giving a neutral but firm excuse ("You're interesting/that's fascinating/nice talking to you, and it'd be nice to talk more, but I need to make a phone call/talk to my friend/get something to drink. It was a pleasure to meet you").

Don't hang on just to be nice. That's misleading and wastes both of your time. Disengage graciously and consider that you're doing both of you a favor. Psychologically, people who can't break away are usually oversensitive to rejection themselves (rejection feels like a blow to themselves). Jackie's mother always warned her, "What goes around, comes around." Set boundaries and stop fearing being punished for rejecting someone else.

When You Get No Response

Remember, dating, like selling, is a numbers game: Learn to welcome "no's," because it means you're getting closer to a "yes." Even the best hitters in baseball get on base only about once every three times at bat—and they also strike out occasionally! If you get a "no" from a person, don't obsess about it. Instead, pick up your marbles and go to another playground where you might be welcome. Immediately turn your attention to others who might be interested.

A common question I'm asked is: "Why is it that a girl seems interested, but when you ask her out on a date or begin to show you're interested, she doesn't want to speak to you?" When people feel awkward or embarrassed, they may avoid talking to you, or you may have jumped the gun interpreting friendliness as interest in dating. If you get no response, accept that he or she didn't mean to lead you on. You can always protect your ego by saying, "It's okay that it's not going to work out between us. Leaving it as friends works out better for both of us."

Don't Blow Up if You're Blown Off

Facing a blow-off, most people wonder, "What did I do wrong?" The answer is: Maybe nothing—but maybe something. Always reflect on what happened, and what you might do better. If you are curious, and have the guts, you can ask for feedback ("I know it's not working out between us, but can you help me by telling me what might be really going on with you?")

What if a "no" makes you fly off the handle? If a woman turned John down, his temper flared out of control. One minute he was a fun-loving flirt, the next a raging bull. Such rejected suitors need to …

◆ Accept that everyone has a right to say no. Don't take rejection personally. Stop and take a deep breath. Then smile and turn your attention to something else that captures your attention and makes you feel good.

◆ Trace reactions to rejection to being spoiled or a need for instant gratification (getting what you want when you want it). Consider patience a virtue.

◆ Identify past events that fuel a current reaction. When one woman rejected John, he was flooded with memories of all the other women who had slighted him. Stay focused on the present.

Dating Data

Research has shown that getting previous hurts off your chest is helpful to physical as well as mental health. A group of people who wrote about their past traumatic experiences for 20 minutes a day for 4 days had fewer visits to the doctor than those who wrote about trivial topics. In addition, those who wrote about their feelings were happier, less anxious, and seemingly healthier than those who described events nonemotionally.

Treat every experience in dating as a learning opportunity rather than as a success or failure. But always feel good about yourself, and trust what you do. Take stock of what happened (not too harshly or judgmentally), not to sink into self-doubt but to make any necessary or constructive adjustments.

The Least You Need to Know

◆ Don't think of a date as a formal outing. Think of it as a casual time to get to know each other.

◆ The same rules of sales that help sell a product can be applied toward dating: Ask questions that lead to a "yes" answer, and consider a "no" response as leading you closer to an eventual "yes" from someone else.

◆ Get as much feedback and learn as much as you can, to refine your style.

◆ Don't take rejection personally. Consider that the road not taken leads you down another (better) one.

12

The First Date (How to Make Sure It's Not the Last)

In This Chapter

- Getting yourself psyched for the first date
- Favorite (and more offbeat) ideas for where to go on the date
- Dating do's and don'ts
- Conversation kindlers and killers
- Turn-ons and turn-offs for men and women
- How to end the date and what to do next

"Cup your hand over your mouth and check your breath."
—first-date rule (John, guitarist from the Dopes)

So you've crossed the first hurdle by asking to get together. Now it's time to follow through with the real get-together—your first date. In this chapter I'll help you get through that with success—and fun—and help you get ready for the next step.

As you prepare for this first date, there's a lot to think about. You have plans to make, and may have anxieties to overcome, and you want to ensure that all goes as smoothly as possible and that you have a good time. This chapter will make sure you do!

Psyching Yourself Up

If your mind instantly fills with images of tripping over your own feet, getting spaghetti sauce on your shirt, or worse, feeling stupid not knowing what to say, relax. A first date is bound to be fraught with some anxieties. Here are some ways to calm down while psyching yourself up:

- Treat the date as simply a way to get to know each other better, have a good time, share an experience, and learn about yourself and each other.

- Remind yourself that your date already likes something about you, or wouldn't have agreed to go out in the first place.

- Don't drive yourself crazy thinking about your upcoming date too much, but as with everything in life, a little planning goes a long way. Think through where to go and what to wear, and make some mental notes about interesting things to talk about. Then put it out of your mind.

- If you are excited about the particular person, it's okay to indulge fleeting thoughts or fantasies about how you want things to go, or how terrific it would be if this is "the one." Then remind yourself to stay grounded in reality, and curb your expectations.

- Resist worrying about what will happen if things don't work out.

- Allow some fleeting thoughts about the frustrations of dating, but avoid over-generalizing that "nothing ever works out anyway."

- Re-read Chapter 8 to build up your confidence. Remember that you are a valuable person and you're fun to be with. If *you* enjoy being with you, others will, too.

As you think about the first date it doesn't hurt to be reminded to pay attention to the basics, like what to wear (be yourself but also consider what your date might like and what's appropriate for the occasion) and good grooming (clean nails, hairstyle, and a dentist's daughter like myself would be remiss without mentioning a clean mouth). I'm all for experimenting, but it can be safer to try out new makeup ahead of time so you know what works, or get a new haircut a few days before the date to give it time to "settle."

Planning the First Date

Once you're psyched for the date, what do you do and where do you go? The key is to go to a place you'll both enjoy and where you will both feel comfortable to be yourselves. The more confident and comfortable you feel, the better time you will have—and the better you will come across.

Keep in mind the purposes of a first date. You want to learn about each other, but you may also want to minimize too much intensity, to ease your anxieties. So while you might want to be alone to some extent, you might not want too much privacy. You also might not want to put your date in too-personal a setting too soon, like meeting your parents or going to a family function.

Of course, the typical first date is a movie and "getting something to eat." This works because you can gradually get comfortable with each other while focusing on the movie (not each other) at first, and then having something to talk about over dinner. But there are other options including a picnic, visit to a museum, or trip to an amusement park. If you're driving yourself crazy drumming up first-date ideas, consider asking your date, "Where would you like to go?" or "What do you enjoy doing most?" Better yet, brainstorm together to come up with something you would both enjoy doing.

Dr. Judy's Dating Do's

Some men and women are afraid to invite someone to an event (such as a friend's birthday party) for fear the other person won't enjoy it. If you get such an invitation, a reassuring response would be, "It doesn't matter what we do, as long as we're hanging out together."

Think Outside the Box

Coming up with something interesting to do has many benefits, like adding excitement to your first date, showing how much fun you can be, and setting the stage for having a good time no matter what your feelings about each other turn out to be. Be creative in coming up with new ideas. What have you always wanted to do but didn't want to do on your own? Ask friends for inspiration, or look at newspapers and magazines for ideas about what's going on around town.

Think of going against tradition. For example, a man who cooks (and washes dishes) is very appealing! New York musician and advertising executive Matt Feinberg admitted he wasn't "a guy who's good at dating," so playing chef for his date gave him a chance to feel at ease, be comfortable in his own surroundings, be creative, and make a woman feel good by doing something to please her.

Use my acronym for the word "CREATE," where each letter is a reminder for how to be on your date: C = creative, R = relaxing and romantic, E = entertaining, A = active, T = talkative, E = exceptional.

Consider these creative ideas:

- A performance by an experimental theater troupe

- A yoga class

- An afternoon at a health club, working out together, playing racquetball, or taking an exercise class

- A more unusual sport, like sky-diving, hang-gliding, ballooning, or bungee-jumping

- A boat cruise or helicopter ride

- A reading with an astrologer

- An appointment for a spa treatment, such as a massage or salt scrub in adjoining rooms

- A rodeo, or dog, cat, or horse show

- An exhibition (gift show, boat show, car show) at a civic or convention center

Dr. Judy's Dating Do's

To make the first date as nonthreatening and non-anxiety provoking as possible, go where you can look at other people instead of just at each other—or talk about them! "People watching" and sharing comments about others give you clues about your date. What does your date like or dislike? Is he or she critical or flattering about others?

Couples on TV dating shows have gone on some creative dates like learning how to lasso, dressing up in a costume shop, or browsing for tattoos. On one show, she taught him ballet and he took her to karate class. More risqué dates involved hot tubs, erotic massages and lap dances, pouring hot wax on each other, body painting, picnicking in a cemetery.

Know Where You're Going and How You're Getting There

Dates can be fun when they're totally spontaneous and full of surprise. But the first date can go more smoothly when the basics are planned—the surprises can come from your interaction and relationship rather than the arrangements. Be prepared about the particulars:

- How you are getting to your destination (taxi, bus, train, your own car, car service)

- How much time it will take (you want to arrive on time)

- What passes, tickets, or identification are necessary

What to Bring

Giving a token gift on the first date is a nice touch, as long as you don't go overboard (too big, too expensive) and look over-anxious to please. A small token you know a person would like (a CD from a favorite artist), or something associated to what you're about to do on your date (a can of tennis balls) are appropriate. Be prepared for different reactions. For example, while bringing a dozen roses can be read as over-the-top, bringing just one might be seen as cheap.

Dating Do's and Don'ts

Finally, you've decided where to go, and it's time for the date. Here are some tips to help things run smoothly and to avoid dating disasters.

Do ...	Don't ...
Feel confident.	Put yourself in uncomfortable situations, such as ordering messy food.
Look your best.	Suggest expensive first dates unless you clarify who's paying.
Smile.	Ogle other women or men.
Address your date by name frequently.	Monopolize the conversation.
Compliment your date.	Lie (about anything).
Listen attentively and repeat things your date says.	Bring up your exes unless you're having a specific conversation about past relationships.
Be honest about whether you're interested in seeing the person again.	Become intoxicated or make unwanted advances.

What Makes a Good Conversationalist?

The art of conversation involves having confidence to speak freely about whatever comes to your mind (without self-consciousness or second-guessing yourself) in a manner that engages the other person to be interested in what you are saying and feel like you are interested in return.

Check out Chapter 16 to determine what type of communicators you and your date are to avoid unrealistic expectations and to have some guidelines on good communication. These include get to the point, ask stimulating questions, and listen without interrupting. Even if you're shy, you might "click" and end up talking for hours.

Some people seem to be born conversationalists. But most people have to practice and learn what makes other people respond positively. Here are some tips to be engaging on your date:

- Talk about subjects that are meaningful to you (cooking, a biography you read about Churchill, volunteering at a soup kitchen) so the other person can sense your passion.

- Ask an open-ended question to get beyond "yes" and "no" and to spark conversation. For example, ask "What's your favorite food?" rather than "Do you like Italian food?"

- Tell an interesting story about what you have done and what it means to you. Maybe you learned a new sport or had an unusual experience.

- Choose a subject that can lead to an engaging conversation (favorite movies, foods, travel destinations).

- Talk about things initially that are positive rather than complaints.

- Use words that are descriptive and rich in imagery (say "sparkling emerald" rather than just "green").

- Avoid slang and worn-out clichés ("you know," "like," "uh") that may be a habit but that are irritating for others to hear.

- Make connections from one subject to another. Use the psychological technique of free association: What does one subject make you think of? For example, if you start with a conspiracy theory about arms sales, you can connect this to the movie *Conspiracy Theory* with Mel Gibson and Julia Roberts, and from there talk about other Mel Gibson movies you enjoyed.

- Keep yourself as informed on diverse subjects as possible. Keep track of the news so you can talk intelligently about major developments in politics, economics, sports, and entertainment.

Dr. Judy's Dating Do's

Keep notes in a special notepad, daily planner, palm pilot, or computer about story clippings and interesting topics you can discuss on your dates. Practice by saying them in a mirror or tape recorder, speaking aloud in the shower, or telling a friend.

- Be surprising. Out of the blue you can interject into the conversation, "Oh, the President of the Czech Republic said in a news conference this afternoon that a poor Russia is better than a rich Soviet Union."

- Pose brain-teasers. Example: A baby fell out of a 20-story building and didn't get hurt. Why not? (Because he only fell out of the first-floor window. I didn't say he had to fall out of the 20th floor, only that the building was that high.)

- Say what you mean. Of course you can (and should) keep certain comments to yourself, but the more you feel comfortable saying what's on your mind, the more comfortable you can become at making conversation.

- A picture is worth a thousand words, so besides just talking, think of taking along something to show your date to illustrate what you're up to or something interesting that you're into, for example, a newspaper article about you or whatever you're interested in, an award you won, or a photo of your latest vacation.

- Talk about how you feel about where you are and what you are doing. For example, you might say, "This is my first calm moment after such a crazy day."

Dr. Judy's Dating Do's

Leave an interesting message on your answering machine. Ask a question or report a news fact. Change it often to keep it fresh.

Pitfalls of Conversation

To refine your technique and really be good at capturing—and keeping—someone's attention, keep in mind the following conversation-busters.

Rambling

Have you been in a conversation with someone and you feel like you can put down the phone, or even walk away, and the person would still be talking and wouldn't know the difference? You're being talked "at" instead of being talked "with." Talking "at" people comes from chattering on about yourself without being connected to the person who is listening. The key is to engage the other person in what you are saying so he or she feels involved. Try these techniques:

- Hesitate while talking to give your date space to jump in and react.

- Stop after talking awhile and ask a question that involves your date. Ask for an opinion ("What do you think about that?"), understanding ("Do you know what I mean?"), or empathy ("Can you imagine how that feels?"). Turn the attention to your date, (ask, "Has anything like that ever happened to you?").

Woo Warning

It's rude to have a long conversation with someone else on your cell phone while you are on a date. If you must answer, make it short. Also, if you and your date go to a concert, movie, or other indoor venue, turn off your cell phone to avoid irritating other patrons. (Many indoor venues require this.)

- Use your date's name every now and then, to make him or her feel special and show that you know to whom you are talking.

- Tune in to yourself. If you sense that you are rambling and your voice is droning, stop talking and give your date a chance to speak. As a radio and TV talk show host and guest, I know that talking even a minute is a long time. And "sound bites" (a quote from a person) on a news show make the point in only eight seconds!

- Ask for feedback. Ask if your date is interested in whatever you are talking about, or wants to change the subject.

The "I Don't Know" Block

Avoid falling into the "I don't know" syndrome. Whenever someone answers a question of mine with "I don't know," I encourage them to come up with any suggestion or response. And guess what, they always can! If a date asks, "Where do you want to go for dinner?" or "What movie would you like to see?" any suggestion is better than none. Imagine the most common question asked in a conversation, "How's it going?" or "What's going on?" Saying "nothing," is boring but also never true—there is always *something* going on. Have the confidence to say anything that comes to you, what you're doing right then, something interesting you did that week, or a feeling that you have.

Touchy and Taboo Topics

Be natural in saying what you want to say, instead of being self-conscious or second-guessing what the other person wants to hear. But a few topics that you might avoid on your first date include:

- **Discussing other attractive people.** This only makes your date feel insecure.

- **Talking about previous dating successes or horrors, or an ex-girlfriend or ex-boyfriend.** This also stimulates jealousy and puts attention on the relationship with other people instead of what is happening between the two of you.

- **Bringing up subjects about which people are very opinionated.** These can be provocative but also risky, in case your date is easy to judge and not easily accepting of opposing points of view. Topics known to touch off fervor include capital punishment, gun control, abortion, and being pro- or anti-war.

- **Launching into sex talk.** This can raise all kinds of anxieties and confusion ("Is he coming on to me?" "Does she always get sexy with guys on the first date?").

If you cannot resist talking about a sexual topic, stick to current events and generalizations about opinions without being too personal ("Do you think that new sex-education bill should be passed?" "Did you read that article about that new sex advice book?").

♦ **Talking about morbid or too-depressing topics.** For example, I have cared deeply about the Jon Benet murder case (the six-year-old beauty queen found strangled in the basement of her home) and can bring up this subject with others, but be sensitive about whether they find the subject too depressing to talk about.

Getting to Know You

The purpose of the first date is to find out about each other. So do something that reveals who you are and helps you learn about your date.

Exercise: Things I'd Like Us to Do Together

The couple that plays together stays together. Do you have shared interests? The purpose of the following exercise is to discover common interests between you and your date. Make a list of the things you like to do, and have your date do the same. Then go through your own lists and assign priorities ("1" for the thing you most enjoy, and so forth). Compare your list with his to see where you overlap. If none of your interests overlap, you may want to reconsider this relationship.

What I Like to Do	What My Date Likes to Do

Exercise: Be a Reporter

The purpose of this exercise is to help you focus on what you really want to know about someone to get better acquainted, and to help you be more assertive about speaking up and asking for what you want. As a psychologist and news reporter, I am used to asking lots of questions. This exercise helps you learn how to ask the right questions to help solve your dating dilemmas.

Interview the person, asking questions as if you were doing a story about him or her, without any emotional investment or fears. Don't jump to conclusions, and get facts as well as feelings. Be curious and ask provocative questions that use the five W's: "Who's your hero?" "What's your dream?" or "Where were you born?" "When did you decide to ..." "Why did you ..." Ask simple background questions (about childhood, schooling, jobs) and then about what's happening between the two of you at that moment ("What did you mean when you said ...?" "How do you feel about ...").

What Works (and What Doesn't) for Men and Women

A series of successful TV specials I did for E! Entertainment TV on *What Women Want* and *What Men Want* addressed many of the issues in this book and especially this chapter. One of the shows covered the stories of women who used a dating service for dates. After the date, I conducted a group session with the men and women together, to discuss what they liked or didn't like about each other—a rare opportunity for feedback, because it rarely happens that you really say what's on your mind!

All three women profiled on the show put a lot of effort into preparing for the date (deciding what to wear, processing past experiences about disappointments). They all formed initial impressions of the men based on the first contact on the telephone about whether the man would be a good conversationalist. One woman was well predisposed to her date because his voice sounded so resonant and sexy (even though she wasn't crazy about him when they met), which shows how you can score initially but still strike out when you meet face-to-face when chemistry and other factors play a role.

The women were very clear beforehand about what turned them on or off. Nice hands were a turn-on to one; dirty fingernails were a sure turn-off to another. All three women cited too-soon sexual approaches as a major turn-off (Kristen recounted her dating horror: "He grabbed me, was in my face, stuck his tongue down my throat, and said, 'Come on, you can do better than this'").

Dating Data

The biggest surprise with the three guys for this show was that they all said that sex on the first date was not a good idea ("except maybe on a vacation when everything is accelerated!").

In *What Men Want*, three guys were selected (for their charm, good looks, and age) to go on a vacation to Cancun, while the cameras followed them on their escapades meeting women. All three men were attracted to honesty, passion, and good communication—not just good looks. Francisco explained further, "I look for some sort of brain first ... somebody who can hold a conversation and have some interests that I have. And then from there, hopefully she's good looking and funny." Matt was looking for a woman with "a good heart and good morals, money, and having a career and all those things in line, who is strong and takes care of herself." Good eye contact and a smile were also turn-ons, while turn-offs included being drunk, smoking, rudeness, embarrassing him, too many tattoos, and not laughing at his jokes.

The whole show corroborated the basic point of this book: Guys don't want to play games. They want to be liked for themselves, and they want a woman to be herself! They want a woman they can be comfortable with, and who has her own life (not clinging on to his).

To Kiss or Not to Kiss

Blatant sexual advances too early in the game are real turn-offs to most men as well as women. Be sensitive about reading a person's boundaries about being intimate: Even a kiss can be a major step.

Read body language to tell if your date is open to being touched at all. Crossed arms, standing away from you, or backing off whenever you make an advance are signs to back off. A green light welcoming physical contact would be touching you, or a positive response if you make physical contact (holding your hand tightly, touching your shoulder, putting an arm around you, too).

If the sparks are really flying, planting a surprise kiss or melting into a kiss after looking into each other's eyes will come naturally. But if that doesn't happen, test responsiveness by making a small gesture (kissing her hand) and seeing whether she smiles (a "yes") or pulls her hand away, frowns, or looks uncomfortable (a "no"). A hug can also test for the responsiveness. Build up to a kiss on the lips by first kissing the neck. The kind of kiss depends on your attraction and passion. It can be romantic and seductive by starting lightly on the side of the mouth and building slowly toward more direct lip contact and more openness. Or you can build the tension until the two of you can't stand the anticipation any longer, and dive into a passionate embrace.

Woo Warning

Singles are sensitive to where a kiss is leading, how far to go, and what the other person expects. Be cautious about making advances, to show you are being responsible in this day and age about avoiding casual sex and sexually transmitted diseases. Never kiss if either of you has a cold sore; oral herpes is highly contagious.

How to Tell if He or She Is Interested

Don't jump to conclusions about a date's interest. Find out the real story. For example, lack of responsiveness might signal no interest, or just shyness or distraction. And if your date doesn't contact you right away, did he or she lose your card or suffer a computer crash?

Observing signs on your first encounter can give you an idea of how much your date enjoyed being with you and interest in another encounter. Here are some signs that things are going well:

- Smiling often.

- Inviting body language—making similar motions as you do (called "mirroring," like putting hand to chin when you do) and assuming "open" positions (facing toward you, arms not crossed).

- Moving close or making contact (holding hands, touching your cheek, or putting an arm around you).

- Referring positively to a future time together. ("It would be nice to do that together.")

- Making eye contact.

- Being enthusiastic about what you are doing, interested in the conversation and keeping it going.

- Complimenting you.

Dr. Judy's Dating Do's

Figure out what your date needs, and show that you "get" him or her. For example, instead of just laughing at his joke, you say, "You're so funny," thereby acknowledging what he really wanted to project about himself—that he's funny.

The opposite of all these would indicate a yellow light about further contact. Other warning signals that indicate that things are not going well include …

- Ending the date earlier than planned.

- Mentioning other relationships, indicating a desire to set up an excuse about having another boyfriend or girlfriend.

- References to being busy, having many commitments, or not being interested in having a relationship (as a preparation for turning down further dates).

- Being preoccupied with other things, such as fumbling with keys, primping, looking away when it comes time to get out of the car or part at the door (times when some intimate contact could take place).

Ending the Date

Saying ahead of time what time you want to be home gives you an easy out if you are not having a good time, without either of you having to make an excuse, or feeling hurt or rejected. And if you are really having a good time, you can always extend the time.

Ending a date early always runs the risk of hurting the other person's feelings. Avoid this by looking for some way that you can enjoy whatever is happening and make it interesting for you, even if you don't want to see the person again. Everyone wants to be appreciated—and is sensitive to rejection. So in ending the date, follow these suggestions:

♦ Point out what you have enjoyed about the person's company and what you did together.

♦ Mention that you have a long drive or something to do in the morning ("I'm having a good time, but I had a more trying day than expected, and have to get up early tomorrow morning, so I hope you don't mind if we call it a day now").

♦ Point out differences between you, your lifestyles, or interests that will make the other person see that you are not a great match.

♦ Mention how you are really going to be busy for the foreseeable future. Emphasizing the long-term is a dead giveaway that you are not anxious for another rendezvous.

If you both had a good time, you won't want to end the date! But you still might feel a little awkward about what to say. Remember my basic principle about dating: Be yourself and don't play games (pretend to be *so* casual). If you really had a good time, say so! Be as warm and enthusiastic as you feel.

If you had a decent time but are not massively enthusiastic about getting together again, find something nice to say about your time together, without making any references to getting together again. Let some time pass for the experience to percolate in your unconscious, to see if you think about the person and want to get together again; if not, you're likely not interested after all.

Woo Warning

Don't end your date with "I'll be in touch" if you know you are not going to do that. Nothing is more miserable than leading someone on and having them wait for a call or check for an e-mail that never comes. It's better to leave someone disappointed about not hearing that promise than making a false promise.

After the Date

No matter how a date goes, I'm a big believer in thanking the person for the date. A woman usually expects to hear from a man the day after a date. Men, on the other hand, usually make contact days—or even a few weeks—later. I recommend calling within three days, whether it's to just say thank you or to indicate further interest. If your date cares, he or she will be happy to hear from you soon, and if not, there's nothing lost.

Another Chance

You can't always tell if you click based on one date. If it was good, maybe your date was on his or her best behavior. But if you didn't, maybe your date was nervous or shy, or the circumstances weren't right. While first impressions do determine how we feel about someone—and even though I've said you should consider your time, energy, and attention precious and not to waste them—there is something to be gained in giving someone another chance. In fact, follow the three-date rule, to give someone three encounters, to get to know each other, and see each other in different situations, and judge more accurately how compatible you are. I'm sure you, too, know stories about people who initially weren't interested in each other, but who were thrown together at events and found themselves clicking.

The Least You Need to Know

- Do something that would be fun and comfortable for both of you, taking into account interests, degree of intimacy, and available time.

- Be creative about where to go and what to do on a first date.

- Be honest about your feelings about how the date went and your interest in each other, making sure not to lead the person on.

- Times have changed: Women as well as men can take the initiative in asking for a date.

- Always thank the other person for the date.

- The initial phases of dating take time and effort and cause anxiety, but hang in there. Your efforts will eventually pay off!

The Second Date and Beyond

In This Chapter

- ◆ Where to go and what to do on date number two and beyond
- ◆ Deciding if this is going anywhere
- ◆ Gifts, housekeeping, and other tips
- ◆ What men think women ought to know, and vice versa
- ◆ How to keep the momentum going

Hopefully the first date worked out and you both think you would like to see each other again. Be prepared that the same anxieties will arise about the second date as you faced the first time around, including making decisions about where to go and what to say. In fact, these anxieties may escalate because the stakes have increased—after all, now you feel more interested in the person and have more fears about whether it will work.

To prevent anxieties from building, remind yourself that you are not "dating" as a formal declaration of a relationship, permanent interest, or commitment to a future together but rather you're merely expressing an interest in sharing another experience. This is the time to think of dating as "hanging out" to feel more at ease about advancing to another stage. Take it step-by-step and day by day. Let things flow instead of worrying. Trust your gut; see if you naturally start thinking about him, wondering how she is, and wanting to share what you're doing.

Asking for the Date

Follow all the same advice as with the first date when it comes to asking for the next get-together, only up the ante a little. Start the conversation with a comment about your last encounter. Refer to something your date said or did last time (that will certainly impress!), offer an honest compliment (to set a good mood!), or relate an interesting experience you've had.

Preface your invitation with the fun you will have ("I know you'll enjoy ...."). Keep topics in the back of your mind to keep the conversation moving, and use the three-step approach outlined in Chapter 11.

Where to Go and What to Do

Where you go and what you do should always be a natural evolution of my basic principle of dating: to enjoy each other's company, and to get a sense of each other and how you approach life. After all, if this relationship develops into a long-term one, you will be doing many things and handling many responsibilities together. Therefore, think of various situations that would reveal how you are. For example ...

Dr. Judy's Dating Do's

Remember that nothing captures a person's heart more than knowing that they were "heard." So, if she told you about her mother being ill, ask how she is. If he said he had a major report due at work, ask how it went.

Dr. Judy's Dating Do's

If you know what worked last time on a date, the tendency would be to play it safe and do it again. It's okay to repeat favorites, but remember that variety is the spice of life!

- Spend time one-on-one but also with other types of people (friends, co-workers, family), to see how you each relate to others.

- Vary what you do. Plan some activities, but also spend unstructured time together, to see how you entertain yourselves without specific plans, and how you make decisions together.

- Vary where you go. Spend time at home to see how you adapt to a homey situation, but also at outside social activities (a bowling alley, putting green, or party).

- Vary times you are together. Meet in the morning, afternoon, and evening to sense the best time for each of you. (Is he is grumpy in the morning or will she keep you up all night?)

- Be indoors (at a museum or concert) as well as outdoors (a picnic or beach).

◆ Include social activities, but also mundane ones to see how well you adapt to doing these together (drop off a deposit in the bank machine, stop into an all-night drug store for shampoo, ask him to help you buy new sheets, ask her to help you fix a leaky faucet).

◆ Come up with ideas on your own and also ask for the other person's suggestions. Welcome disagreements (you want Italian food tonight but your date craves sushi) to see how you negotiate and resolve differences.

Remember my two cardinal principles of where to go: Make it a setting you both feel comfortable in, and one that builds on your interests. If she told you how much she enjoys art, check the newspaper for exhibits or openings coming up. If he told you his favorite sport, call up for tickets.

Review the idea list of first dates in Chapter 12 for your second dates and beyond. Here are some additional suggestions:

◆ Do laundry or errands together on a Sunday afternoon.

◆ Make a social visit to family. Go together on a family picnic, take your parents out to dinner, or visit your grandmother on a Sunday.

◆ Visit an aunt or grandparent in a nursing home or retirement village, to get a sense of how you each deal with aging.

◆ Visit a friend who has just had a baby.

◆ Visit a sick family member to see how you both handle illness.

◆ Host a dinner party to see how you both share responsibilities and prepare for guests. Togetherness is heightened as you work as a team for others. You also get to meet each other's friends, see how you each treat friends, and if all your friends get along.

◆ Go with him or her to an appointment.

◆ Attend religious services together.

◆ Cook a sensuous meal. Choose suggestive textures, smells, colors, and tastes such as crunchy string beans, tangy sauces, or red tomatoes. (Be sure to find out if your date is health-conscious, vegetarian, or has special dietary restrictions so you don't turn him or her off with greasy hamburgers, too-salty appetizers, heavy cream sauces, or too-sugary cakes.)

◆ Do something for the other person that she or he needs or would like (teach him/her a new computer trick!).

♦ Attend a wedding together—or a funeral (really!). Sharing sad times is as revealing as happy occasions.

Dr. Judy's Dating Do's

Different types of music affect different moods and emotions by stimulating certain brain chemicals and muscular reactions. If you like country and your date likes classical, appreciate each other's choice. Listen to your collection to select CDs conducive to a date. Go through racks at a music store together. Pick out compilations that set the tone for romance.

Woo Warning

Be on time for dates! If meeting at a restaurant or club, know whose name is on the reservation to be seated if you arrive first, and be clear about where you'll meet (at the table, bar, or corner of the club).

♦ Spend a Saturday afternoon volunteering together (taking a homeless child to a park or working at a soup kitchen).

♦ Go shopping together. Since most men traditionally don't enjoy shopping, choose something he needs or enjoys, like "window-shopping" for a new computer gadget.

♦ Watch a video at home together. While I know this can be a popular suggestion for initial dates, save this for later dates because coming over can imply pressure for intimacy and trigger feelings (however unfounded) about not being "taken out and treated." Choose a video with a positive message about relationships (*Crossing Delancey* shows how nice guys can finish first; *Selena* proves love can survive obstacles). Research even proves that scary movies or horror flicks stimulate chemicals in the body that encourage intimacy.

♦ Take a class together. Learn drumming, dancing the tango, wine tasting, or computer skills. Try a class about relationships!

♦ Get a massage together.

Much later in the game you can plan a short overnight trip. This can involve some activity (antiquing) or a sport (such as skiing, which involves preparation and time). Or take him or her along on a convention trip.

If you're a single parent with kids, once you're comfortable with a new beau, the two of you can take your children on an afternoon or early evening excursion (to a park or for a bike ride). There are plenty of restaurant chains in cities across the country with amusement arcades with interactive games and simulators that kids (and adults!) can enjoy. (See Chapter 26 for more on dating when you have kids.)

Bearing Gifts

Small tokens are a great way to show your interest and make the other person feel good. Find out what your date likes. Thoughtful but inexpensive gifts include a CD from a favorite artist, souvenir from a city you visited, T-shirt from an event you attended together, or book that has meaning to both of you. Think of something that he would use or see often (a pen with some inscription, a paperweight for the desk) that would make the person think of you.

Where to Meet

In the old days, a gentleman caller would always collect a lady at her place. Suggesting any other rendezvous would be insulting. She would never dream of getting herself anywhere on her own. Of course, find out if either of you wants to follow tradition. But these days, anything goes. You can meet anywhere comfortable for both of you, like at work if he or she has to stay late, or at a mutually convenient place considering time and distance. She can even come to his place.

If your date is coming to your home, review your place with an eye for having company. Create a mood. Adjust lights and shades. Clean up yourself, or get a service to do a thorough job. Tidy up the bathroom and kitchen. Make the bed and throw any scattered clothes into the closet, then close the door so the bedroom is not visible. Go over essentials: fluff pillows, toss papers in the closet, sweep dust balls off the floor. If you can't put them away, hide piles of things (magazines, videos, CDs, mail) under a pretty piece of material. Also, put away too-obvious photos, memorabilia, and evidence of other lovers when you expect a date at your house. This avoids unnecessary jealousy, insecurity, and questions.

Woo Warning

If you really don't want anyone in your place, arrange meeting elsewhere or be ready before the appointed time so you meet outside (but making anyone wait too long is rude).

Who Pays?

When you start going on several dates, the issues about who pays can shift from the routine you have set up on your first dates. As you go out more often and spend more money, you might want to share more equally in some of the expenses. For more on this, see Chapter 14.

Getting the Go-Ahead or Putting on the Brakes

Along the way, there will be signs about whether you are interested in—and suited for—each other. Think of these as traffic lights. Green means it's safe to go ahead. Yellow means caution, that it might turn to red, a sign to stop. I talk about this traffic light metaphor also in Chapter 25.

Green light, go if …

- ◆ He or she asks what you would like and does it.
- ◆ The amount of time you talk together increases.
- ◆ The things you share become more intimate.
- ◆ He or she says "sweet" things (you're gone only a few hours and are missed).
- ◆ You think about each other when you're apart.
- ◆ You both put other people on hold when either of you calls.
- ◆ You leave free time (from work or other appointments) to see each other.
- ◆ You wonder what each of you is doing when you're not together.
- ◆ You get a twinge of possessiveness or jealousy.
- ◆ You are amused by things that might have annoyed you in others in the past.
- ◆ You think about having a picture of him or her.
- ◆ You develop experiences as a couple ("your song," "your place to eat").
- ◆ You feel comfortable sharing feelings.
- ◆ You listen attentively to each other.
- ◆ You do thoughtful things for each other (scraping the ice off her car, leaving him his favorite breakfast at his door).
- ◆ You enjoy each other's company, even "doing nothing."
- ◆ He or she asks what you did that day, and is interested in hearing your experiences.
- ◆ Neither of you has a desire to date others.
- ◆ Flirtations from others don't make you flirt back.
- ◆ He or she puts a toothbrush for you in the bathroom.
- ◆ You aren't afraid to do and say what comes naturally.

- You express affection freely to each other.

- You're willing to spend time with each other's friends or family.

Yellow light, proceed with caution if …

- One of you makes all the approaches or invitations.

- One of you is hesitant to make definite plans and leaves things until the last minute.

- You get together only if there is nothing better to do.

- Some things your date says don't ring true.

- You find yourself being unnatural, playing games, or being dishonest.

- Dates are refused.

- He or she lies.

- He or she plays games.

- Dates are often broken.

- You get excited about meeting that new person your friend wants to fix you up with.

- You find yourself not feeling special or thinking, "He says that to all the girls" or "She's the same way to every man."

- He or she seems unresponsive when you are together, or attention to you is inconsistent.

- He or she doesn't show any affection toward you in front of other people (beyond being shy or not liking public displays of affection).

- He or she doesn't tell friends or family about you.

- He or she rarely compliments you or returns compliments you give.

- He or she doesn't ask what you're doing (on evenings or weekends).

- He or she doesn't call when he says he will.

- He or she won't make any sacrifices or change any plans to see you (especially if a certain date is important to you).

- He or she always seems too busy to see you.

- He or she says "I need more space." Give it. Remember that your time and love is precious.

- He or she doesn't offer affection (holding hands, hugging).

- He or she is critical.

- Everything is on his/her terms (where you go, when you go out) and never at your request.

- You don't "feel" emotion from—or for—him or her.

- He or she makes too many references to sex too soon.

Woo Warning

If you find yourself still looking at others, don't immediately think it means your date is not the one for you. Healthy males and females can keep on looking until the day they die.

The more of these warning signs that apply, the less likely it is you are truly interested in each other. Of course, it's possible that other things are getting in the way, but generally, if many of these warning signs are present, it is best to turn your attention elsewhere.

You can usually gauge someone's interest by his/her actions. But if you're unsure about someone's intentions, ask and get feedback. Set things straight early in a relationship. Say something casual, like "I had a great time. We should do it again sometime, don't you think?"

Getting Double Messages

What do you do when you get double messages? Rocco likes a girl he's dated a few times, but she's giving him double messages. Sometimes she's nice when she sees him on campus, and other times she ignores him. She told his best friend that he calls her too much. This may "feel" like double messages, but really the message is quite clear: Back off. Rushing into something too fast makes the other person feel suffocated and crowded. Give her space—get involved in other interests so you don't become overly attached.

Clicking or Clunk?

Everyone has his own pace and comfort level for intimacy and independence. Some people need time to let a relationship grow, while others jump right in and go for broke. Some drag their feet, suffer fears, or endlessly sit on the fence. If your styles clash, you won't be on the same wavelength. Keep alert to each other's pace in developing a relationship.

To truly hit it off, your love scripts must intertwine. For example, Kiesha was totally taken with her new man who had a stash of cash. She dreamt of long romantic weekends in the Islands at five-star hotels, so when he suggested, "Let's go to some cheesy motel for the night and be naughty," her fantasy was crushed, she felt insulted, and she stopped returning his calls.

Is This Going Anywhere?

If you are really enjoying each other, you will likely feel right about continuing to be together. As soon as you start wondering about whether you are wasting your time, you might be. The more dates you have, the more you will also be deciding whether this person is "the one." While this is a natural reaction, it is best to take each date one at a time and let things evolve at their own pace without imposing definitions or expectations about whether it's forever. Like the old song says, "You can't hurry love." You have plenty of time to make that decision after months of seeing each other.

Sometimes the fire is a flash in the pan and when you really get to know the person, you realize you are not right for each other. By the opposite token, you could appreciate things you didn't notice at first. That confused Jody at first. She asked me, "I don't usually like men with round cheeks, a beard, or a hairy chest, but I met a man who looks like that and I think I'm falling in love with him. How can that be, and won't I fall out of love with him eventually?"

Like Jody, nearly all women and men have a concept of what constitutes a desirable mate (see Chapter 2). While women can still specify details about men they find physically appealing or unappealing (hair, height, build), they can more easily than men suspend such judgments when confronted with a suitor who does not fit that type yet who still captures their heart. Remember the truth of the idiom that looks fade. Identify those qualities that you appreciate, and keep concentrating on those.

 Dating Data

Instead of affection diminishing, appreciation of someone can actually grow. Someone you initially may not find physically attractive can appear more attractive over time, as the person treats you well and intimacy grows.

Cutting It Off

"My definition of dating these days is caller ID and call-block," quips my friend, TV producer and reporter Susan Cingari. She said it in humor, but caller ID is not a bad idea; that way, you know who's calling and whether you want to pick up. No matter how you do it, rejecting someone is not fun for anyone, so please be kind. If you believe, as I do, in karma, then whatever you do to others eventually comes back to you. Acknowledge how you enjoyed meeting the person, appreciate specific things about them (humor or intelligence), and then say something that is honest and nonblaming about why you can't continue the relationship. Never say you don't like them (that can hurt forever), but point out how both of you would be better suited for different partners. See Chapters 25 and 26 for more on getting on with your life after rejection.

Making Subsequent Dates

Once you've established that you're into each other, you have to set the pace for how often you make contact and how often you get together. This is the tricky part: keeping track of how and where you both stand on whether you are free to date others, or if you are seeing each other exclusively. What number of dates (three dates, or consistent dates for three weeks), events (family functions, meeting close friends, staying over), or sexual activity defines commitment for you both? Make sure you both have the same criteria for this. Nothing is more painful than one of you thinking the other owes you exclusivity. And nothing is more common in dating than getting hurt if you think you're "seeing each other exclusively" but the other person still wants to play the field.

Dr. Judy's Dating Do's

As long as you don't deceive anyone, you can date as many people as you like (to boost self-confidence, feel less desperate, and meet many interesting people while learning about yourself). But you might prefer to concentrate on one person at a time to see whether you are "enough" for each other.

Woo Warning

You are being obsessive or becoming co-dependent if you beep or call several times a day and the other person gets increasingly busy or short in response. Control your urges. If you get a clear message to back off, respect that. Stalking reflects a serious psychological disorder. And if you're the one being stalked, don't hesitate to tell the other person to back off.

Take it slowly and don't expect exclusivity until it really becomes clear that the two of you are getting more serious. One test of the other person's interest is to mention that you're going out with a "friend"; if he of she asks more questions or seems curious, he or she likely cares about whether you date others (if not, he or she may also be too anxious to ask). You can always have a discussion about it. Wait until a time when both of you feel relaxed and have private time. Start out talking about what exclusivity means in general, and then bring up a situation between the two of you (ask, "Are we agreeing to see each other only, or are we still dating other people?"). Listen to the answer and respect the other person's needs. The one who wants to have more "space," or isn't "ready" to get more serious, should set the pace, whether you like it or not. You can never force anyone to like you or want to see you.

The more you see each other, the more contact you may have over the phone, Internet, or in person. Trust your instincts about when to call, beep, e-mail, or send a text message. If you get the sense that you are being demanding, do something else to get the attention you need at that moment (get busy with your own work, responsibilities, or a pleasurable activity) to keep your attention focused elsewhere.

Men, Women, and Dating

Men and women definitely approach the dating scene differently (as you'll see in Chapter 17). Here are some guidelines for both men and women to consider at this stage of the game.

What Men Need to Know: The Woman's Point of View

DO:	DON'T:
Be romantic and sensitive in your words and actions. Send cards. Bring small gifts (flowers or thoughtful trinkets).	Compare her to other women.
Listen attentively. (Eye contact is critical here; if on the phone, ignore your call waiting.)	Rush things.
Agree to do things with her family and friends.	Be a player or flirt with other girls.
Build her trust by being faithful and truthful, and always "being there."	Imply she needs to lose weight.
Spend time cuddling.	Expect or demand sex.

What Women Need to Know: The Man's Point of View

DO:	DON'T:
Take the initiative.	Expect him to profess his devotion so soon.
Understand his need to be alone or withdraw once in a while.	Push him into a commitment or an exclusive relationship.
Take things slowly.	Get overemotional or take everything personally.
Let him have a night out with the guys.	Snoop.
Accept him without judgment.	Nag him into talking about his feelings.

Dating Data _____

In a newspaper article, authors Ron Mitchell and Sacha Mornell wrote about accumulating "date equivalents" to rack up the number of contacts necessary for a woman to feel comfortable before she gets intimate with a guy. A telephone contact is equal to 0.5 dates, making two long phone conversations equal to one date. Or you can leave a voice mail message at her job late at night so she starts work with a nice message from you; call or e-mail after a date when you know she won't be home yet; or call when you know she's away on vacation or on a weekend, and say you're thinking of her.

After the Night Is Over

As with after the first date, always say something nice about the time you spent together. Don't make false promises about what comes next if you're not interested. But if you are interested, then go ahead and say so. Your date will welcome the encouragement! Follow up with a casual phone call, e-mail, fax, cell phone call, or message on the machine saying something like, "I had a great time." Comment on something you shared. Keep the contact going. Forward a joke (just the really funny ones, please) or inspiring e-mail (like from beliefnet.com), being careful not to overdo it. Send a fun card (there are free ones on the Internet, or make one yourself) or write a personal note with something poetic or interesting. This is the time to start revealing your unique personality even more.

Time In Between

Now that you've gotten to know each other a little better, you're either getting along or still not so sure. In these early stages, be aware of the following:

♦ Don't jump to conclusions too fast. Follow my six-date rule if you're at all interested. Give someone six dates to really reveal him- or herself so you see each other on bad hair days and in different situations. Over time, you'll be able to better judge character and compatibility.

♦ Stay grounded in reality instead of sliding into the fantasy of a dream lover. Be careful not to plan your vacation with that person already in your mind, think you're set for New Year's Eve, or start shopping for a wedding dress.

- Keep busy with your own life so you still have interesting things to share with one another.

- If you don't feel interested in accepting other dates, don't—but also don't expect he or she will do likewise.

The Stages of Hooking Up

There are many stages between casual dating and getting serious. There's more to say about commitment in Chapter 22, but for now, notice these 10 stages:

1. The first look. At first glance, you sense initial attraction. Research shows it takes 15 seconds to make your initial decision about whether you are interested.

2. The first flush. When you're face-to-face, you get a fuller sense of how you interact and whether you feel good being around each other and can talk to each other.

3. Feeling "in like." You enjoy being around the person and are curious to find out more about him or her.

4. Feeling lust. This is the flush of adrenaline that may make your heart pound. Your skin tingles, and you can't wait to feel their arms around you or their lips on yours.

5. Falling in love. You've spent time together, and you notice he has that savoir-faire that makes you melt. He orders wine and you're impressed he knows the vineyards. She talks to your friends and you feel the thrill of pride over your catch.

6. Getting over humps. You first imagine you could wake up every morning looking at her without makeup, or you decide you can fall asleep every night next to him even though he snores.

7. Speaking words of commitment. Telling each other you could be "the one."

8. Practicing "coupledom." You spend a weekend playing house, making his bed, cooking her breakfast, and taking your nephew to the zoo. Now you think you might be able to do the marriage-and-kids thing together.

9. You may move in together and see how you really get along.

10. You can get through the rough spots, where you might feel tinges of being bored with him or you're worried that she doesn't look as hot to you that day. Still, you hang in there and it gets better again.

The Least You Need to Know

- ◆ Choose things to do that you know you both enjoy.

- ◆ Keep thinking about enjoying what you do instead of becoming involved too quickly.

- ◆ Be sensitive to cues about whether you are getting along.

- ◆ Always be gracious about appreciating each other's company, even if it's not going anywhere.

- ◆ Be prepared to take things slowly; be aware of each other's pace and comfort with intimacy and the stages of commitment.

Chapter 14

Money Matters

In This Chapter

- ◆ Recognizing your attitudes about money
- ◆ Keeping a dating budget
- ◆ How to talk about money and decide who pays
- ◆ When finances fuel or extinguish sex appeal
- ◆ For love or money: sugar daddies and sugar mommies
- ◆ How to marry a millionaire

The best things in life may be free, but sooner or later in dating, money is going to matter. Just how much finances figure in your love life will depend on your attitudes, values, needs, lifestyle, and desires.

I'm sure you know stories that back up statistics that show that people can break up over disappointments or disagreements about money. That's why it's important to know the priority you place on money in your life, the symbolism you attach to it, and how you use it. Knowing the same for anyone you date is crucial in order to predict how compatible you can be.

Your Attitudes Toward Money

How you deal with finances during your dating depends on your and your date's attitudes toward money. Attitudes are beliefs that we develop, and thoughts that stick in our mind and govern our behavior. For example, if you're a woman who grew up thinking that the guy should always pay for the date, you could get mighty angry if he doesn't snatch up the bill. Or if you're a guy who has that attitude, and you're short on cash, you might not even ask someone out!

Of course you're entitled to your attitude, but it would be a shame if you had some preconceived notions and they got in the way of your starting, or continuing, a potentially good relationship. So let's review your attitudes toward money, with the intention of seeing how these affect your dating behavior.

Beliefs usually start in childhood and then get adjusted by experiences as we grow up. Our peers' attitudes also affect us; when girls ogle a guy's fancy car, for example, they perpetuate valuing guys for their possessions.

Dating Data

Women are becoming wealthier, because of higher numbers of women working, the maturing "baby boom," and mortality figures that favor women living longer than men. Although they still earn less on the dollar than men in comparable jobs, the U.S. Department of Commerce statistics show women make up 41.5 percent of all individuals with assets over half a million.

Examine what you learned about money from your parents or other significant figures, or experiences when you were growing up, and how they affected how you act toward money now. Write down your thoughts in the following space. For example, let's look at two women. Georgette grew up in a family that had little money, but her father worked hard and taught her that if she got a good education, she could get a high-paying job and make more money than they had, and live a good life. That inspired her to go to business school and start her own successful business. By the opposite token, Danielle's mother told her that she should get a decent job but marry a man who can give her a good life, and as a result, Danielle judged her dates by how well they could fulfill that prophecy.

Roots of My Money Attitude

What my father taught me about money:

_____

How it affects my choice of dates now:

_____

What my mother taught me about money:

_____

How it affects my choice of dates now:

_____

What another significant figure taught me about money:

_____

How it affects my choice of dates now:

_____

Thinking of someone I admire for the way he or she handles money, what I can learn about managing my own money:

_____

What I learned about money from dating experiences:

_____

My stereotypes about money (for example, men should pay, or women should share equally):

_____

My underlying psychological needs or conflicts about money (for example, I should be taken care of, or I have a hard time accepting when someone pays for something for me):

_____

Monitoring Your Money Mind

There are many phrases about money that have become part of our daily lexicon. Which ones can you think of? Look over the following table and check which phrases you relate to. Fill in any others you can think of. What do these phrases say about you and how you feel about money, life, partnership, and your values? If you are not happy about thinking this way, you can always work on changing your attitude. In one technique, as soon as you say the phrase, see a big stop sign in your mind or say "stop" aloud, and replace the phrase with something else that you prefer. Or, instead of reading the phrase as it is, replace it with the opposite or another related one that you prefer.

Which phrases does your date believe? How many do you feel similarly about? If you feel differently, how does that affect how you think, feel, or behave toward each other?

Our Money Attitudes

	I Would Say:	My Date Would Say:
Money can't buy you love.	❏	❏
The best things in life are free.	❏	❏
Money isn't everything in life.	❏	❏
Put your money where your mouth is.	❏	❏
Money is the root of all evil.	❏	❏
Money makes the world go round.	❏	❏
The only thing that matters is money.	❏	❏
Everybody's always after your money.	❏	❏
You get what you pay for.	❏	❏
The rich are better than us.	❏	❏
There are some things money can't buy.	❏	❏
All that glitters is not gold.	❏	❏
I deserve the best money can buy.	❏	❏
_____	❏	❏
_____	❏	❏

The Indecent Proposal Test

When Robert Redford propositioned Demi Moore in the movie *Indecent Proposal*, her dilemma ignited a controversy around the question: Would you have sex with a handsome stranger if the person offered you a million dollars? Most women and men I've asked on my radio show were unequivocal: They would go for the bucks and convince the mate it's in both of their best interests. What would you do, faced with this situation? Would you have the one-night stand and take the money, or decline? Would you tell your spouse about the offer? What would he or she recommend you do?

Your Money Style

Just as in Chapter 15 where I talk about your love style, you also have a style about how you handle money. Which of the following statements describes you and your dates? Rate yourself on these characteristics, placing a mark along the continuum from one end to the other. Ask your date to do the same, using another color pen, or mark where you think he or she would answer.

Money Style

I'm a real risk taker	— — — — — — —	I watch carefully what I spend
I'm overly generous	— — — — — — —	I'm very tight-fisted
I'm reckless and irresponsible	— — — — — — —	I'm responsible
I keep detailed records of how much I spend	— — — — — — —	I spend whatever I like

Compare how you and your date(s) rated, and discuss your differences. You don't have to be the same in how you deal with money. If one of you is a careful record-keeper, the other doesn't have to be. Decide whether you want to change. Being reckless about spending is not a helpful trait! Being overly generous may reveal a need to earn love or respect, when it would be healthier to be only somewhat generous.

Dr. Judy's Dating Do's

Dating TV shows have set new standards in how people prepare for dates, including the practices of buying new clothes, new hairdos, and bringing gifts. Find out what your date likes so you can be sure to please without blowing your budget.

Money as a Barometer of Sex

Economics drives our ego. Feeling financially flush can lead to feeling flush with sexual excitement. By the opposite token, a blow to your account can take its toll on both sexual desire and performance.

If a man associates money with power, and can only perform when he feels powerful, his sexual desire and prowess is going to be at the mercy of his salary. Any dips in his bank account will make him feel he also doesn't amount to much in bed. While women have traditionally felt more or less sexually attracted to men according to their wealth, women are now extending that measurement to themselves as well. As they become more enmeshed in measuring themselves by their earning, they find themselves similarly falling prey to sexual problems suffered by men.

To prevent these problems, separate sex from money and power. Clear your mind regularly from money worries so you're free to be turned on. Remind yourself continually of your value as a person and a sexual partner.

Having "The Talk" About Money

You might easily fall into a pattern about who pays, for what, and when, that works for both of you. But if anger or resentment builds, before you throw in the towel on the

Dr. Judy's Dating Do's

Always explore your own and your date's attitudes towards handling money before you kiss off any potential mate. Have courage to talk about these attitudes, to see if you can make changes or compromise.

relationship, consider having a talk about how to handle finances. I know this can be very difficult and embarrassing, or you may worry about your date's reaction. Maybe you think you are attacking the other person's personal worth, or revealing that you have mercenary values. Recognize these hesitations and have the conversation anyway. Holding back discussing such issues may only drive you apart anyway. Be honest and aware of how this discussion indicates how well you trust each other.

How Much Is This Going to Cost?

Anticipate dating expenses beforehand. This will be evident as soon as you plan where you go and what you do. For example, when going out to dinner, what type of restaurant will it be? Edward said, "I just heard about a great new restaurant started by a famous chef and designed by the architect who built the best restaurant in Hong Kong," guaranteeing it's at least $60 a person for the meal. How much different would this be if he said, "I really like that really out-of-the-way place on the other side of town that isn't too fancy but the food is really good." Your mental calculator would be ringing up maybe up a bill one tenth that amount!

Even the typical date of movie and something to eat is not cheap these days. With the average movie at $10 a ticket, and an after-show bite to eat at $15 a person, you're looking at $50 at least for a simple night out.

Most people live on a budget, so keep track of expected and real expenses for your dates. Ben had a good suggestion, "I can easily excuse myself to the bathroom and put things really fast into my palm pilot so I have a record right away of what I'm spending." Here's a sample of items for your dating expense record. Put an amount under each column for what you paid and what your date paid for three recent dates. Fill in any other expenses you can think of at the end of the table.

Dr. Judy's Dating Do's

A man might suggest an expensive date at first to impress you, but that's really stretching his budget. Why not give him a little out, by presenting a less expensive alternative. If he instantly sighs with relief and goes for it, you know you've helped him out of a financial crunch.

Dating Expenses Record

	Date 1		Date 2		Date 3	
	Me	*My Date*	*Me*	*My Date*	*Me*	*My Date*
Phone calls (cell phone time can add up!)						
Food						
Events (tickets, entrance fees)						
Transportation (car, taxi, parking)						
Clothes (anything special to wear)						
Gift						
Preparations (haircut, manicure, massage)						
Unexpected costs (a spontaneous ride on a horse-drawn carriage; having a caricature done by a sidewalk artist while taking a walk in the park)						
_____ _____						

Here are some tips on handling finances over time:

♦ Decide on your dating budget for a reasonable period of time, depending on your income. Estimate an amount just as you would for rent, phone, or other expenses. Of course, it might vary over time, unlike monthly bills, because you might go out more one month and less another month.

Dating Data

Wise money management has become increasingly important in the current economy, with increasing options to educate yourself, through TV channels devoted solely to money matters, innumerable courses and media advisors, and reasonably priced investment opportunities.

♦ Estimate how long you have been dating a particular person. Figure out your long-term spending account, and then vary dates from more to less expensive ones, so you can stay within a long-term budget. For example, go to an expensive restaurant every third time, but in between, order take-out, or just have fun stopping in to a drive-through!

♦ If you're not dating the same person, decide on how much you will spend on one person and what you have left in your dating budget for an unexpected new date.

Let's face it. Whether you like it or not, you're both going to be figuring out how much you each can afford on your dates. Some indicators include suggestions about where to go (a walk in the park versus dinner and a show); where you both live; suggested transportation (bus or taxi); talk about lifestyle (hanging out or sailing the Pacific); and personal responsibilities (alimony, two homes, ill parents).

Who Pays?

Anything goes when it comes to who pays these days. Early in dating you will make one of several choices: your date pays, you pay, you split the expenses (the old "going Dutch," which could mean you each pay for yourselves or you pay for different parts of the date), or you take turns paying (an option increasingly common these days, "I'll treat you this time, you get it next time").

Here are some guidelines to follow about who pays:

♦ Whoever invites the other person out pays for the date.

♦ Whoever has more money pulls more weight paying.

♦ Whoever doesn't pay offers to contribute—and should be prepared to follow through with the offer if accepted, without being angry or resentful.

Bring cash and credit cards (if you have them) to cover what you expect to pay, with "emergency" money in case something comes up or vendors accept only one form of compensation. Even if you are being "treated," be prepared to take care of emergencies (he loses his money, her credit card is declined, or you want to split early and have to get home on your own steam).

To avoid the problem of too-expensive dates, plan a few activities that don't cost much. For example, go to free concerts in the park, take a drive, visit a museum, or hang out with friends.

The tradition where the guy always pays has changed, to where the couple can make new decisions. There are several reasons these days why more women offer to pay:

> **Dr. Judy's Dating Do's**
>
> Even if one person earns more than the other, the lesser-earner should offer to pay sometimes—the offer may be declined but will be appreciated. Make up for it by preparing a surprise of something you've pre-paid for.

- ◆ More women are earning more money, and so have greater financial resources.

- ◆ Some women earn more money than men these days, especially if the woman is older than the man.

- ◆ Paying her own way gives the woman some emotional benefits, like feeling independent, powerful, generous, or enjoying role reversal ("wearing the pants in the relationship").

- ◆ Paying her way separates money from sex, like for Cherise who admits that she still feels she owes a guy something when he spends a lot of money on a date. "I hate to say it," she said. "But if he just paid $200 for a meal, and he wants to make moves and have sex, I feel a funny obligation. That's why I feel much better if I pay my way, or he doesn't spend a lot, so I don't have to play if I don't want to."

Woo Warning

Old attitudes can die hard—be aware of how they affect your dating. Even though women are expected to contribute more to the financial aspects of dating, most women prefer men who pay, and some resent if he lets her pay, thinking she should "be taken care of" and "treated." And men may still operate with the belief that "I pay, she plays," expecting sex in return for paying for the date.

Money Needs

Some men and women are happy when their basic needs (shelter, food, clothes, and some entertainment) are taken care of. Others want a lavish lifestyle and if not able to provide that for themselves, they seek to "marry up" (to find a spouse who can bring them into a higher socio-economic status). A small number of women are willing to "marry down" (settle happily with a husband of a lower socio-economic status). Reflect on how much money you think you need, and how much you want, and whether recent dates measure up.

Talking About Money

Meeting a date's expectations about what a date costs, and how fancy or homegrown it is, may greatly affect how you feel about each other. Even though you'd like to think that *who* you are is more important than *how much* you spend, the truth is that people's attitudes can be triggered by money. The best way to prevent attitudes from wrecking your potential relationship is to talk about any problems. This takes courage. Surveys show that talking about money is as intimate a topic as talking about sex. As your relationship progresses, issues about finances become more important, especially as you decide about a future together. You will want to know ...

- What lifestyle do you each want? Will you be happy living simply or in a lavish home with expensive outings?

- What are both your present earnings?

- What are your future earning potentials?

- What are your financial responsibilities (alimony, child support, debts from college or other expenses, tithing or contributions to any organizations)?

- What are your collateral incomes (contributions from parents, inheritances)?

Read more about this in my book *The Complete Idiot's Guide to a Healthy Relationship* (see Appendix A), which explains how once you make a serious commitment, you need to make financial disclosures about the financial trio: what each of you *earns, owns,* and *owes.* The "Dozen Dollar Decisions" include key talking points about money, like "Will you have separate, or joint back accounts?" "Will you have a prenuptial agreement?" "How will you decide what you buy, like a house, car, stereo?" "Will anyone contribute to your expenses?"

The right time to address the subject of money is as soon as it starts gnawing at you. This might be on your first date, or it could be later. Just don't let it wait too long to get some answers about what's bothering you. Many a married couple has been brought to the brink of divorce over money troubles, so settle these issues long before getting to the altar. Resentments build quickly, and understanding finances can save the relationship. For example, he might not suggest a nice place—or to go out at all—if he doesn't have the money, leaving her thinking that he doesn't care about her when really he is ashamed or simply cannot afford it. Also, consider the date according to your date's cultural background before you make any judgments. Is it usual in his country to take a walk along the riverside, have a nightcap at a local bistro, or plan an evening at a show and expensive restaurant?

Be prepared that your date could be offended (you'll be able to tell by a chilly silence, or a defensive remark, like "That's not something to talk about"). Say something like, "That sounds like an expensive evening …" and wait to hear the response. If you think the date is not fancy enough, you can also be subtle in your tone and words, like suggesting, "It would be nice to do something special" and see what the response is.

Dr. Judy's Dating Do's

Gauge money conversation on the depth of your commitment. In the beginning of dating, don't ask details about finances, but the more serious you get, the more acceptable and essential (while still though maybe not comfortable!) it is to discuss finances.

For Love or Money

As I mentioned in Chapter 2 about love criteria, money might buy you love in some cases, or not matter in others. You have to know your date's priorities in life. It's true, some people are money-hungry and there are male as well as female gold-diggers. One woman I know refuses to date any man who does not give her expensive gifts and take her on pricey vacations. Similarly, another woman who is proud to say, "There is no such thing as an ugly rich man," advises all her young female friends who fall for guys who are cute that they should get over that, shut their eyes, and think about whether the guys can keep them in high style. She further disputes the romantic notion that love can reach heights if the guy's bank account dips.

Self-described "male feminist" and noted author Warren Farrell disparages these types of women. In his book *The Myth of Male Power*, Farrell describes how these pecuniary performance pressures strain men's egos and cause stress, physical illnesses, and even early death. Farrell and others champion the woman who judges a man by his personality more than his portfolio, and point out that these women have a greater chance of spiritual happiness than those who choose a loveless mate who simply can pay the bills. Of course, it's all a matter of what matters to you, for your personal happiness.

While people don't usually mention money when asked about the top qualities that attract them to a date (as I mentioned in Chapter 2), it's another story when I ask about the importance of love and money. Which matters more to you: love or money? There was even a TV show of that title, where the guy picked among 20 girls, but then the winner had to choose between him or a million dollars.

On a scale of 0 to 10, with "0" meaning not at all and "10" meaning a lot, rate how much money and love matter to you in the following table. When you rate "love" think of the global feelings and actions that implies, including feelings, relationships, romance, and caring. Then take a different color pen and ask a date to do it, or take your best guess and mark what you estimate your recent dates would say (fill in their names on the chart).

	You	Date 1 Name:____	Date 2 Name:_____	Date 3 Name:_____
How much money matters in picking a mate	——	——	——	——
How much love matters in picking a mate	——	——	——	——

Examine your scores and those of your dates, and identify any patterns. Do you consistently pick dates who are "into" money, or do you go for dates who are into love? How do your ratings compare to those of your dates? Do you tend to go out with others interested more in love or capital gains?

Qualify your answer by considering the attitudes you reviewed in the previous exercises. Why do you rate this way? Maybe you already have enough money and so look for love. Or maybe you believe that money can't buy love and the only thing that matters in life is love. Also consider how your ratings and choices of dates change with your circumstances (if you come into money, or feel strapped).

Examining these trends is not meant to make you judge yourself or others, but simply to help you to understand your values and priorities. How do you feel if a date seems more concerned with financial assets than feelings? Maybe your match balances assets, like the stereotype of the wealthy guy who's not at all physically attractive but always has a tall leggy "arm charm" who is waitressing to make ends meet but makes him feel good.

In a survey I did with one of my graduate classes, the class averaged a score of 67.3 out of 100 on how important love was (ranging from 35 to 88), and 32.7 out of 100 on how important money was, making love twice as important as money. Of course, a psychology class would naturally consider relationships important, but their comments did include mentions about the necessities of money (to finish school, start a family).

Here are some explanations from those who rated love higher than money:

◆ "My grandfather taught me that family and devotion to marriage means everything, so I have to give love a 70 but I know it takes money to get by these days."

◆ "Love gets an 85 because without love your life is empty."

◆ "Love means 80 to me and money 20 because I come from a poor country and learned that love is important."

◆ "My family is well off so they can help me, so I can afford to say love is 75 to me and money only 25."

Explanations from those who rated money higher than love:

◆ "I have to give love a 35 and money a 65 because money is tough now. I'd rather have a soul connection carry me through life than a full wallet, but only if I had a lover to help with my financial burdens now, could love matter more."

◆ "In a perfect world, love would be 100, but money is freedom, so I give it a 55 and love a 45."

The Old Sugar Daddy and the New "Sugar Mommy"

You're surely familiar with the term "sugar daddy"—the older man who pays all the expenses for a younger woman who lives a life of leisure. Many women do not look kindly upon fellow females who "live off" men, even if they might admit jealousy of such an "easy life." Or they disdain the idea, valuing the self-respect and freedom that comes from taking care of themselves financially, so they don't stay with a man for security, and know they can manage if the relationship breaks up.

The age of the career woman has created the corollary for the sugar daddy: the sugar mommy, where the woman supports the man. Celebrities have done it, like Cher and her then-bagelmaker boyfriend, and Elizabeth Taylor and her now-ex husband construction worker. The stigma attached to these unions has lessened, and some men even find it an appealing position!

Paying the bills can be a woman's insurance against rejection. As one woman said, "When I was married to a rich guy, I feared losing him and the lifestyle. Now that I have more than the guys I date, I feel like I won't be wiped out if it's over."

Jacqueline makes a six-figure salary and picks men who are out of work. Despite her friends' protests, she pays for the guy's meals, buys them expensive clothes, and even paid for her last boyfriend's child support. She came to me for therapy to understand her pattern and came to realize how taking care of a man makes her feel powerful. As she said, "I like to make men dependent on me like all those times I have been dependent on them. So I can ask a man to do things for me, because he's owes me, instead of me owing him." Getting what she wanted by paying spilled over into sex, as she said, "I pay so I expect him to please me sexually."

Dating Data

Men may even find it sexy when the woman pays. He enjoys that she is expressing her power, and he likes the feeling of being taken care of.

Woo Warning

The increase in the number of fiscally secure women allows more possibilities for "gigolos," the guy who takes advantage of a woman by living off her means. The dysfunctional nature of such co-dependency emphasizes the need for each person to be responsible for taking care of him- or herself without leeching off the other, in order to maintain self-respect and a healthy relationship.

The pattern became a problem because ultimately Jacqueline ended up hurt anyway. After spending so much on her last squeeze, he ended up cheating on her; worse yet, with a woman who offered him access to money and professional opportunities. Other problems can develop. A sugar mommy can start a relationship enjoying splurging on the guy, but end up resenting him, feeling used, and ultimately seeking more traditional roles.

Be aware that couples can compete over money, just as over career success. Whoever earns more could be perceived as having more power to make decisions, or expect more respect. If she earns more than he, he could feel threatened and emasculated, and she could feel dominating or unfeminine. Separate who charges from who's in charge.

A Dirty Dozen Tips on How to Marry a Millionaire

You know I encourage you to value personal worth, but we have to acknowledge a trend toward materialism in society today. The pursuit of money is partly caused by recession after a booming market, and reflected in the popularity of TV shows like *The Millionaire* and *Joe Millionaire*. The classes I lead at various seminar centers on "How to Marry a Millionaire" are always packed. I start out challenging people not to judge others' worth by their wealth, but then I do give advice on how to get what you want.

If money is what you're after, here are some tips on how to find that wealthy mate:

◆ Go where wealthy people go, like yacht clubs, pet shows, private dining clubs, auctions, polo grounds, wine tastings, expensive gyms, stockholders meetings, happy hours in high-finance neighborhoods.

◆ Check society columns in newspapers to see what's happening that you could go to. Go to plays, art openings, lectures or foundation events at museums, zoos, and parks that wealthy people would support or be members of.

◆ Save money to buy a ticket to a fundraiser. Look for ones where you can go to the cocktail hour or after-party admission that is far less expensive than the dinner cost. Get there early to take full advantage of the reception where people are mingling. Find someone to introduce you around. If you stay for dinner, call ahead of time to find out where you will be seated (request a table of singles).

◆ Take a course in some subject that rich people would participate or be interested in, like antiquing or building a custom car.

◆ Take up a sport that rich people would likely be doing, like sailing, skiing or golf.

◆ Network with friends who might belong to some club where they could take you as a guest.

◆ Stay abreast of news that would interest rich people (read *The Wall Street Journal*, follow stock prices, read books on the *New York Times*' best sellers list.

◆ Work as a volunteer or create a fundraiser event for a charity or organization (hospital, university) that celebrities and wealthy people would attend or be featured at. (This is how Paul McCartney's wife met him.). Make pitch calls or solicitations.

◆ Write an article for an upscale magazine and interview wealthy people you want to meet.

◆ Join associations likely to have wealthy members and business people. Go to annual meetings, conferences and conventions.

◆ Read high-class magazines like *Travel and Leisure*, *Wine Connoisseur*, *Architectural Digest*, for talking points and ideas on events and places to go.

◆ Get a job where you would interact with wealthy people, like running a boutique, managing a 5-star hotel, or selling real estate. One female flight attendant quit working for commercial airlines and joined a private jet company so she could meet a rich man (and she married a millionaire private plane owner). Carolyn Bessette Kennedy met the American Prince JFK Jr. (may they rest in peace) when she was a publicist/personal shopper for fashion designer Calvin Klein and he came in to buy some clothes.

Your attitude and how you present yourself matter. Here are five tips on how to *be* rich:

- "Think" rich. Don't imagine yourself as a pauper or you will come across with low self-esteem.

- "Live rich." Even if you don't have the money to support a fancy lifestyle, save whatever you can and splurge when the opportunity arises.

- Act rich. Carry yourself with confidence as if you are a "somebody." Be natural but act like you belong.

- Dress rich. Buy classy clothes, even if not expensive. A few nice outfits are better than a closet-full of mediocre attire. Look for bargains at designer discount stores or resale houses. Pay attention to grooming, with a good haircut, trimmed nails, clean shave, appropriate make-up (not overdone) and polished shoes. A nice piece of costume jewelry can be just as presentable as real diamonds and rubies.

Dr. Judy's Dating Do's

The best tip of all on how to get millions is to make it yourself instead of pursuing a wealthy date. The satisfaction and security are far greater!

- Talk rich. Make sure your accent is sharp and your vocabulary broad, and be prepared to talk about timely topics from the economy to arts and sports. Read varied newspapers and magazines. I'll never forget how my father used to quiz me on vocabulary when I was a kid; he would write words on 4x6 index cards so I could study them. Searching the thesaurus for new words is still one of my favorite pastimes.

The Least You Need to Know

- How you deal with finances on a date depends on your and your date's attitudes toward money.

- Be aware of your own and your dates' values concerning the importance of money. Separate your ego from economics, and assess your value as a personal, as well as financial, partner.

- Be clear about the basis for making decisions about who pays for what on dates.

- Don't be afraid to discuss issues about money before, during, or after your date, to clarify how to handle finances and avoid misunderstandings.

- Decide whether love or money is important to you in a mate. When looking for a wealthy mate, go where people with higher financial resources would go. But always feel your personal worth.

Part **4**

Is This "It" or Do I Keep Looking?

Dating should be fun and bring you happiness. If your dates are bringing you not joy but gloom, fear, and insecurity, then they're not right for you … and it's time to figure out what's going on so you don't make the same mistake the next time around.

In this section, I'll help you understand different personality types, why people act the way they do, and whether you indeed have found a good match. You'll learn about the importance of communication styles and the differences between the ways men and women approach love. You'll learn how to recognize, and handle, different or sometimes difficult personality types, and how to put a stop to unhealthy hook-ups. And when you just can't figure the person out or you're just not happy, you'll learn when and why to move on—or take a needed break!

Chapter 15

Are You on the Same Wavelength?

In This Chapter

◆ Getting to know yourself and your date

◆ A quiz to test four dating personality types

◆ Dating game questions

◆ The Noah's Ark test

◆ Matching by your senses

This chapter is about finding a date whose lifestyle, personality, and dating expectations are compatible with your own. While no date will ever be perfect, there are certain types of people who make better matches. When two people are running on the same track, the connection can be blissful. But when love trains collide head-on, or when their tracks diverge, the pain and disappointment can be overwhelming.

From psychology to astrology, theories abound as to why certain people get along, and others clash. While no theory tells the whole story, many offer useful clues about human behavior and compatibility. I've adapted certain personality theories to come up with the quizzes in this chapter.

Keep in mind that these are simplifications of some very complex theories and assessments. Use them as fun guides in your search for a lifelong love, or at least a pleasant dinner date!

Basic Dating Rule: Know Your Love Target!

Janet came to me for therapy to help her figure out why all her relationships turned sour. Janet is the spontaneous type. An artist, she loves to wear colorful, sequined dresses, and tends to move around a room like a jackrabbit. At a party at an art gallery that represents her work, she met the gallery's accountant, Al. Stunningly handsome, he was wearing a starched shirt and a dark suit, and spoke slowly and deliberately—unlike Janet, whose sentences tumbled out a mile a minute. Drawn to Janet's energy, Al followed her around all evening and then offered to drive her home. He lingered at her door as they said goodnight, and Janet, sensing his passion, grabbed him wildly. Standing in her foyer, they embraced passionately.

Janet thought about Al all week until she finally saw him again at another business function. Sidling up to him, she whispered in his ear, "I'm mad for you." To her shock, he pushed her away and muttered, "I don't want you to do that," as he walked away.

Devastated, Janet needed to make sense of Al's behavior. How could he be so hot one minute, so cold the next? I explained to her that while Al was so attracted to her "wildness," it probably frightened him—as did his own loss of control. If there was ever to be anything more between them, Janet would have to tone down her behavior and proceed more slowly.

This doesn't mean that you should adapt yourself, chameleon-like, just to get a date. But if you are attracted to someone whose outward style is radically different from your own, you may have to be more flexible in your approach. Sometimes it's easier to win over a person if you approach them in their style—even if it's a little against your nature. Al, the starched-shirt accountant, was upset that Janet came on to him during a business meeting, thus his rude rebuff. If she had been more sensitive to his nature, the results might have been different.

The Personality Style Quiz

The following quiz will help you assess your own style and that of your love interest. The questions come from a quiz that I adapted from the brilliant work on brain style by my friends at the Ned Herrmann Group. Answer the questions as they best apply to you. Then answer them as you think a date would (or give him or her the quiz). Most of us are a mixture of personality types, but the indications from the results offers some useful guidelines on compatibility. I've used this quiz to help many men and women over the years, and I know it works!

Dating Data

Over 30 years of research have shown that most people fall into one of four main personality categories, reflecting dominance in one of the four quadrants of the brain. Brain dominance determines how we think, relate to others, choose jobs, and fall in love. Once you determine which type you are, you'll have a better chance of determining who you like and don't like—and why. And once you know another person's basic type, you have an advantage in influencing or pleasing that person.

1. **The Personality Test.** My best qualities to attract someone are that I am …

   a. Smart and rational.

   b. Able to be counted on and get there on time.

   c. Romantic and a good talker.

   d. Spontaneous and a barrel of fun.

2. **The Love Test.** My feeling about love is …

   a. You have to keep your wits about you.

   b. You should go slowly and keep your emotions in check.

   c. It's the best feeling in the world.

   d. It's magical, especially if you take risks.

3. **The Money Test.** When it comes to spending money on a date, I believe in …

   a. Analyzing the best decision.

   b. Sticking to a strict budget.

   c. Spending on friends.

   d. Splurging for something special.

4. **The Restaurant Test.** I would rather eat in a …

   a. Highly recommended restaurant.

   b. Old-fashioned place I've been before.

   c. Romantic spot.

   d. Gazebo or hot-air balloon.

5. **The TV Clicker Test.** On TV, I would rather watch …

   a. *L.A. Law* reruns.

   b. The Learning Channel.

   c. *Oprah.*

   d. The Discovery Channel.

6. **The Perfect Date Test.** My idea of a perfect date would be …

   a. A stimulating conversation or debate over a new movie or current events.

   b. Clear plans of what to do and something I enjoyed in the past.

   c. A romantic dinner and intimate conversation.

   d. Doing something new or going somewhere different or exotic.

7. **The Sex Test.** When it comes to sex, I like …

   a. Being in control and performing well.

   b. To stick to proper times and places.

   c. Feeling close or like soul mates.

   d. Fantasies and being playful.

8. **The Future Test.** When I consider a future together, I need to …

   a. Know I have made the right decision.

   b. Feel secure.

   c. Feel warm and wonderful.

   d. Picture lots of excitement.

Record the number of a's, b's, c's, and d's you selected in the following table.

Your Score	Your Date's Score
a's _____	a's _____
b's _____	b's _____
c's _____	c's _____
d's _____	d's _____

The Four Basic Personality Types

No one personality type is inherently good or bad, desirable or undesirable. The challenge is to understand your own tendencies and those of your partner. If you are not in a relationship, you can use this information in your search. For instance, if you are basically conservative but would love a more spontaneous mate, you may have to adapt your style to attract this type of person.

Use your quiz answers to assess where you and your date fit into these four broad personality types:

◆ **Thinkers** (mostly "a" answers): Analytical, rational, logical people who love to win arguments and solve problems. They often choose professions such as banking, law, or engineering. Thinkers like to be right and know the facts. Don't come on with a barrage of emotions. Instead of saying, "This will be crazy" (a Creative response), or "I feel good about this" (what a Relater would say), ask, "What do you think?" Thinkers can be controlling, something to watch out for.

◆ **Conservatives** (mostly "b" answers): Practical, organized, detail-oriented people who go by the book and value predictability. They are often administrators, planners, or computer operators. Conservatives can seem picky and unimaginative, which may be frustrating for Creatives, who like taking risks. Or they might seem cold to a Relater. You have to appreciate their discipline and punctuality. If you need security, they're a safe bet. Initially, at least, be predictable and punctual yourself, to make them feel safe.

Dr. Judy's Dating Do's

Personality type is just one factor in the great mate equation. Compatibility is another. Remember that the key to compatibility lies with my three A's: acceptance, appreciation, and adjustment.

- ◆ **Relaters** (mostly "c" answers): Emotional, expressive, sensitive people who value personal relationships and communication of feelings over facts. Psychologists and teachers frequently fall into this category. Relaters love relationships, and talking about feelings. If you're interested in this type, get ready to talk a lot and dote on feelings. You'll win his/her heart if you ask, "What are you feeling?" and give lots of hugs and attention.

- ◆ **Creatives** (mostly "d" answers): Imaginative, free-spirited, impulsive people who thrive on experimentation and taking risks. They are often artists, CEOs, or entrepreneurs. Creatives are exciting even if they sometimes seem "too much" or a little wild. If you're attracted to this type, you're in for a ride, and can be stimulated to let your own imagination run free. Don't expect this type of person to focus on details or take "It can't be done" for an answer. Enjoy their fantasies and have fun!

Notice how your answers and those of your date overlap, and where they diverge. For example, if you both score the same on the relaters dimension, it means you probably have a fairly equal desire to express emotions. If your score is high on the creative scale while your date's is higher on the conservative scale, the two of you may be out of synch much of the time. If you are aware of your differences, you will be in a better position to understand your partner and work through the difficulties that are apt to arise.

While the cliché is that opposites attract, in fact it is common that "like" initially attracts "like." For instance, creative types who are into fantasy and adventure are more likely to enjoy dates who share their interests. But in the long run, all this similarity in temperament might get boring or create friction—for example, a creative man may wish he'd ended up with a conservative woman, or vice versa!

Woo Warning

Opposites may at first attract, and then repel. For instance, a thinker may be attracted to a relater for her warmth and outgoingness but as the relationship progresses, he may accuse her of being overly emotional. The very traits that are endearing in the beginning of a relationship may be the same ones that drive you apart—if you let them.

Lindsay is a poignant example of how understanding differences in style can help you avoid devastation in dating. This sweet, shy guy in his late 30s came to one of my seminars where I explained these brain styles. Weeks later I saw him again and he told me how he had been fixed up with a friend and for their date and she suggested they go to an amusement park. Frightened of the crowds and rides since childhood, he politely said he would prefer a quiet movie. She became completely disinterested, and ended the date quickly, which he never would have understood, he explained, had he not been familiar with the brain style quiz he learned in my seminar. It helped him understand that there was nothing "wrong" with him, and that their types simply did not mix. She was obviously the imaginative, risk-taking, creative "d" type, while he was the more organized, cautious, conservative or "b" type.

Coming to Your Senses

Our senses play a large part in why we choose dates and partners. Just as some of us are more creative and some of us more emotive, some of us are more focused on scent and others on touch. Once you know which sense is dominant in your love interest, you can use that knowledge in your seduction. Also consider these types when giving a gift. For example, give scented candles to a date who is scent-oriented.

Think back over your recent relationships. What is it that you first recall about your partners: the touch of their skin, their particular scent, the sound of their voice, their eyes, the feeling of closeness? If your dominant sense is visual, you'll probably create a picture of a person in your mind. If your dominant sense is aural, you are more likely to recall a voice or the songs you listened to when you were together. Kinesthetic types focus on how things feel—his strong arm muscles, her soft, silky hair. Some of us are most sensitive to smell, with a particular scent producing an instant flood of memories.

How can you tell which sense dominates in people you know well or barely know at all? Pay close attention to the words they use. Visual-type personalities use words to create pictures: "I see …", "Let's look at …", "I imagine …", and so forth. In a restaurant, they may reach for a pen to sketch on the tablecloth. If your love interest is visually oriented, choose eye-catching clothes and try gazing lovingly into her eyes.

Aural-type personalities might use phrases like "I hear that …", "I say …", "That sounds like a good idea …", "Something tells me …", and so forth. They may touch their ears when you're talking, or close their eyes so they can hear you better. If your love interest is more attuned to sound, try seducing him over the phone. Before you make the call, rehearse detailed descriptions of what you're doing and feeling. Have music playing when he comes over.

Dr. Judy's Dating Do's

Be sensitive to your date's reactions. For example, you may be the spontaneous type, but if your date is a more formal, conservative type (even if he's attracted to such forthrightness), temper yourself and present an idea calmly to let him get used to it.

Kinesthetic types are touch-oriented; they literally take a hands-on approach and concentrate on how things feel. They frequently use words that describe touching ("I can't put my finger on …", "I'm touched that …"), or textures ("This feels like …"). They shake hands readily and hold on longer, and find opportunities to touch you whenever they can. They may rub their chin or stroke their hair as they talk to you. They may also have a difficult time sitting still and move around a lot. If your love interest is a touchy-feely type, wear clothes that beg to be touched, such as silk or fur. Occasionally offer a gentle touch on the hand or shoulder.

Scent-focused types pay attention to how things smell. They'll sniff the food, your perfume—and probably you! Perfume, flowers, incense, and scented candles are obvious devices for attracting someone whose dominant sense is the sense of smell. But since the wrong choice can be a turn-off, ask your love interest about favorites.

The Noah's Ark Test

There are countless tests for determining compatibility. Some are scientifically based, such as the Personality Style Quiz, based on personality styles, earlier in this chapter. Others are more playful, based more on common sense than on scientific research. These fun tests are a useful way to encourage openness between you and a date. For example, consider the following hypothetical situation.

Imagine the world has come to an end. There is one boat: Noah's Ark. You can take just one animal as your companion. Which of these animals would you choose: a horse, tiger, sheep, or peacock?

The horse symbolizes a career, the tiger symbolizes power, the sheep symbolizes love, and the peacock symbolizes pride. Following this, a person who chooses the horse might be most focused on their work, and might tend to put relationships on a back burner. Someone who chooses the tiger might need to exert a lot of control over your relationship. Be prepared to give the person who chooses the peacock a lot of attention, compliments, and flattery, and the one who chooses the sheep a lot of affection.

The Dating Game Quiz

Classic TV shows such as *Love Connection*, *The Dating Game*, and MTV's *Singled Out* use simple questions and hypothetical situations to help couples find out whether they are well matched. Here are some questions like ones from these shows to help you assess your styles and preferences, as well as your date's. If you're not sure about asking your current love interest to answer these questions, take an educated guess at his or her answers.

For each of these aspects, underline the one that you prefer and put a check mark over the one your current love interest prefers:

Which do you prefer?

Q: Body: slim and trim, or muscle-bound?

Q: Sleep style: wrap-around or "Move over, baby"?

Q: Lifestyle: fireside chats or disco inferno?

Q: Commitment: one and only, or play the field?

Q: Underwear: silk boxers or cotton briefs?

Q: Eating: raw veggies or raw meat?

Q: Dazzle me with Einstein brains or beer stein?

Q: Career goals: Wall Street or Easy Street?

Q: Vampires: real romantic or blood-sucking freak?

Q: Snoop Doggy Dogg or Snoopy the dog?

Q: Let's go: Venice or Vegas?

Q: In the morning, sleep in, or "rise and shine"?

Q: E-mail me or call my cell phone?

Q: Strip clubs: sleazy or sexy?

Q: Bungee-jumping: daring or deranged?

Q: Wonder Bra or no bra?

Q: Lie to break a date, or go anyway?

For the following situations, write in the space provided how you and your date would respond.

Situation	You	Your Date
I caught you with another guy, and now your head is in a guillotine. What would you say to get out of it?		
If you were a dessert, what would you be? (The guy who won the date on this one said "chocolate mousse.")		

Situation	You	Your Date
You're on the *Oprah* show. What's the topic?		
I keep a secret diary. What would the entry read on the night I met you?		
What was your childhood nickname and why?		
If you could be a famous character, who would you be and why?		
If you met me at a crowded club, what would you do to get my attention?		
It's Valentine's Day and you wrote me a love poem. Recite it.		
If you were an ad campaign, what would the slogan be?		

Feel free to come up with your own questions to help stimulate conversation and display your creativity, as well as cue for specifics you want to know about your date.

What's Your Sign?

It has become cliché to ask someone, "What's your sign?" But interest in astrology is reviving. Even if you're a skeptic, there could be something to be learned from the 12 astrological types. Your sun sign can give you clues about why you like a certain person, what a date *may* be like, and what *might* appeal to him or her. At the very least, it can spark conversation between you.

New York astrologer Jenny Lynch, who runs an Internet dating site based on astrological profiles (www.sexyspirits.com), says the best time to date is when, according to your chart, Venus (the planet of love) is being influenced by positive aspects from the Sun or planet Jupiter. It all depends on how the planets are positioned and affected by each other. For example, Lynch says, Uranus will bring someone exciting, Saturn brings long-lasting relationships, and Neptune can bring in a soul mate!

The Least You Need to Know

- Learning about your own (and your date's) love style can increase your chances of finding a compatible match.

- No personality type is inherently good or bad, desirable or undesirable. The challenge is to understand your own and your date's inclinations.

- You can be attracted to people who are like you—or opposites *do* attract.

- Sometimes it's easier to win over a person if you approach them first in their love style.

- Tests and quizzes about personality and behavior—no matter how cursory—can be fun, give you valuable clues about you and your dates, and be a good way to get you talking.

Chapter 16

"Can We Talk?"

In This Chapter

- ◆ A quiz to determine your communication type
- ◆ Getting a nontalker to open up
- ◆ How to read his or her mind
- ◆ What to share and what not to share
- ◆ Communication do's and don'ts

In a roomful of potential mates, who's the one you'd feel most comfortable with? Likely it's the one who seems "on your wavelength"—someone you can talk to. Good communication is the key to a good relationship. Whether you're the silent type or a talker, you have to feel that you can relate to and are understood by your partner—you need to "speak the same language."

However, people do have different styles of communication. If you date someone whose style is different from yours, it is possible to adapt—as long as you know your own style, and what you're adapting to!

A Communication Quiz: Are You the Boulder Dam or Niagara Falls?

What kind of communicator are you? Find out your communication type by taking the following short quiz:

1. You've just had a big fight with your friend when your date calls. He tells you that he has just lost his job. You …

   a. Tell him all the details about the argument you had with your friend first.

   b. Warn him that you're upset, but then drop it to listen to him.

   c. Listen and pretend nothing happened to you.

2. You've been dating for a while and have a minor disagreement that you feel could erupt into your first big fight. You …

   a. Need to blow your stack and say everything that's on your mind.

   b. Don't want to talk about it until you both cool down.

   c. Want to forget about the disagreement completely because you feel there's no point in talking about it.

Dr. Judy's Dating Do's

Paying attention and noticing details are also qualities of good communication skills. It's a tremendous high to feel "heard" by someone. For example, while Andy and Melissa were riding in the car, she got excited when her favorite song came on the radio. The next day, he surprised her with the CD containing that song.

If you selected answer a) to both situations, you have the need to spill out your feelings. I label these kinds of people as Niagara Falls communicators—people who need to pour out their emotions to relieve their tension. Niagara Fallers clash with the other extreme, Boulder Dam communicators—those who answered both situations with choice c). These people don't like facing and revealing their emotions, either because they're too frightened of their feelings or because they feel it's a waste of time. They usually have problems being intimate because they don't want anyone or any feelings to get the better of them.

Though they are opposites, Niagara Falls and Boulder Dam communicators may be drawn to each other. Boulder Dammers look to Niagara Fallers to unleash or vicariously express their feelings, and Niagara Fallers look to Boulder Dammers to help them control their troublesome outbursts. But ultimately, a match can lead to unhappiness, as the Dammers get too uncomfortable and the Niagara Fallers get too frustrated.

Steamship communicators, those who answered b), are sturdy communicators who aim to be reasonable. They hold a steady course so that they are never running the rapids of uncontrolled Niagara Fallers, but are also never stagnated like the Boulder Dammers. Because they have a little of the two extremes, they can get along with either type of communicator.

Two Boulder Dammers and two Steamships usually get along better than two Niagara Fallers. This is because Niagara Fallers often blow up easily, leading to fights with no one there to referee.

Talkers Versus Silent Types—Which Is Better?

"When my boyfriend and I fight, is it better to talk it out right away, or talk about it later when we both cool down?"

The answer to this question depends on your communication style. That style is determined by how you deal with feelings and anxiety. Some people need to get their feelings out and have an argument resolved right away, or their tension grows. As soon as these types of people have let off some steam, they feel relieved and more connected, and their anxiety is reduced. For others, talking about something right away is what makes their tension grow, so they need a cooling-off period before they can communicate. Neither style is right or wrong, it's just a matter of understanding what works for you and your partner. Then you can adjust and accept each other's style of communication.

When You Won't Talk

If you are the silent one, why are you afraid to say what's on your mind? Are you afraid that you'll be judged, sound silly, or be misunderstood? Are there feelings or memories you don't want to face? Or are you afraid of getting hurt if you open up?

To increase your communication, try this exercise. On a piece of paper, write down some thoughts or experiences you'd love to—but fear to—share. Writing them down is an important step to clarifying the experience, feeling the fear, and possibly sharing the feeling.

When He Won't Talk

It's the biggest age-old complaint women have about men: They don't talk about their feelings. What's new—and this is good news—is that men are making progress. The Internet has been a great help in this department, because men have had to express themselves in written form—so they're getting better at it!

The bad news is that men still have a ways to go. Women tend to interpret a man's silence as deadly. Often they ask, "What are you thinking?" when they really want reassurance: "I'm thinking of you." Rather than saying, "You never talk to me," it's better to say to your male partner, "I'd really like to talk about (something specific)" because men respond better to specifics and clear requests about what they can *do*.

These communication issues don't apply just to men. Interestingly enough, I hear some men these days making the same complaints about women in their relationships. For example, Brad told me, "My girlfriend gets off the phone too quickly. I want to talk to her but she hangs up so fast, and I get really frustrated." One reason for this is that as women become more independent in their financial, social, and sexual roles, some have taken on more of the traditionally male ways of communicating. Also, there are some women who—like the male stereotype—just don't like to talk.

Dating Data

Women and men are conditioned at a very young age on how they should communicate. Tradition often still reigns, where girls are taught to openly express their feelings while boys are taught to hold in their emotions. Girls tend to spend hours on the phone talking to their girlfriends about their problems while boys are taught to solve their problems on their own. Unfortunately, too, some people today still perceive emotional men as being "weak."

The advice in the following situations applies equally for him if *she* won't talk, as for her when *he* won't talk.

"My boyfriend is afraid to express his feelings and has a hard time admitting them. What should I do?"

Be gentle, kind, patient, and reassuring. Some people are scared to reveal their feelings. It makes them feel vulnerable, exposed, and out of control. Reward your mate when he does make an effort to express himself by saying "Thank you. I love it when you say how you feel." Or, "I know that was difficult for you to say, but thank you for doing it." Or ask him about his experience in a reassuring way: "Now that you've said that, how do you feel about it? You may have expected some disaster or that you would be hurt. But, see, nothing like that happened."

"My boyfriend has a hard time expressing his feelings. But he did admit that he's scared to because he was hurt once before. What can I do to make him less frightened?"

First of all, appreciate the effort it took for him to tell you that he's scared, and that he was hurt before. Those are two big confessions, and reveal a tremendous effort to open up. Reassure him that everyone has been hurt sometime, and that being with you will not mean a repeat of the past. Tell him that he can recover slowly by building up his trust again. You can even agree on a label for his feeling—for example, call it the "fear factor." Make it humorous. Every time he feels it, have him alert you. Then both of you can turn it into something funny, like, "Oh, the fear factor is rearing its ugly head again."

"My boyfriend sends out mixed signals about whether he really wants to be with me. When I've confronted him, he's withdrawn. I'm afraid if I confront him again, he'll get tired of me and really break it off."

It's one thing to be a different kind of communicator from your mate, it's another if you feel threatened by trying to communicate. Don't suffer from anxiety. If you need an answer to a question—get the answer! If you push and he ends your relationship, what kind of future would you really have with that type of communicator anyway?

Is Your Date a Good Communicator?

Take the following quiz to discover how well your date communicates with you.

Picture the following scenarios:

1. You tell the guy you're dating that you're scared to get involved because you once had a bad experience where you got really hurt. He …

   a. Changes the subject, figuring it's too hurtful for you to talk about and he's really not interested anyway.

   b. Turns the table around and talks about his dating experiences.

   c. Asks you what happened.

   If he changes the subject, (answer a), you should find out why. Is it because such openness makes him uncomfortable or because he isn't interested (both are bad signs)?

   Is he afraid you'll be too hurt to discuss the subject (a better reason but still an avoidance of your feelings)? If he always turns the conversation to his experiences, (answer b), he's too self-centered to care about you. The best answer is c, because he's showing that he has empathy. Hooray for those dates who ask questions, say, "Tell me more," care about finding out about the real you, and are able to show it.

2. You tell the guy you're dating that a friend of yours is miserable because she was dumped by her boyfriend a few weeks ago and you're still upset for her. You then mention her name a few times in the next conversation you have with him. He …

    a. Says he doesn't remember what you said about her before.

    b. Asks you who she is.

    c. Asks you whether you want to ask her to join you the next time you go out.

Remembering what someone told you and doing something about it is a sign of a good communicator and shows the person really cares about you, as in choice c. However, choices a and b may show that the person either doesn't concentrate on what you say, or isn't interested enough.

3. You call your girlfriend on her cell phone and she's on the Internet e-mailing back and forth with another friend. You say it's an emergency. She …

    a. Asks you to call her back later.

    b. Puts you on hold and comes back eons later to your line.

    c. Gets off the other line to talk to you.

Placing priority on the relationship and making the other person feel important is a sure sign of good communication and caring. There's nothing more exciting than thinking that you come first, no matter what. Answers a and b are not unacceptable, but a c answer reveals her good character, raises your self-esteem, and strengthens your bond together.

4. You tell the woman you're dating that you were hurt by something she did. She …

    a. Tells you that you're too sensitive.

    b. Denies that she did anything wrong.

    c. Apologizes and asks what she did to hurt you.

Defensiveness, as in answer a, and denial, as in answer b, shut down communication and sabotage closeness and openness. Someone who can accept your feelings and examine their own behavior, as in answer c, is the best choice.

5. You tell the guy you're dating that you would like to spend more time with him. He says …

    a. "We already spend a lot of time together."

    b. "Just like all women—it's never enough."

    c. "Okay, but why? Do you feel like we're not close enough?"

Pointing out whether someone is right or wrong, as in answer a, doesn't get to the heart of the matter. Generalizing, as in b, further negates the person's feelings. Choice c shows that the person is not being defensive, but rather is truly open to what is really troubling you.

6. You're trying to tell the guy you're dating how you feel about something he said. He …

   a. Gets impatient because you're not spitting it out fast enough.

   b. Asks you what you mean.

   c. Finishes your thought for you.

Intuition, as in c, is another high state of communication. People really in synch with each other can anticipate each other's thoughts and can finish each other's statements. It's an exciting and affirming experience—but not one you should expect. Nor should you think that if someone cannot do that with you, he doesn't love you. Answer b shows that the person is patient and is trying to understand you—a good sign, and certainly better than answer a, which shuts you up and shuts you out.

Woo Warning

When pointing out something you don't like about a person, it's important to say what you *do* like first. Be careful not to criticize your date; criticisms only make people defensive and deflated. When the brain creates a positive image,

Mind Reading

When two people are in sync, they can often tell what the other is thinking and feeling before it's said. The feeling is exhilarating when she can finish your sentences (assuming, of course, she's respectful enough not to interrupt), or he says he knows exactly what you mean. But reading each other's mind is not always possible, nor does it mean you're not right for each other.

"What are you supposed to do when a woman wants you to automatically know everything she's thinking, and then gets angry when you don't?"

You tell her that if she cares about you, she should share her feelings with you and not play mind games. She needs to be more open and assertive when expressing her thoughts and feelings, without expecting you to automatically know her needs.

Some people were indulged by their parents when they were children—their every need was anticipated. As adults, these men and women expect their lover to do the same, and are quick to lose patience with mates who are not intuitive to their every feeling. They need to learn to be patient, accept that their lovers are not their parents, and learn how to communicate their needs without resentment.

Although you may think you're terrible at "reading" people, you're probably better at it than you think. I use an exercise in my classes to prove that everyone is capable of being intuitive. Find two other people to do this exercise with you. Person A thinks of a situation and assumes a body position consistent with the experience. Person B mimics the body position of Person A and concentrates on what that feels like, and reports on what Person A must be thinking. Person C monitors and adjusts Person B's position to match Person A's position as closely as possible. It's uncanny how often Person B is right in reporting what Person A is thinking.

The exercise proves that concentrating on the other person's emotions and getting into his or her mental as well as physical "space" can help you tune in to others (since a large proportion of the messages of what someone means is communicated through body language).

How Much Should You Share?

Some books about dating tell readers to "hold back" on some of their feelings and not to give away anything. As in playing poker, they advise you to keep your cards close to your vest. But you've probably noted from my advice throughout this book that I don't agree with this type of game-playing. If you feel that you have to resist being yourself, the relationship is not right for you. A good relationship is one where you feel you can ask your partner anything, speak your mind, and do what comes naturally. But hold on. There are certain limits to what you should share:

- ◆ Don't talk about past loves unless you are perfectly sure that your date won't feel jealous or threatened. Evaluate why you are discussing the past (are you trying to foster jealousy or boost your own ego?).

- ◆ Don't talk about others you may be dating at the same time. This only stimulates competitiveness, disinterest, or judgments that may backfire on you, making the person drop out of a crowded playing field.

- ◆ Don't confess to something in order to selfishly get over your own guilt. For instance, suppose you told your date that you were busy at work, but really you had a date with someone else. Always assess what the impact of such confessions would be on the person you're seeing. Of course, you should think about—and resist—betrayal beforehand, but once the damage is done, why throw salt on an open wound? Learn to forgive yourself. Don't expect a hurt person to absolve you and make you feel better.

Handling Touchy Situations

Even the touchiest situations can be dealt with if you know how to communicate effectively. Here are two examples:

"How do I tell the guy I'm dating that he's cheap?"

Have a general discussion about money and what it means to both of you. Consider using an icebreaker so that he's not put on the defensive. Ask him to explain his fears about money. What did he learn in childhood about handling money (he could be copying his father)? Money can also be symbolic of a person's security, so discuss those deeper feelings.

"How do I tell my girlfriend, who has been under a lot of stress lately, that she's put on weight as a result of using food as a stress-reliever?"

Losing weight involves changing your lifestyle, exploring your emotional needs, and adopting an eating and exercise plan. You may suggest to your girlfriend that she's using food as a way to relax or to comfort herself, and that you'd like to help her find other solutions. Face up to your true motives (worry about her feelings or her health) or fear of what others will say about you being with her. Offer support and reassure her that you love her for who she is, not for what she looks like. Suggest that you exercise and eat more healthily together. Never drop hints about how heavy she looks; it will only damage her self-esteem.

> **Dr. Judy's Dating Do's**
>
> One way to show a person that you've been listening carefully is to repeat what the other person said. For example, if your date says "I'd like us to be closer," you say, "So you want to be closer." Then follow it up with a question like "What do you mean by that?"

Guidelines for Good Communication

There is no one right or wrong way to talk and express yourself. Learn to trust yourself and your style first. Any attempt at communicating will be appreciated and is a step in the right direction. Here are a few points to keep in mind:

◆ Talking is an ongoing process. You can't always cover a topic all in one conversation. If that's the case, end the conversation with: "We can continue this at another time."

◆ When expressing yourself, be as honest and straightforward as you can without beating around the bush. Write it down to help you focus. Get to the point and be clear about what you want to say or ask.

◆ Be open to questions. Give permission to your date to ask you anything.

◆ Be a good listener. Learn to listen without interrupting or telling your own story—hold back responding until the other person has finished a thought. (This is one of my favorite pieces of advice.)

◆ It's okay to be embarrassed. Some topics are difficult to discuss. Admit that you feel this way.

◆ Say up front what you think your boyfriend or girlfriend might fear when trying to discuss a topic. Preface the discussion by saying something like, "I don't want you to be hurt" or "I don't want this to scare you."

◆ Practice admitting difficult things: "I'm hurt by what you did."

Dr. Judy's Dating Do's

When asking a question or putting in a request, your best chance of getting what you want is to ask without expectations or demands (called "nondemand" requests). Simply state what you'd like without implying punishment or guilt-inducing feelings. This way the other person is free to give willingly or refuse without being defensive.

◆ Not knowing what to say is okay, but you can always come up with some explanation or answer. Nothing is more frustrating in a conversation than to hear a person say "I don't know," or worse, say nothing at all. You can say "I'm not sure why this happened, but it could be because …" Or you can ask what the other person thinks or feels.

◆ Know what's motivating and affecting you. Getting to the bottom of an issue is like peeling the layers of an onion. Talk is often a smokescreen for something else. What is your real need (to be loved, listened to, reassured)?

Words can be reassuring by easing your mate's fears, and can be alluring by promising pleasures to come. In order to get to these benefits, keep in mind the following do's and don'ts:

◆ DO relax. Anxiety ruins your concentration and confidence. Take deep breaths every time you feel like ending a conversation out of fear.

- DO listen to your date.

- DO be prepared for repetition. If the issue comes up again and again, it hasn't been resolved. Instead of complaining that your date is nagging, ask "What is really going on here? Why is the subject still bothering you?"

- DO be patient. Give the person time to express himself.

- DO admit that both of you have differences, which is okay.

- DO expect to feel uncomfortable. It's not always easy to confront issues.

- DON'T think you have to solve everything at one time.

- DON'T run away from a conversation. Talking is not always easy. Don't let your anxiety get the best of you. If you have something to say, say it.

- DON'T insult your date with vulgar terms and put-downs. It's disrespectful and cheapens not only your date but yourself as well.

- DON'T criticize, judge, or make fun of what your date has to say. You both have to feel comfortable sharing.

The key to having good and open communication with someone is to make him or her feel secure, loved, and respected. Speaking your mind and sharing feelings creates a bond that's sure to deepen your relationship. Doing this in a mutually respectful way also raises your self-esteem—and your partner's.

The Least You Need to Know

- Good communication is the key to a good relationship. It requires attention, acceptance, and appreciation.

- Understand and accept other people's communication styles, especially if they are different from your own.

- You can get nontalkers to communicate more by offering a lot of encouragement and compliments for when they do open up.

- Always be respectful, open, and honest.

- Give sharing your best effort.

Chapter 17

Men and Women: Not Such Different Planets

In This Chapter

- Left- versus right-brain tendencies
- Why men and women talk and love differently
- Debunking gender stereotypes
- Complaints women have about men and how to solve them
- Bridging the gender gap

Best-selling author John Gray summed up the differences between the sexes with this catchy metaphor: Men are from Mars and women are from Venus. But men and women these days are bridging the gap between those planets.

Eastern philosophy acknowledges those differences; not to imply gender but rather qualities of "masculine" and "feminine." The Chinese "yin-yang" symbol shown on the next page depicts the masculine (yang is active, positive, sky) and feminine (yin is passive, negative, earth) aspects of nature as two contrasting, but complementary, parts of a circle. Their interaction is essential to maintaining harmony and balance in the universe. It is important to note that passive is not negative nor is active positive, nor do these qualities only apply respectively to women or men. (For a full description of what this all means, refer to my book, *The Complete Idiot's Guide to Tantric Sex*.)

In the past several decades, many men and women have come to see that it is important to "own" both "masculine" and "feminine" parts of themselves. Many men these days are trying to become more sensitive, while women are making great strides in becoming more assertive and independent. Yet certain differences persist, and it's helpful to explore in this chapter how these differences play a part in the dating and mating world.

Left-Brain Versus Right-Brain Approaches to Life

It's easy to make gender generalizations: Men are stubborn, women are clingy. Men love violent movies; women prefer romantic comedies. These are cultural clichés that are slowly changing. But there is still some tendency that men and women communicate differently.

Dating Data

The Virginia Slims Opinion Polls taken over many years indicated that certain sex role stereotypes persisted. Women commented that men would rather get lost than stop and ask for directions, are bad cooks, monopolize the remote control, and can't find things around the house without a woman's help. Marlo Thomas once joked that hubby Phil Donahue always asks her where his shoes are, "as if my womb had sonar for his shoes and socks."

Research at the Ned Herrmann Group, with whom I've been associated for many years, suggests that most men are more predominantly left-brained, with their cognitive style being more logical (they tend to focus on problems and solutions). Women, on the other hand, tend to be more right-brained, with more of an emphasis on communication and emotion. This left- or right-brain dominance affects all kinds of everyday interactions and exchanges. The following table describes many of the ways in which right- or left-brain characteristics can show up in everyday life.

How Differences in Brain Dominance Affect Behavior

Left Brain	Right Brain
Values power, being in control	Values love and communication
Is motivated by being right	Is motivated by togetherness and harmony
Hates being told what to do	Accepts direction
Relates well to objects and things	Prefers relating to people
Likes to prove things	Likes to improve things
Comfortable with gadgets and hi-tech equipment	Comfortable with gab groups

Brain differences help explain why many men won't ask for directions (he needs to be right), and why many women get upset when men want them to get off the phone too quickly (she likes to talk). Women like to improve things, and will offer to help a guy without being asked (as a sign of love). But guys need to prove themselves, so they may interpret a woman's offer of help as an implied criticism (he's just not good enough). That's how your communication can get so confusing and why so many TV shows about singles show bubbles indicating "what he really means" in contrast to what he is saying.

Communication Styles

Here's how those differences show up in the way men and women talk to each other (based on my own work and that of Herrmann, Gray and linguist Deborah Tannen in her book *You Just Don't Understand*). Use these observations as guidelines to expand your possibilities: If one column describes you, consider the usefulness of the other.

 Woo Warning

What do most women list as their top complaint about men? According to my own and numerous other surveys, one of women's biggest complaints about men is that they don't talk enough about feelings!

How Men and Women Communicate Differently

What He Does ...	What She Does ...
Speaks to make a point	Speaks to share feelings
Says "I"	Says "we"
Interrupts	Invites others to speak
Takes credit when things go right and blames others when things go wrong	Gives others credit and takes blame on self
Talks about facts	Talks about feelings

When a problem comes up, there are three basic factors or steps in discussing it: the problem, the feelings about it, and the solution. Men tend to skip step two, while women tend to dwell on step two. Therein lies the potential conflict.

For instance, a guy is always late and the woman finally says, "I'm really upset that you're late. It's like you don't care about me." He says, "You got to understand, my boss is forever dumping last-minute projects on my desk that I can't walk out on." To which she responds, "How hard is it to pick up the phone? You could call." And he responds, "Have you seen my cell phone bill lately? You'd know why I don't call."

The guy is focusing on his work and defending his actions, while the woman cares more about how his not showing up makes her feel. In her view, if he cared enough about her, he'd get there on time. It would be easy for the discussion to stalemate right here. His next response might go something like this: "You're being ridiculous. I was swamped, and the time got away from me. Don't make me as the bad one just because I want to get ahead." You can imagine the downward spiral from here.

Both parties need to step back and follow my three A's: acceptance, appreciation, and adjustment. He needs to acknowledge her hurt and disappointment, and get to the bottom of what she really means, emotionally. In return, she needs to understand and avoid being overly emotional so he doesn't turn off and stop talking.

Assertiveness and Power

Assertiveness and power are no longer considered exclusively male traits, with more and more men choosing to express traits traditionally thought of as "feminine," and more and more women embracing the so-called masculine trait of assertiveness.

> **Dating Data**
>
> Survey results show that men are just as interested in romance as women, with their top three romantic fantasies being candlelight dinners, sunset walks on the beach, and shared bubble baths.

In many cultures, men have traditionally been more assertive than women, going for what they want. Women, on the other hand, have tended to be more passive, waiting for things to be given to them. The women's movement has helped change this dynamic somewhat. In the past, an assertive woman was labeled aggressive, or even a nastier term. While times have changed, I still find that women need encouragement to be assertive, and need to take more initiative to ask for what they want.

Traditionally, it is believed that men hold the power in life and in relationships. But feminist and male movement leader Warren Farrell, a good friend of mine and the first male President of the National Organization for Women, takes a controversial stance. In his book *The Myth of Male Power*, Farrell points out that men have only the illusion of power. He goes on to say that men are historically the ones who sacrifice their lives in war, suffer more physical illness from work, feel more pressure to perform sexually, get trapped in frustrations that leads them to become abusive, and die younger.

Also, anthropologists and scholarly authors point out, as in Merlin Stone's book *When God Was a Woman*, that some ancient cultures were matriarchal (ruled by women).

ACEing It

How do assertiveness and power factor into the dating game? Well, it's useful to recognize the different ways in which men and women approach life. This recognition can help both men and women achieve the three A's (acceptance, appreciation, and adjustment); the three C's (confidence, compliments, and compromise); and the three E's (encouragement, energy, and empowerment). All these put together—ACE—is your key to self-fulfillment and satisfying relationships.

Coping with Problems and Stress

Traditionally, men and women react differently to problems and handle stress differently, as described in the following table, according to the "six F's" of possible problem-solving behaviors (that elaborate on John Gray's "four F's").

Men	Women
Fight: Take the offense, blame, judge, justify themselves to feel they've won	**Fold**: Give in and assume blame
Flight: Withdraw (going into their cave)	**Fake**: Put on a happy face
Focus: Focus on what to do	**Flood**: Overwhelmed by emotion

Women like talking about problems; it makes them feel better to express their feelings about things even if they don't reach a solution. Men, on the other hand, feel frustrated until they do something to solve the problem.

Tom was stressed out at work, and started to obsess about it so much that he neglected his girlfriend, Tanya. She felt increasingly hurt, and kept asking him, "Let me help you feel better." But Tom just answered, "I'll call you when this project is finished." Tanya then got so paranoid, she was convinced Tom was seeing someone else, because if the situation were reversed, she would want to be with him so he could help make her feel better. Tanya complained so much that Tom eventually told her, "You're always so demanding. Let's give it a break." She wanted reassurance, but it all spun out of control.

When things reach this kind of stalemate, what can you do? The healthiest approach is for both people to face separate needs and feelings. Don't get to the point where the straw breaks the camel's back and you break up.

On Commitment

Men as well as women can certainly be possessive, jealous, or obsessive in love. But traditionally, it has been men who are more skittish about commitment. However, I have heard more and more stories from men complaining about the women they love. Either the woman is cheating, or she's ambivalent about commitment, like this example, "I met this perfect woman last week and fell madly in love. Now all I do is think of her and I can't stand thinking of her with anyone else, but she says she wants us to keep seeing other people." I'll explore this further in a later chapter on commitment, but it certainly shows the tables are turning.

Men love like yo-yos: They want to run to the end of the rope to express their independence, with the confidence that the rope will snap back to the secure base of the woman's love, which is more like a favorite blanket or teddy bear—always there to offer warmth and comfort. Women's love, on the other hand, is usually more stable. Women are usually ready for commitment at a younger age, partly because they have been prepared for commitment by their upbringing, conditioned through life to share, sacrifice, and compromise. As a result, women often feel taken advantage of in relationships, especially if a man acts like he will always "be there," or if she simply reads more into it than he intends.

Dating Data

National surveys over time conducted by the Virginia Slims Opinion Poll revealed that 4 out of 10 women find men selfish and self-centered. The most recent survey further reported that almost half of the women polled think men are still more interested in their own sexual satisfaction than that of their partner, only slightly improved from five years ago.

Traditionally, women are caregivers who tend to subjugate their own needs to the needs of others. In contrast, men tend to focus more on their own needs (thus appearing inconsiderate without even realizing it). These stereotypic roles are changing in modern times.

Thus, when a woman is despondent about a guy breaking up with her, I encourage her to assess the situation. Does she still think she has to have a man to be happy? Was he really ready to love? Does he have the emotional and intellectual capacity to give, devote, share, listen, and care?

Debunking the Sex Stereotypes

Melissa asked me whether it was okay to have phone sex. She described how she talked to her boyfriends on the phone, repeating hot graphic fantasies, such as, "You grab me and put your hard throbbing member in my mouth." I asked her, "That's getting right to the heart of the matter fast. Is that what you really want to say?" "No," she answered, "I'd really like to say something more romantic, like 'Lower me gently onto the bed and we'll embrace longingly, our lips lingering lovingly over flesh afire with desire,' but I know guys wouldn't go for that. They prefer the raw stuff!"

Melissa's experience was certainly helping to reinforce sexual stereotypes. But many of these ideas about men's and women's sexuality today are myths, based on outdated ways of thinking. Here are some typical examples:

STEREOTYPE: Men's sexuality is rated "NC-17," while women's is rated "R."

IN MODERN TIMES: Many women enjoy wild uninhibited sex, and many men enjoy romanticism.

STEREOTYPE: Men get more satisfaction from sex than women.

IN MODERN TIMES: There is no question that men have traditionally had an easier time having orgasms. They tend to climax more quickly than women, and are comfortable with more types of partners, and under more varied circumstances (in a car, a stairwell, or just while making out). Most women need longer, more direct stimulation (from both a physiological and emotional point of view). Part of the reason is that a man's genitals are more exposed, allowing easier access.

In addition, women tend to be less comfortable with their bodies—less than 50 percent of all women admit to masturbation, compared to 96 percent of men (some think the remaining 4 percent are lying). Only a third of all women surveyed experience regular orgasm during intercourse; most report that they can only achieve orgasm in certain ways. But once a woman learns to be more comfortable with her body, she can have as much satisfaction as a man—and this can be escalated by her emotional investment.

Dr. Judy's Dating Do's

WOMEN: To help him be more romantic, reassure and appreciate him every time he says or does something sensuous. Alternate telling him "hot" things with sensitive things. Read novels or watch videos together with romantic story lines to give him ideas. Trade off by enjoying a hot fantasy of his.

MEN: Encourage her to be more comfortable talking about hot sex scenes. Recite them for her as you'd like to hear her say them. Accept her embarrassment. Trade off by enjoying a more romantic fantasy of hers.

STEREOTYPE: Men always want sex—no matter what, who, or where.

IN MODERN TIMES: Survey results indicate that it is a myth that men are always clamoring for sex. I've talked to some men who don't want it as much as their female partners. Or they feel that their lack of constant desire means that something is wrong with them. Men are brought up thinking that an unquenchable desire is manly (making them mourn the passing of their teen years, when raging hormones seemed to create incessant desire), when in reality that expectation only creates pressure.

Additionally, it's traditionally easier for men to get sex than it is for women—there are more outlets, legitimate and illegitimate. Thus, for many men, sex and emotion were often separate entities (since they could fulfill the need for sex with very little emotional investment, and be less choosy about who, where, and when).

You might be surprised to hear that many men these days tell me they don't want to have sex right away on a date—particularly if they really like her. Holding back is a sign of their respect, and need for time to be sure about their mutual interest. Nor do they want sex without any involvement. More men are valuing sex *with* intimacy and meaning.

STEREOTYPE: A man who sleeps around is a stud; a woman who sleeps around is a slut.

IN MODERN TIMES: Social mores are responsible for cheering the man who sleeps around, but jeering the woman. Fortunately, this stereotype is dying out, as society, and women themselves, accept the notion of sexual freedom and experimentation.

STEREOTYPE: Women are monogamous, but men can't be.

IN MODERN TIMES: Surveys have suggested that women can have the same problems with monogamy as men! By the end of the last decade, despite the fear of AIDS, some surveys estimated that up to 8 out of 10 married men, and half of all married women, have had some kind of affair.

> **Dating Data**
>
> In some animal species, the females are the infidels—they like to upgrade their mates to find the most fertile males and those that are most capable of caring for their young.

STEREOTYPE: Women can easily have multiple orgasms, but men can have only one per sex session.

IN MODERN TIMES: Research has shown that while the stages of the male and female sexual response are the same (excitement, plateau, orgasm, resolution), the timing is a little different. Women can traditionally linger longer in the excitement and orgasm phases, leading to multiple orgasms. Fortunately, men can train themselves to control their timing instead of always ending in a quick release. And by learning so-called tantric love techniques, they can not only last, but have as many sexual highs as women.

STEREOTYPE: After sex, men like to just roll over and fall asleep.

IN MODERN TIMES: The physical exertion and orgasmic release during sex can certainly produce relaxation conducive to rolling over and falling asleep, but there is no reflex that makes a man do that. Better explanations include fatigue, force of habit (guys learn as adolescents to have a quick release at bedtime), stress relief, and even escape from post-orgasmic intimacy.

Chemicals released in the brain during sex may have a sedative effect (for women, too)—but consider that increased blood flow and heart rate have stimulating effects. Women often want more sex even though their partner is finished, often because they did not have orgasm (which can cause discomfort, restlessness, or unquenched desire), but also to enjoy more closeness or the afterglow.

STEREOTYPE: Men are more capable than women of having sex without love.

IN MODERN TIMES: Here is one that still has some residue of truth, since I still hear from and treat women who want intimacy but give in to having just sex just to get or keep a man. Men, on the other hand, are much more capable of having purely sexual relationships, saying: "It was nothing, it was just sex." This attitude produces a kind of sexual bribery, with women feeling that they have to give in if they want anything back. But in this new millennium, more women are allowing themselves the freedom of sex without commitment, even though, deep down, they expect and desire more emotional involvement than men do. And as I have said, more men are refusing to have sex just for sex's sake, and are admitting that they find such behavior to be "empty." They want to make love when they truly feel love.

STEREOTYPE: Between the ages of 20 and 30, men just want sex, while women are looking for love. By age 40 or so, the opposite is true.

IN MODERN TIMES: There is reason to believe this stereotype. As men age, they are not as ruled by their hormones, and their lifestyle is not as conducive to casual sex, so they do become more interested in relationships. Studies at Florida State University and the University of Kansas suggest that men's sexual motives vary with age. For men under 25, physical release is the key; for men over 30, love takes precedence over pure pleasure. Physical changes account for some of this shift (it takes an older man longer to get an erection and more time to "rebuild" between erections). But in recent years, men have started reevaluating traditional sexual attitudes and have become more attuned to sensuality and romance at all ages.

It is true that as women age, they become more confident, more willing to express themselves sexually, and more open to sexual experimentation—including sex for sex's sake, without deep emotional attachment. But women of all ages would certainly prefer sex in the context of love.

STEREOTYPE: Guys rush through foreplay, and head right into intercourse.

IN MODERN TIMES: Too often, men do what comes naturally—the quick build-up and release. And too often, they don't understand how women in general, and their partners in particular, like sex. But modern men welcome lingering in love—and need some guidance. So if a man is insensitive to your needs and desires, educate him! Show him what you like, and express your appreciation when he gets it right.

STEREOTYPE: Men love watching two women go at it, while women are turned off by the idea of watching two people together sexually.

IN MODERN TIMES: Men have traditionally been more open to unusual sexual practices. Also, society has revered the beauty and sensuality of two women together. In addition, men get turned on thinking that the two women are really putting on a show and warming up for them. However, surveys indicate that an increasing number of women do entertain fantasies about watching a couple (men, women, or a man and a woman) have sex. This is probably the result of women in general becoming more experimental and open about their sexual desires. (But keep in mind that thinking it does not mean you have to do it, and remember that scenes in your mind are not the same as in real life, when people's feelings become complicated.)

While differences exist, there are still some trends and efforts that bring the male and female sex drives more in synch. This is possible. Women do take longer than men to get sexually aroused to the same point (because of differences in the male and female sex response cycle), with the result that women tend to need more time, and respond to slower, more sensuous touches (remember the popular Pointer Sisters song line, "I want a man with a slow hand"). Yet women today allow themselves a wider variety of love-making, with more active, vigorous activity. Similarly, though men have shorter response cycle times, making quicker, faster stimulation more common, an increasing number of men are learning the pleasures of more leisurely love-making.

> **Dating Data**
>
> Dating coach Myreah Moore says that women should date like a man. In her book, *Date Like a Man*, Moore says men like women who eat and who make a lot of noise in sex. Says Moore, "Stop dating like a woman to find a husband, and date like a man to have fun."

The Gender War and the Movement Toward Peace

The "war" between the sexes has raged in the past few decades as women have strived for equality in all areas of life, and troubled times are still ahead. But as men and women accept themselves and each other more, harmony is becoming more evident.

I still hear so many complaints from women about men, and from men about women. As I've suggested, women frequently complain that they'd like men to listen more attentively; be more communicative and honest; be less selfish, pushy, and obsessed with sex; and help out more around the house. Men want women to be less emotional, and to stick to the facts at hand during an argument.

According to surveys, women's complaints about men have changed very little over the years. Only half the women in a major poll reported being satisfied with the man in their life—a slight improvement five years previously. When women were asked to list the things in life that please them, men rated fourth—after children, friends, and motherhood.

Interestingly, men thought they were doing better than women thought they were. Three-quarters of the men surveyed said they are better able to express their feelings and are more understanding of women's needs than they were years ago, but fewer women agreed. Additionally, men thought they questioned the need to act "macho"; yet over half of the women said the "macho man" lives on. Over half of the women surveyed also thought that men are self-centered and commitment-shy while few men believed this to be true.

Sex roles have blurred, and 7 out of 10 men and women surveyed admit to being confused. Some women admit to wanting to be a woman of the modern age when it comes to career (equal job opportunities, pay, and power as men), but a woman of the 1950s when it comes to love (being taken care of and being provided for).

Reaching Détente in the Gender War

Here are some ways for men and women to better understand each other:

- Accept differences and communicate needs. Your partner is not a mind reader. You've got to express your desires, your frustrations, and your pleasures.

- Adjust to your partner's needs and requests. Within reason, accommodate to each other's ways.

- Appreciate that men have made progress. Despite the many complaints that women have about men, I must note that overall men have changed. My professional experience, as well as many survey results, suggest that there is a "new man," similar to the one women have been demanding. He's more able to express his feelings, even with other men. He's more involved with children. And he agrees that he shouldn't make all the decisions.

As callers to my radio call-in advice shows over so many years have revealed, there are an increasing number of men with those proverbial cold feet who have warmed up. They want to make a commitment and are asking for help to do so. Or they can't find a woman who wants to settle down. Or they're the ones who feel used for sex. On some phone calls, if I didn't hear a distinctly male voice, I wouldn't be able to tell if it was a man or woman saying, "I'm shy. How do I meet someone?" or, "I got dumped and it hurts so bad." Men are owning up to their problems, like the guy who admitted that he criticizes his girlfriend because, "I guess I feel inadequate."

Dr. Judy's Dating Do's

How can we eliminate sex role stereotypes? Retrain your brain! As soon as the thought comes into your head, snap your fingers (to interrupt it) and change the thought to, "Men and women can both be sensitive, assertive, nurturing, logical, and so on ...."

I always try to point out similarities I notice between men and women, instead of always emphasizing differences—because they're real, and to cross more of that divide. Women need to understand that men have the same feelings, but just handle them differently. A little understanding will make both men and women feel less helpless and more empathic.

Role-Reversal Exercises

"I never heard of a couple breaking up because they understood each other." My long-time friend and men's movement leader, Warren Farrell, opened his seminar one summer about "Resolving the Gender War" with that very line. Try to put yourself in your partner's moccasins—that's the surest way of reaching a true understanding.

Farrell's seminar (open to the public, drawing about 20 people) was held at Esalen, the New Age center high in the mountains of Big Sur (where Indians had walked in real moccasins for centuries). It had been several decades since my last visit (I was a typical "flower child" from the East, curious about the West Coast "enlightenment" hype), but one step onto the property was enough to transport me back into the '70s feelings of innocence, openness, and trust—states I still believe are crucial to resolving misunderstandings between men and women.

At the seminar I attended, we performed role-reversal exercises, which you may wish to try. The exercises were designed to promote understanding of the opposite sex's way of thinking and to help shake us from our traditional ways of behaving.

First, the dance. We picked partners, and each woman led her male partner, controlling his every move. He had to follow and look at her with awe (what Farrell calls "awe training"). One man said, "It feels wonderful to let someone else be in charge for a change." Another was more skeptical: "I didn't like following. I'm used to being the one in control." A few women enjoyed leading, but most preferred looking up to the man.

Then, we were asked to reconstruct dating choices in adolescence. We started by thinking about the person we would have loved to have asked to the prom. Most women thought of guys who were good-looking and successful (the jock or student government leader). The guys also chose good looks. But leadership? Yawn.

Next came the male beauty contest—a lesson about being a "sex object." The five biggest "studs," as judged by the women in the group, were herded into a large room. As they stood before us, the emcee, a woman, called each of their names. The women, clapping and hooting for the ones they liked best, whittled the group down to the top two "pieces of meat," who then competed on talent and brains. One women asked, "How do you feel about birth control?" Another asked, "What would you do if your girlfriend had to move for her job?" For the talent contest, one guy sang and the other stripped. The stripper won the contest, judged by the women's howls—perhaps proving that sexual seductions have more power than tamer talents.

Next came the "success-object" contest. The women lined up in rows according to income, with those earning over $55,000 in the front row and those making $5,000 or less in the back. The idea was for women to feel the sting (or satisfaction) of being judged by their bank account—as men often are. Money, instead of looks, became the criteria for their being chosen, and the exercise gave women a sense of how men struggle in the dating selection process.

Then came the role-reversal date. The women had to ask a guy to lunch. The men were told to say yes or no, depending on the woman's ability to support him and children. The men in the group realized that the woman who would normally be their first choice based on looks was not necessarily the same one they'd pick as a provider.

We also played opposite roles on the "date." My date, Brian, asked me questions about my work, and listened with apparent rapture while puffing out his chest. Mimicking a guy, I chatted on, and paid the check. Back in the group, we shared our experiences. One woman nearly cried. "I sat in the last row because I make no money and the three guys I asked out all turned me down. Now I know how devastated guys feel." A guy confessed, "It was horrible, worrying if I was 'pretty' enough."

Finally came the tolerance lessons. After we'd walked in the opposite sex's shoes, we were asked to close our eyes and think about what we'd learned. Had we learned tolerance and empathy? Could we put our lessons to work with our co-workers, family, and friends?

In typical Esalen style, we hugged each other and clapped for ourselves. And we were given a task for the future—to truly encourage equality, we must help train boys for caring and girls for financial independence; we must learn to communicate and cooperate rather than compete. Farrell added his favorite message: "Women cannot hear what men do not say." Just as the women's movement empowered women to speak up and ask for what they want, men need the same encouragement. When both sexes learn to listen to each other, we can have the loving dialogue that will end the gender war.

The Least You Need to Know

- ◆ Differences in men and women's brains, as well as in their upbringing, account for some of the differences in communication.

- ◆ To get past arguments that can lead to a break-up; accept, accommodate, and appreciate your differences.

- ◆ The traditional gender war is far from over—but there have been many gains where men and women have understood and incorporated each other's behaviors.

- ◆ Walking a mile in the other person's shoes can help you understand the other sex's dilemmas and give you new insights and behaviors that bring men and women closer together.

Chapter 18

Dating Disasters and Dilemmas

In This Chapter

- ◆ What to do when he or she doesn't call
- ◆ Breaking out of the "dating daisy chain"
- ◆ Dangerous liaisons to look out for
- ◆ The ugly trio of feeling used, abused, and foolish
- ◆ What to do with a cheater
- ◆ Abusive relationships

It would be wonderful if all of dating was a smooth, happy road. Unfortunately, there are bound to be bumps and some painful collisions. In this chapter, I'll alert you to some of those problems, so you can be prepared.

But you still have to put yourself "out there" because there *are* some good rides! As you read on about possible dating disappointments or even horrors, remember two pieces of my advice: (1) continue to put yourself "out there" despite some setbacks, and (2) maintain a positive attitude and high self-esteem. Think of your most precious possessions (your car, childhood teddy bear, best suit) and how you wouldn't want those to be smashed or dragged through the mud. Now think of your heart and handle it as gently, even if others don't. Be your own best friend, and expect others to treat you similarly.

Unmet Expectations

When dating, people inevitably make assumptions about what the other person feels or needs. These assumptions can lead to misunderstandings, resentment, guilt, and disappointment. Prevent these feelings by keeping track of your realistic and unrealistic expectations.

When Laura invited Dave to her best friend's wedding weekend activities, she was hoping to be with someone she could feel close to on such an intimate occasion. Overcome by the feeling of love in the air, Laura wanted Dave to hold her hand and look at her admiringly. Instead, Dave was chilly towards her and later admitted that he had fallen for another girl the week before and assumed that Laura just needed an escort.

Laura's experience teaches a few lessons:

- Know the person well before you get into a situation that stimulates fantasies that this could work out.

- Have no expectations, since whatever happens between two people is unpredictable, and since some people react poorly to demands. You'll get more if you're in "nondemand" mode.

- Be clear about the "deal"—what you both want out of time together. Does he just want a good time? Is she looking for romance?

- Be honest about other relationships you each have. Ask "Have you met someone else?" If his or her mind, heart, and sexual energy are elsewhere, the relationship becomes confusing and possibly emotionally devastating.

- Be aware of your "love script"—the role you want the other person to play. Sometimes the person is either not aware or not interested in your plans, making the outcome upsetting for both of you.

The "Why Doesn't He (or She) Call?" Dilemma

Michael dated a woman a few times. On one date he thought they were having a ball "car dancing" (dancing in the car at a stoplight). When he dropped her off, he told her how great he thought she was and what a great time he had, but he could see her eyes glazing over. An amateur cartoonist, he sent her a cartoon to ask her out for Valentine's Day, but she never called. "How can she blow me off like that?" he wondered.

People can have a good time, but that doesn't necessarily mean they're really into you. It seems outrageous, but even though you can talk, laugh, and be physically close (or have sex), it doesn't imply a next time. That person may have had a good time, but was not into you. It's sad, but something you have to realize and accept. Of course you can end up feeling used and foolish, questioning yourself ("What's wrong with me?"), blaming yourself ("I should have been more attentive or less demanding"), or resolving never to love again.

Instead, consider other explanations that have nothing to do with you. The other person could be pre-occupied with other things, a loner (who really doesn't relate to others or fails to follow through on plans), immature (who doesn't know common courtesy), or noncommittal (who can't keep up a relationship beyond a one-night stand). If you've had sex, maybe your date doesn't view sex in the same way as you do (for you it might be connected to love, for him it's just sex). Resolve (wisely) not to jump into bed so fast, until you know the person better and can better predict their post-sex responses.

Whatever the reason, don't obsess about it. Treat dating as a learning experience—you can learn as much from "failures" as from "successes." If you feel used, then you gave much more than you received, and you need to make sure next time that you get your needs met, too.

Woo Warning

It's dangerous (and futile) to hook up with someone to try to change that person. People can change, but only if they want to. Look at every relationship as a mirror. If you're trying to change someone, you're really trying to change *yourself* through that person.

The "Dating Daisy Chain"

Groucho Marx once joked, "I wouldn't want to belong to any club that wants me as a member." It's a common scenario: Every girl James wants doesn't want him. But every girl who does want him, he doesn't want. I call this the "dating daisy chain." This scenario can have three explanations: low self-esteem (you think if someone wants you, he can't really have good taste, because deep down you don't feel worthy); self-sabotage (you ensure that you never get what you say you want); or a twisted love antennae (you're attracted to the wrong ones, the ones who don't want you). In any case, even if you *say* you want it to work out, you might not really *want* to find someone if it never works out!

It's not uncommon to go through many relationships, repeating a pattern, until you finally realize what you're doing. Think of dating as a tabula rasa—an empty canvas— where you choose the colors and shapes. Or consider it your own drama, where you're the producer, director, and all the actors. Refer to Chapter 2 for the exercise on writing the movie of your dating life. What leading lady/man are you going to cast? What is the script? Are you in the dangerous *Fatal Attraction* or the more tender *An Affair to Remember*?

The "Forbidden Fruit" Syndrome: Going for the Unavailable and Unattainable

Kimberly's dilemma is not uncommon: "I'm only attracted to men who have girlfriends or who are married. If they're single, I think there's something wrong with them." Being stuck in a no-win situation reveals a need for a challenge to prove you are desirable and attractive. Both men and women get caught in this trap, going for someone who is clearly unavailable and unattainable.

Dr. Judy's Dating Do's

If your dating disasters seem repetitive, strive toward less pain, quicker exits, and wiser choices.

To get out of this trap, examine your fears of getting involved, your need to compete (perhaps traced back to childhood sibling rivalry or Freudian dynamics to win one parent from another), or your need to test your attractiveness by stealing someone else's partner. Take up more constructive challenges—how about racecar driving or rock climbing!

Remember that people are on different wavelengths and have different needs. For example, Derek thought his last girlfriend was "the one," but she told him she wanted to work on her career and didn't have time for him. If you find yourself in this same situation, it means that you're wrong for that person at that time. As unromantic as it may sound, love has a lot to do with convergent needs—the two of you being in the same place at the same time.

Attracts Only When Already Taken

Vinnie wants to know why women always seem to like him when he has a girlfriend, and avoid him when he's free. The answer is simple—some men and women act more confident and carefree when they're involved, so naturally they become more attractive. In contrast, when they're not dating someone, they feel insecure and desperate, exuding unpleasant vibes that repel others.

Living with Ghosts of the Past

We carry with us ghosts of past loves that infringe on current relationships. If you've been hurt before, you might anticipate being hurt again, or protect yourself by hurting someone else. For example, April stays away from dating because three past relationships failed and she doesn't want to get hurt again. Tom got hurt in the past, so now he acts badly toward women before they get a chance to hurt him. Healthy love requires ending these vicious cycles and entering each relationship without acting out past love scripts.

Be cautious if an ex-lover calls to relive the past. He or she may have changed and want another chance, or feel nostalgic, or want to use you to fill an empty need. Find out the real intentions to protect yourself.

Les Liaisons Dangereuses

Although the thought of having a dangerous liaison may seem adventurous and exciting, it may also be exactly that—*dangerous.* Watch out for these potential disasters:

- Flirts who catch you in their web to use and manipulate you for their own ego, or who have some ulterior motive. As John said: "I work with a woman who says she dreams about me kissing her. But she has a boyfriend. What should I do?" Teases like this woman try to catch others in their spider web. If you're drawn in, take note of your own vulnerability to get attention.

- Flirtations with associates, friends' partners, and boyfriends' or girlfriends' parents. As Trish said: "My friend's husband followed me into the bathroom at a party and we had a quick one. I have a hard time facing her now." Examine your own apparent need to mix into a relationship or family (Ask yourself, "What went on in my childhood?"). Learn to control your urges and to think of others and the consequences of your actions before seeking immediate gratification.

- Messy relationships in circles of friends. Tom is attracted to his ex-girlfriend's sister who is dating a friend of his, but Tom's ex wants to get back together with him. Sidestep out of this whole mess, since it's loaded with land mines of jealousies and competition.

- Dating several friends. Theresa asked me, "I'm dating three guys who are all friends. Is there anything wrong with this?" Dating friends can give you a sense of power—that others want you so much that they'll sacrifice friendships for you. Recognize your need for "ego food," and don't be surprised if one day you're the one left out in the cold. Ask yourself what's more important: years of friendship or a new date?

♦ Putting dates through unreasonable tests and traps that end up backfiring. For example, one woman put a note on her boyfriend's car as though it was from another woman (it said, "I look forward to seeing you"). When her boyfriend didn't mention it, she decided he was untrustworthy—when in fact he assumed it was a mistake and didn't want to upset her. Her test led to an unnecessary and unfair test of his devotion.

♦ Juggling several people at the same time. Sometimes it's good to enjoy your popularity, proving you're desirable, and sample many types of people to decide who you really like. But if you're caught in too many complications, start lying, and break agreements, it's time to stop two-timing.

♦ An obsessive attachment to bad boys or bad girls. Bridget can't get no-good guys off her mind, even though she feels used by guys who have girlfriends and call her for late-night sex and expect her to have sex with their friends. Roger said: "My ex-wife made me feel worshipped, but then dumped me—several times. Then, I met this new girl and fell in love but she's always drunk and high on cocaine. I left her several messages to meet me somewhere, but she never came or called." Roger saw a pattern, but wasn't willing to stop it. When you see you're "doing it again," take heed and decide to do it differently this time. Therapy can help you break this pattern. Check out my 10-step program in my book, *How To Love A Nice Guy* (see Appendix A).

♦ Rejected lovers seeking revenge. Some people feel the urge to be mean and to hurt others back when they're hurt. Mark was on that verge. "I was seeing this woman and brought her flowers and perfume, and then heard rumors that she's two-timing me. What can I do to get her back?" Don't spread bad energy, punish others for the ill will of one person, or defend yourself by becoming belligerent and rude to all partners. Tune your love antennae better to draw nicer people to you.

Woo Warning

Demands for affection can become overbearing for a partner. Back off to give the other person a chance to willingly initiate attention.

When Nothing Works Out

David sat next to me in the booth at a Florida restaurant, talking about the sadness of his divorce and how he had dated women but none had worked out, leaving him depressed, disgusted, and discouraged. I had to remind him not to lose heart. Of course, love is not easy to find, and patience is necessary. Don't generalize that "Nothing ever works out," blame yourself, or decide you're a loser.

But do take responsibility. Leslie asked me: "Guys always break up with me after one month. I'm tall and attractive and I have a strong personality, and a friend said they could get intimidated. Is that true?" Yes, too-strong behavior can be intimidating. Leslie can change her behavior, and experiment with being less "strong" and see how it affects others, or she can enjoy who she is and accept that some men will be intimidated.

 Woo Warning

People pack on pounds easily when they're frustrated about dating. Food becomes a substitute for love. Instead of eating, do something else to make yourself feel better. Call up friends, start a hobby, get active!

The Ugly Trio: Feeling Used, Abused, and Foolish

When you give your heart innocently and unselfishly, but then feel used, abused, or foolish, it's devastating—but it is a learning experience. Brad had been dating Nanette for nine months, and had just asked her to move in with him. When his phone bill came, he noticed calls to another state. Since the phone company claimed they were legitimately made from his phone, Brad called the number. A man answered, and when Brad asked for his girlfriend, she was there—with another live-in boyfriend. Marla had been seeing Peter for six months. Since he was a struggling photographer and she was making good money as a TV producer, Marla paid for everything, including fancy restaurants, Broadway shows, and movie tickets. One night, at a party, Peter seemed to spend a great amount of time with a magazine publisher who came from a wealthy family. Marla dismissed it until months later, when Peter claimed that he was spending weekends with his sister (whom Marla didn't know he had), who was stricken with cancer. Later, a friend told her that she had run into him several weekends on the publisher's yacht, and that they were "an item."

Brad, Marla, and hundreds of others want to know, "How could I have been so blind?" Even the smartest of daters can let their guard down, deny evidence, and be temporarily hoodwinked by a double-crossing dater who keeps an innocent other hooked while looking out for a better "deal." Learn to interview partners more carefully and to be sensitive to troublesome clues early on. Trust your instincts (Marla had been puzzled to suddenly learn that Peter had a sister, but had unfortunately dismissed her doubts), and tune your love antennae for someone with more honesty and integrity.

Julie recounted another common woe: "Though this guy and I only went out on a few dates, we had really intimate conversations on the phone three times a day where he called me pet names, and his voice had a sexy tone like a boyfriend's. Then all of a sudden, he disappeared. I am in terrible pain. Why did he do this? Should I call him?"

It's painful and confusing to be pursued but then summarily discarded. When you open your heart in good faith, but then get shut out, you can suffer emotional trauma (self-doubt, fear, and insecurity) as well as physical symptoms (tightness in your chest, constriction around your heart, shortness of breath, disinterest in your work, fatigue, and sleeplessness). Many women and men in Julie's situation question whether they are desirable or lovable. Reassure yourself, and trust that you had reason to believe that this person cared for you. It may not, however, have been as primary in importance for him or her as it was for you. Learn some lessons: Did you miss early cues that it wouldn't work out? Is he or she really a player?

Friends may advise you to never call this man until he calls you, or that you should dismiss him entirely to protect your pride and prevent desperation. But if you are suffering, consider calling not as disgrace or defeat, but for resolution and closure. Ask for feedback about what was really going on, to help you in your future relationships. You might be surprised that the withdrawal could have nothing to do with you, but rather, something else was going on in that person's life that you weren't aware of.

Play fair and kind in the dating game by not being a hit-and-run lover, who, like a hit-and-run driver, leaves blood behind. Why have someone else's bleeding heart on your conscience? And remember, what goes around comes around. Keep your dating karma (your energy in life) clean.

Skeletons in the Closet

Keeping secrets can be destructive for a relationship, but telling all at the wrong time, too early in the relationship when trust is not established, is also unwise.

Secrets You Should Tell

Most of us have secrets we'd be afraid to tell others. Some are ethically necessary to tell, like if you have a sexually transmitted disease. In other cases, intimate sharing can create strong bonds, showing your trust. Sometimes fears are unfounded. For example, Sandy said: "I'm 28 and still a virgin. I don't want this man I'm dating to know. I'm embarrassed and I don't want him to think he's conquering me."

Some men love to know that they're someone's "first." Sandy needed to face her feelings (embarrassment, fear, worries about how she'll perform), and get over them. Instead of being embarrassed, she can be proud, keeping in mind that sex is not about power, or about a guy owning her but about two people sharing body and soul while maintaining their own integrity of self.

Secrets You Should Not Tell

Some people "freak out" when they discover a partner's keepsakes or secrets. Keep in mind that everyone is entitled to personal belongings. If your partner's keepsakes upset you, examine your own insecurities: Are you jealous that you don't have similar memories or important past relationships? Is your current relationship fragile?

Dating Data

Most people keep memories of past loves: gifts, letters, cards, or photos. These can be reminders of your history, proof of how far you've come, things to show future family and friends about who you are, or reassurance about your attractiveness. Just be sure these keepsakes aren't excuses or escapes from moving on. Monica Lewinsky's now-infamous semen-stained dress has heightened lovers' paranoia that keepsakes can be used against them, as hers led to President Clinton's impeachment hearings.

There are often secrets that men and women have, that they're unsure whether they should tell. Chrissie wondered, "I live with a guy, but we haven't had sex in ages. So two or three times a week I sneak out of bed in the middle of the night while he's sleeping and go to his best friend's house. Should I tell him what's going on?" And Chad said, "I got drunk at a party and ended up spending a lot of time with two girls. I love my girlfriend, but should I tell her?"

What you don't know won't hurt you—sometimes. Before you reveal a secret that is potentially damaging to the relationship, consider the following:

◆ Examine your intentions. What do you want the other person to give you? If you want absolution from guilt, consider getting that in church. If you want to hurt your date, examine why you're bitter. Sometimes, as in Chrissie's case of sneaking out and cheating, you may unconsciously want to be found out.

◆ Consider other ways to get what you want. If you need more love or attention, ask for it directly. For example, Kiniesha might get her boyfriend to give her more attention by asking for it instead of threatening him that others guys she dated before would give her what she wants.

◆ Anticipate the impact of the confession on the other person and on the relationship. Be considerate. Sharing some sensitive past sexual experiences may make your present partner obsess endlessly about it. When Jake told Alice about his exciting past with an uninhibited woman, Alice couldn't stop counting her orgasms with him and feeling she came up short.

Confronting Cheaters: Changing Them or Changing Yourself

I get heartsick from hearing so many stories like "My boyfriend cheats on me and lies, but I still love him." Loving someone who treats you so poorly is a sure sign of low self-esteem and a lack of understanding of what true "love" is. Decide that you don't deserve to feel anger, depression, and distrust. Clarify your relationship, and decide whether you can come to a new agreement about fidelity, or whether you should break up. If you decide to stay together, rebuild trust without wallowing in bad memories, disappointment, or generalizations that all men or women are rotten and deceitful.

Greg's story is typical: "I'm going away to college and I told my girlfriend I would be true to her, but I know I'm going to get there and there'll be so many other women. What should I do?"

Some people pledge fidelity even when they know it will be difficult because they don't want to lose their "steady," and they want to be free to date others. In other words, they want to have their cake and eat it, too.

You probably know by now how strongly I feel about keeping agreements. Rather than break an agreement, it is wiser to be honest about changing it. Your partner may be relieved and might also want some freedom. If not, it's better to deal with disappointment up front, and clarify your relationship, rather than cheat and face betrayal and hurt. Forcing partners to promise faithfulness doesn't make them genuinely feel it. And making an "exclusivity contract" before you're ready can make you feel resentful, frustrated, and suffocated. One option is to agree to see others, without torturing each other about any details, unless another relationship becomes significant enough to change your relationship. You might get so upset by the thought of your lover seeing other people that you genuinely want to make more of a commitment to each other.

Dr. Judy's Dating Do's

Think before you act. Consider the consequences of any sexual encounter. Some men and women who are very open and sensual may never stop being interested in others even when they love one person. This doesn't mean they are bad or unsuited for love—what matters is controlling yourself so that you don't act on every attraction.

Snooping

Some people want to know about a date's life without asking, and find snooping irresistible. Amanda dug around in her boyfriend's closet and found a book of letters, including one from a girl that said, "I don't care about Amanda's feelings, what happened between us was great and we can't fight it." Steve read his girlfriend's diary and found entries about her fantasies about other guys he knows. MaryBeth's boyfriend said he was going away on a business trip, but when she listened to his answering machine she heard his ex's voice saying, "I'll see you at the appointed place."

Checking credit card receipts and computer e-mails is a common "investigation." A few go further, like Lauren, who spied her boyfriend Jack kissing one of her friends and started carrying around a camera. The next time she saw them together, she snapped a picture of them and had it enlarged. She confronted Jack, and after he lied about the incident, she whipped out the telling photo. Certainly this technique precluded his lying, and made Lauren feel better that she wasn't being a fool. In most cases, however, it's more mature to confront the person rather than snoop around gathering evidence.

Long-Distance Love

"Out of sight, out of mind"—is it true? Or does absence make the heart grow fonder and distance lend enchantment? Many men and women ask me if long-distance romances can work. They can, if you keep sharing (by phone, fax, letters, e-mail), plan reunions in enough time to satisfy both your needs for closeness, and keep clarifying your commitment status. But distance can lead to unrealistic expectations and fantasies, and "out of sight" can lead to "out of mind" if the time intervals are longer than your tolerance and need for closeness; if you neglect reassuring each other; and if you develop too-separate lives, interests, and relationships. When Ricky had to move to another state for work and asked his girlfriend to come with him, she refused—not wanting to leave her job and family—and the relationship was doomed. Clearly, being with him was not as important to her as the other anchors in her life. Ricky needed to give her an ultimatum to join him, or to let her go. When a long distance love doesn't survive, it wasn't solid enough to last and so all is for the best.

Abuse: Stop It Before It Gets Worse

Pay close attention to how you're treated in dating. If you're being treated poorly in the dating stage, it won't get better—and will likely get worse—over time. Don't stand for mistreatment or abuse, whether it's physical, sexual, or psychological. Also, note how past abusive experiences (date rape, harassment, and incest) affect your current relationship, in terms of being hesitant to trust and commit. Here are some general guidelines to keep you from being trapped in an abusive relationship:

Dating Data

The majority of abuse victims are women, but men can also be abused or harassed. This was dramatically shown in the movie *Disclosure*, where Michael Douglas played an employee seduced by his female superior played by Demi Moore.

◆ No one deserves to be abused.

◆ No one has the right to touch you or demand sex from you.

◆ You're not to blame for being abused.

◆ Protect yourself from abuse by being assertive, avoiding dangerous situations, and avoiding alcohol and drug use.

◆ Report any abuse to authorities.

◆ Seek professional help (through hotlines, support groups, or therapists).

Woo Warning

Avoid destructive and dangerous power relationships involving sexual favors. If you are threatened with sexual harassment, tell the person his approaches and demands are unacceptable—and illegal. Contact the Human Resources department where you work, school officials, or the National Association of Working Women at www.9to5.org.

How Do You Know if You're in an Abusive Relationship?

If you are being abused in a relationship, it still is possible that you care for the person, especially when they act kindly or lovingly in spells. You might even tend to deny that you are in an abusive relationship. The following can help you recognize the signs of a destructive union:

◆ Are you being put down/criticized/controlled?

◆ Are you ever forced to do anything despite saying "no"?

◆ Does your partner apologize for treating you poorly but do it again?

◆ Do you wish you could get out of the relationship but feel trapped?

◆ Do you have a history of similar relationships?

Psychological Abuse

More people are aware of abuse when it involves physical blows or forced sexual acts, but not when it erodes self-confidence and self-esteem. But psychological abuse can be just as damaging, and even more difficult to recognize because it may be subtle at first. For example, in the beginning of their relationship, Patrick would just butt in whenever Pam spoke, criticizing and contradicting her. But over time, his behavior became nastier—telling her to shut up in front of people and calling her stupid and even worse names.

Date Rape

In the '50s, dates were simple: a hamburger and coke at the local diner, a movie, and home by 10. Today, those simple days are gone. Dates are costly—not just in money, but in safety! Dating violence has become a serious problem, ranging from hallway harassment in schools to date rape affecting all ages. Most rapes are committed by people who are known to the victim rather than by strangers. When messages are unclear, approaches can lead to traumatic sexual attacks. Some infamous cases (like those involving William Kennedy Smith, who was acquitted, and boxer Mike Tyson, who was convicted) have brought date rape to public attention.

Know what constitutes such "acquaintance" or "date" rapes, and that they are unacceptable. Avoid situations that could lead to danger (like drinking at wild parties). Don't buy into sex-role stereotypes that girls owe boys sex or that sexually active girls ask for or deserve rape. Choose healthy relationships and love, and communicate clear sexual intentions. Some colleges have even mandated asking and giving permission for various acts ("Can I kiss you?") at the risk of suspension.

Avoid dating where one person has power over the other to extract sexual favors, a hotbed for harassment. Vivien's attraction to her boss is tainted by the fact that he can offer her a promotion over others more qualified. Georgia is considering dating her high school soccer coach who has offered to put her on the starting team. These types of relationships are a set-up for disappointment, and are not "true love" that is based on equality and mutual respect.

Dating Data

Surveys show that one in four women, and up to one in seven men, has been abused. A research study on my radio show revealed that over a third of callers admitted to some kind of abuse while dating. A recent study published in the *Journal of Adolescent Health* found a high prevalence of dating violence for gay and straight adolescents, reinforcing the need for violence outreach and prevention for all teen groups, with bisexual females at the highest risk.

Why People Stay in Abusive Relationships

I've mentioned that often I hear complaints like that from Lajoia, "He cheats on me and treats me so poorly, but I *love* him." It gets worse, like what T.J. described to me, "When I get into fights with my girlfriend she hits me hard and once came at me with a knife. Friends say I should dump her but I love her." Despite the pain of abuse, some women and men choose to stay in abusive relationships, clinging to excuses such as the following:

◆ "He was my first." People often get addicted to their first love or to the first person they had sex with. They want desperately to believe in the fantasy of a beautiful first love, and are unwilling to face reality that it has turned ugly.

◆ "We've been together so many years already." Granted, it's hard to turn your back on years with someone, but think of it as an investment. When you've sunk money into a stock that keeps going down, there comes a time when you have to cut your losses and sell, instead of hoping and praying that some miracle turn-around will happen.

◆ "I know he or she can change." People addicted to bad relationships (called "co-dependent") have a problem themselves if they are willing to sacrifice their own happiness and life in order to save an abusive or addicted partner. You need to concentrate on saving yourself.

◆ "I'm afraid to lose him." Think about losing your self-esteem instead and convince yourself there will be someone else who will love you in a healthier way.

◆ "If I leave, he'll kill me." When your safety is threatened, get out immediately and get help (from therapists, police, domestic violence hotlines and shelters). True love does not mean being controlled by another person or living in fear.

Getting Out of an Abusive Relationship

Ending abuse is a sign of positive self-esteem, saying "I will not put up with this" and "I deserve better." But it can be very difficult to get out of an abusive relationship when you have limited financial, social, or emotional resources, or really care about the person. Break free of an abusive relationship by doing the following:

- Realize that you have a choice.

- Do not believe threats from the abuser that you are undesirable or unworthy.

- Face ghosts from your past when you may have been treated poorly, and separate these from your present—when you deserve to be treated well.

- Repair your self-esteem. Practice affirmations: "I will only be spoken to in loving terms," "I deserve to be treated well."

- Take responsibility for your choices. Ask yourself "Why do I allow this person in my life script?" "What do I need to teach myself?" Remember, the people we are attracted to reflect something about ourselves.

- Tune your love antennae to those who will treat you well. Grammy-winning singer/songwriter Alanis Morrisette told me that after years of being treated poorly by a man, she can now tell within 15 seconds of meeting someone whether that person will treat her well or not. While it's not always possible to spot an abuser right away, since most people are on their best behavior at the start of a relationship and others become abusive when they drink, learn to develop the skill of observing people as much as possible to determine their potential for abuse.

- Trust that you can make it on your own and believe you deserve better.

- Stop making excuses for the person who is treating you badly, and for yourself for staying in the relationship. Sympathy is sweet, but self-destruction is stupid. Abusers have a serious problem, requiring professional help.

- Realize that you help the other person by refusing to be abused. Only when you stop putting up with the abuse does the abuser have a chance to get help.

- Get support from family and friends to stay away from such abusive dates and make healthier choices.

- Seek professional help to turn powerlessness into empowerment, and to turn being a victim into being a survivor.

- Consider legal action to bring the abuser to justice and to further restore a sense of personal power.

- Each time you choose to treat yourself well, you are building stronger self-esteem and will ensure that the next suitor treats you well—as you deserve to be treated!

The Least You Need to Know

♦ Resist making assumptions about other people's feelings or needs.

♦ Always maintain self-esteem, no matter how bad the date was, or how badly you feel.

♦ Examine your dating patterns carefully—they may reveal a great deal about your own personality.

♦ Think twice before having a dangerous liaison. It may be disastrous to both you and others.

♦ If you were cheated on, see if you can rebuild trust with that person, or trust in your next relationship.

♦ Stop any kind of abuse before it has a chance to escalate. It won't get better, and you deserve better.

What's Up with This Person?

In This Chapter

- ◆ How to recognize different personality types
- ◆ Coping with depression and mood swings
- ◆ Dealing with addictive or unhealthy behaviors
- ◆ When and why to end the relationship

We've all run into them—ones who cling or are too stand-offish, ones who are over-emotional or not emotional enough, the sad sacks, and the ego-maniacs. Is there any way to do a "quick read" on a person before plunging into a possibly ill-fated romance? In this chapter, I describe some basic personality types, and provide clues that will help you figure out what you might be in for. The more aware you are of what makes someone tick, the better prepared you'll be to either accommodate their flaws and eccentricities—or run!

As I've mentioned earlier in this book, a key to success in dating lies in using the three A's: acceptance, appreciation, and adjustment. But sometimes, despite your best efforts, a person's problems might be far larger than you want to take on. If the person you are seeing has insight into his or her own problems and is willing to work toward change, then it might be worthwhile to hang on. But don't get into situations where you fool yourself into thinking that you can change a person—especially one who refuses to acknowledge a problem and has no desire to change.

Narcissistic Types

There's a long-standing joke that describes the typical narcissist: "Enough about me. Now tell me—what do *you* think about me?" Narcissists are so self-involved and self-centered that they see all lovers and friends simply as extensions of themselves. But they are also very seductive, and will use endless charm and flattery in pursuit of their own happiness. "God's Gift" comes in male and female varieties.

For example, Kathleen was mesmerized by Al, with his dashing looks, red Porsche, fancy suits, and impressive talk about his promising future as a famous movie star. An aspiring actress herself, Kathleen fell for his constant flattery and was seduced by his talk about how great she'd look by his side when he won his Oscar. Kathleen felt her Prince Charming had finally come. But at an industry party, Al met another aspiring actress who fed his grandiosity even more than Kathleen. Taken with this new admirer, Al began to pick on Kathleen, pointing out how her dresses were getting tighter, and how bags were beginning to show under her eyes, until he finally dumped her for his new "arm charm."

Al is a self-centered exhibitionist, obsessed with flattery, demanding adoration and attention. He exaggerated his own success, and as if to prove it, he also exaggerated the success and beauty of the people he dated. Narcissists are so taken with themselves that they are only attracted to others who flatter, embellish, or enhance their image in their own or others' eyes.

While they may seem self-confident, narcissists crave attention because their egos are so fragile. They (and their love interests) become victims of their own "hero-zero" mindset, vacillating between feeling like the best and the worst.

Ask these questions to help identify a narcissistic type:

- Does the conversation always revolve around him?
- Does she lose interest when she's not the center of attention?
- Is he grandiose, constantly referring to himself in the same breath as superstars?
- Does he make you feel like a million bucks with constant flattery?
- Does she have a pattern of supposedly "ideal" loves who end up disappointing her with some fatal flaw?
- Is he a show-off, courting compliments?

◆ Does she fall apart in the face of criticism—for example, if you mention that she looks tired or has made a mistake?

◆ Does he fly off the handle if he doesn't get special treatment (the best table at the restaurant, the best seat in the theater)?

◆ Does she use people to get what she wants, only to discard them when she doesn't need them anymore?

Five or more of these characteristics mean you may have a narcissist on your hands. Most psychologists say that true narcissists are among the most difficult patients to treat—so you have a big challenge on your hands. If you're looking for attention, commitment, and devotion, you won't find it here.

Over-Emotional Types

Joanna was the life of the party, always attracting the coolest guys in the room. But inevitably, after a few get-togethers, her dates would begin to feel uncomfortable. Joanna liked to grab her date's arm—a little too tightly. She also liked to gaze longingly into her man's eyes, with a look that indicated she was expecting affection in return. Within a date or two, she would turn the talk to their fabulous future together—despite the fact that they barely knew one another.

Women like Joanna (and some men, too) love high drama. Their emotions spill out quickly, which makes their dates wonder about the genuineness of it all. On the upside, they can be charming and engaging; but on the downside, because they're so driven by their need to be taken care of and loved, they can try to make others responsible for them, becoming helpless and dependent, clingy, and suffocating. Such histrionic women often seem "wild" in bed, yet ironically, many are unable to achieve orgasm because of their fears of really letting go.

These emotional types are trapped by a desperate need for love. In psychological terms, they look for a lover to help recapture the comfort of the early mother-child union.

Ask these questions to help identify an over-emotional type:

◆ Does she cry at the drop of a hat?

◆ Does she squeal with enthusiasm when meeting a casual acquaintance?

◆ Does he ask often "Do you love me?"

◆ Is she a chronic flirt?

◆ Does she fly off the handle (for example, if she caught you flirting with another woman, would she throw her glass at you)?

- ◆ Does he talk too soon or too often about how perfect you are for each other?

- ◆ Does she always ask other people's opinions of what she should do?

- ◆ Does she have a history of abusive relationships?

- ◆ Does she always seem to be helping or "saving" others?

- ◆ Does he seem overly sensitive about rejection?

Many people who crave love so intensely are suffering from what's called hysteroid depression (a mixture of over-emotionality and depression). With treatment, these people can develop a stronger sense of self and a greater ability to fulfill their own dreams and needs.

Dating Data

The ancient Greeks thought that histrionic females had exaggerated emotions because they were afflicted with a "wandering womb." Freud believed sexual trauma in childhood was a better explanation.

If this description fits you, learn to enjoy yourself and your life instead of looking for a lover's approval and admiration. "Re-parent" yourself by picturing yourself being both the little child and the parent giving you the attention you need. Check your emotions before you let loose, and purposefully under-react. (When you exaggerate emotions, you actually push away your true feelings.) If you break up, focus on simple facts of the situation ("He met someone else," "We went our separate ways") rather than exaggerations ("The world has come to an end," "I'll never find anyone else").

Passive-Aggressive Types

Pam had been dating Tim for four months when she complained to me, "I can't figure him out. On one hand, he says he's more relaxed with me than with any other woman, and I can ask him anything, but then when I do, he complains that I'm like every other demanding woman. When I try to talk to him about his mixed message, he says that nothing's wrong and walks away."

Pam's lover is a typical passive-aggressive type who gives double messages—come closer, move away. Such a person can leave you on an emotional seesaw between hope and frustration. The "aggressive" part of the person is seething with unexpressed anger, while the "passive" part expresses that anger in subtle ways, such as with "innocent" remarks and little digs that are really intended to hurt.

These types often use the "silent treatment" to thwart confrontation. They pretend to cooperate but then don't do what you ask, and shift blame to you, making you feel guilty for being demanding or angry. Because they are terribly conflicted about intimacy, aggression, dependency, and competition, they can't express love and either sleep around or completely withdraw from relationships.

Ask these questions to help identify a passive-aggressive type:

- ◆ If you complain that he's late, does he claim you're too demanding or that it's your fault?

- ◆ Does he refuse to say "I love you" because he says you should know how he feels?

- ◆ When you get angry, does she give you the silent treatment?

- ◆ If you walk ahead of him, does he complain you're rude, but if you hold his arm, does he protest you're crowding him?

- ◆ Does she pout unless she gets her way?

- ◆ Does he promise to make love to you when he's in the mood, but he never is?

- ◆ Does she agree to pick up dinner or make a phone call, and then forget?

- ◆ Does he forget your birthday, anniversary, and dates, but always come up with excuses?

- ◆ Is she always lagging behind, dawdling, or running late?

If you fall for this type, think about whether you also have a tendency to stifle anger. If you stay with this person, resist doubting your perceptions about situations, and resist the pressure to blame yourself. If your mate backstabs or twists the facts of a story, state your feelings and the facts clearly and unemotionally. Call him on unexpressed anger, and don't let yourself be abused.

Dating Data _____

In his book *Living with the Passive-Aggressive Male*, Scott Wetzler describes three types of women who fall for passive-aggressive men: the Victim, who willingly suffers humiliation for scraps of attention, thereby losing his respect; the maternal Rescuer, whose cleaning up after him earns his resentment instead of the appreciation she seeks; and the Manager, whose need to control attracts his dependence but incites his rebellion against feeling trapped.

Obsessive Types

Whenever she's out on a date, Jackie is totally distracted with worries that she's forgotten to turn off her computer, which, she's convinced, will blow the machine's memory. Larry is so worried about germs that he can't even contemplate a goodnight kiss without going into a panic.

Both Jackie and Larry display degrees of obsessive behavior. Obsessions range from simple self-doubt to more serious distortions (such as thoughts about being contaminated). Many of us know what it's like to have rituals or patterns. For example, Jack flies off the handle if his girlfriend moves anything on his desk, even something as simple as a memo pad. Kris wants to look so perfect on her dates that she irons her dress over and over, making her late. Jason always thinks he left the lights on when he leaves his apartment and goes back three times to check. For certain people, rituals become overwhelming and interfere with normal functioning and relationships.

Woo Warning

It's a good idea to suggest that a person get a psychiatric consultation if any behavior becomes too extreme.

Ask yourself these questions to help identify an obsessive type:

- ◆ Does she repeat phrases compulsively (such as "Don't you think …")?

- ◆ Is he a neat freak (CDs all in line, books alphabetized)?

- ◆ Does she constantly doubt herself?

- ◆ Does he have to repeat certain acts in a particular way (such as locking all the doors in sequence)?

- ◆ Does she check things (her car, keys, schedule) over and over?

- ◆ Does he count things repeatedly?

- ◆ Does she repeat herself and goes over details endlessly?

Obsessive or compulsive people are driven by a need to control—their lives, their emotions, and the lives of others. Some obsessive types can become extremely successful in positions of power (in politics, business, money dealings), which can be very attractive. On the downside, because they are controlling and are threatened by feelings, they can be rigid, stuffy, and detached. The need, but inability, to control (oneself, one's emotions, one's life, or others) can lead to serious problems, like alcohol and drug abuse or eating disorders.

Insecure or Paranoid Types

Gordon complained that his girlfriend was always accusing him of seeing other women, which was simply not true. He went on to say that when he came home, she examined his clothing for hairs and other indications that he'd been with someone else. While she'd always been a little insecure, he felt that she was getting completely carried away with her suspicions and accusations. Was it something he was doing? I told Gordon to face her accusations honestly. If his girlfriend truly has no reason to doubt him, he must insist that she stop accusing him and work on her own self-esteem and inner security, lest she destroy the relationship once and for all.

Many people throw around the term "paranoid," but chronic distrust can be a serious problem. Here are clues for recognizing overly suspicious, paranoid types:

- He makes false and frequent accusations that you are looking at someone else.

- She accuses you of trying to make her "feel bad."

- He is distrustful of others and over-generalizes beyond reason ("All women are after one thing: money").

- She is excessively guarded ("You can't be too careful about people these days").

- He has frequent doubts of others' loyalty.

- He reaches irrational conclusions ("I saw you talking to that man, which is proof that you're cheating on me!").

- She is preoccupied with hidden motives and meanings ("You and your friends seem to have a secret signal to quiet down when I walk into the room").

- She easily blames or takes offense ("You purposefully ruined my night").

If your date displays this behavior, don't blame yourself, or constantly try to prove or defend yourself. You don't have to settle for a person whose problems are too large to take on.

"Slick Ricks" and "Too Good to Be Trues"

Beware of fast-talking, smooth operators, with great lines and too-good-to-be-true promises—they just might be taking you for a ride. You read about such sociopaths all the time in the tabloids—from gigolos who con unsuspecting, naive, and lonely women out of their savings, to polygamists, who keep a string of wives and families.

Sociopaths are often delinquents, thieves, liars, and poseurs (one notorious guy performed surgeries, though he had never gone to medical school). But they are also often bright, charming, and exciting. They're good at seducing others, but inhumanely aggressive once their prey submits. Many harbor a deep resentment and hatred for one or the other sex, and some threaten to unleash a violent rage.

Catching on to these people (most of whom are men but who can also be women) is difficult because they're good cons. And changing them is nearly impossible, since true sociopaths feel no reason to live by the rules that govern the rest of society and, therefore, feel no guilt or pain for hurting other people. Be suspicious of slick lines and of someone who sounds too good to be true (the handsome "high-roller" with no visible means of support but lots of slick schemes). Remember the adage: "Fool me once, shame on you; fool me twice, shame on me."

Depression

Who hasn't felt depressed at some point in life? You know the symptoms—you're "down in the dumps," you have trouble sleeping, you're eating too much or too little, you've lost interest in activities. Such feelings usually pass. But depression that lasts more than a few days, or is accompanied by feelings of doom or despair, is a different matter. For example, Scott told me at one of my workshops, "I've been dating this woman for five months, and at first she just seemed a little sad about things, but lately she doesn't eat when we go out and even said that she thinks life's not worth it. What should I do?"

> **Woo Warning**
>
> Many singles today take anti-depressants of various types in order to overcome the depression and anxiety that stop them from enjoying dating and life in general. Research has shown that a high percentage of people taking certain types of these medications develop sexual problems (decreased sexual desire, impotence in men, and anorgasmia in women), while other anti-depressants (Remeron, Wellbutrin) do not adversely affect sexual functioning.

Depression can be a serious illness that requires attention. If you are seeing someone who seems depressed (not just "blue"), urge him or her to talk with a professional. Psychotherapy, sometimes with medication, can help.

Don't blame yourself for a partner's depression, but if you find yourself chronically attracted to depressed people, look inward. Use my "Mirror Law of Attraction" and ask yourself if you're also depressed or need to help someone who is. Face your own problems instead of picking dates who let you hide behind their problems.

Mood-Swing Types

When Joe started dating Marta, he was taken with her passion. If she loved a film, she would describe it as "awesome," and would go on and on about how much she loved it. On the other hand, if she disliked a movie, she'd be totally unable to discuss it reasonably, calling it "repulsive," and commenting that anyone who'd like it must be a total idiot. While the strength of Marta's opinions at first intrigued Joe, the attraction began to wear thin as he began to realize that with Marta, there were no shades of gray. She had a long, checkered career history, with jobs that started out with promise but ended in disappointment—and it was the same with the men in her life.

People like Marta seem pretty normal at first. They seem to function on an acceptable level (or even at a high level), but on the inside they feel like lonely, terrified children. They cling to a partner one minute, but push him away when they become terrified of being "swallowed up." This dramatic inner battle becomes totally confusing to an unsuspecting partner, who doesn't seem to be able to find a happy medium in the relationship.

Woo Warning Many dates begin with dinner, lunch, or some other event where food takes center stage. But for the thousands of people with eating disorders (either anorexia or bulimia), a simple meal can set the stage for all kinds of interpersonal dilemmas. Eating disorders involve the need to control one's feelings and life, and those who have them need treatment.

Ask these questions to help identify this mood-swing type:

- Does she cling to you as if her life depended on it, or at other times push you away angrily?

- Does he either love or hate people in extremes, calling them the best or the worst (or switching from one extreme to the other)?

- Does she seem to use people?

- Does he fly into a rage or withdraw if the slightest thing doesn't go his way?

- Does she have an addictive personality, relying on drugs, shopping, alcohol, food, or gambling?

- Is he "accident-prone"?

- Is she endlessly confused about "who she is," or does she frequently say she doesn't know what she wants to do in life?

♦ Does he seem unable to spend an evening alone?

♦ Does she experience dramatic mood swings?

If you date a person of this type, expect a roller-coaster ride of emotions—you may be on a pedestal one minute and in the doghouse the next. If you have the stomach for it, strap in for a bumpy ride. Sometimes the disorder is a chemical imbalance that requires psychiatric attention and/or medication.

Attention Deficit Disorder (ADD)

Sara complained about her recent boyfriend; the relationship was going reasonably well, but she frequently felt hurt by his inattention. She told me that even when they were holding each other while watching TV, he'd suddenly jump up to make notes in his daily planner, or he'd decide it was time to reorganize his CD collection. "Am I so boring that he has to escape?" she asked. I pointed out that it sounded as if her boyfriend was suffering from Attention Deficit Disorder (ADD, or ADHD). More often recognized and treated in children, millions of adults also have ADD, but usually go undiagnosed. They can be creative, quick, unconventional, spontaneous, lots of fun, and full of energy—thus make exciting dates or excellent workers. But they may also fall apart in unstructured situations in dating, becoming easily distracted or unable to concentrate.

Dating Data

ADD is a neurobiological disability that tends to run in families. Symptoms can be triggered by fluctuations in hormone levels, as well as by increased stress levels and frustration. Medication and psychological counseling can help.

If you date someone like this, don't take his distractions personally. Identifying and understanding a problem is half the battle to overcoming it. Forgive your date and try to improve your communication. Talk about the problem and schedule private, intimate time that won't be interrupted by distracting tasks. Rather than referring to him as hyper or exasperating, tell him you appreciate him for being so energetic and stimulating.

Addictive Behavior

If you find yourself falling in love with a drug addict, whether the drug of choice is alcohol or narcotics, keep this simple thought in mind: You cannot "save" an addict. The only addicts who clean themselves up are those who take steps to help themselves. If you are seriously involved with an alcoholic or drug addict, join a support program (like Al-Anon) and start living your life—for yourself.

Rehab counselors may recommend that recovering addicts refrain from commitment to new relationships for a year while they reestablish their life. Be prepared that recovery is a "one-day-at-a-time" process and can be an emotional roller coaster.

Many people are also adding "smoking" to their dating criteria list, rejecting those who do. "I hate that ugly thing hanging out of his mouth," Charlene said. She added, "If he needs something to suck on all the time, why doesn't he stick a pacifier in his mouth?"

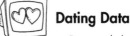

Dating Data

Research by Dr. Stan Grof shows that addicts can overcome drug-taking by using a technique called holotropic breathing (continuous inhaling and exhaling that is deeper and faster than your normal pace), which helps you reach deep states of consciousness, insight, and awakening. More information is at www.holotropic.com.

No doubt smokers are hooked on nicotine, but psychologically you could say they are stuck in the "oral" stage of Freudian development, where the child has to have something in his mouth to feel secure. The smoking habit is one of the hardest to kick, so if you fall for one who smokes, be prepared to lend tons of support while he tries to kick the habit, or accept it if he won't change.

Deciding Whether to Stick It Out

It's wonderful to be understanding and sympathetic when you fall for someone with a problem. But it's important to know when to cut your losses and cut yourself loose. If you're in extreme pain, danger, or you are being abused, you need to get out. Also bail out if your partner's behavior is getting you in trouble.

Remember my "Mirror Law of Attraction"—we tend to attract people who reflect our own needs. Examine what your partner's behavior means to you or tells you about yourself. Are you living vicariously through your lover? Are you co-dependent, sacrificing your own well-being to save the other person? Are you hiding behind your partner?

The Least You Need to Know

- If a date displays unusual or disturbing behavior, there is likely an explanation for it, based on personality types.

- You can't change people; they have to want to change themselves.

- If the person you're dating acknowledges problems and is willing to change, it might be worth staying in the relationship.

- We attract people who reflect our own needs. Consider what your date's behavior says about you.

Chapter 20

Dating Time-Out: Taking a Needed Break

In This Chapter

- ◆ When it's time to take a break
- ◆ Examining your reasons for not dating
- ◆ How to resist pressures to date
- ◆ Benefits of taking a time-out
- ◆ What to do when you're not dating
- ◆ How to get back into the dating scene

This is a book about dating, so you might ask why, Dr. Judy, would you include a chapter about *not* dating?

Because even though it *seems* like everyone is dating, they're not! And not dating is what some singles may want—and need—to do. And because real people have asked me about doing just that—taking a break from dating.

Here are important issues and advice about that time off.

Why Take a Time-Out from Dating?

Dating takes energy. You put yourself on the line. You muster up the gumption to ask someone out, or you go out and have to be on your best behavior. Then there's the aftermath; you can feel great if it works out well, but more often than not, you end up confused, wondering about the future, or worse yet, frustrated and fed up.

Then there are times when you just don't have the time or interest to date. Or you feel that things just aren't working out right now and you want to step aside and regroup.

My most important advice to you at this time: Give yourself permission to take a "dating time-out." Every athlete needs some time off the field after being tough in the game. Give yourself the same needed break. Just like you need sleep to regain your bodily strength, you need downtime from dating to regain your physical as well as mental strength.

You don't have to date if you don't want to! Some of you may sigh with relief at that thought.

Give "Dating Time-Out" a Positive Spin

Instead of thinking that you're stepping out of the game for a while because of failure to find anyone you like, think of it as a positive choice. By embracing a no-dating-for-now stance, you can take time to enjoy other experiences and find out more about yourself.

How Much Time Off?

Dating abstinence means taking a break. What's an acceptable amount of time for that break? That's up to you, and you don't have to decide ahead of time. Trust that you will naturally come around when the time is right for you. Deciding ahead of time only puts the very pressure on you that you are trying to avoid in the first place.

Examining Your Reasons

While I'm giving you the go-ahead to take a dating break, I do encourage you to examine the reasons for it. Why? Because there are a few instances where getting out of the game can reveal a problem that you should pay attention to.

Legitimate reasons you might need time-out include ...

- ◆ You're frustrated with dates that haven't worked out and feel discouraged

- ◆ You've got lots of other things on your mind, like schoolwork or work projects

♦ You feel run down and tired

♦ You have a family crisis you have to deal with

♦ You were hurt by someone and need some time to recover

♦ You've shifted your priorities

♦ You're fed up with peer pressure to date

♦ You've just broken up with someone and you don't want to throw yourself into dating on the rebound

Troublesome reasons you take a time-out include …

♦ You're trying to escape what seems to be inevitable failure

♦ You're smarting so much from a past hurt that you vow to never date again

♦ You develop a deep hatred for men or women because things have not gone your way

♦ You feel really insecure about yourself

Woo Warning

While I am highly supportive of your being hard-working, consider whether you are working so hard that you are avoiding taking advantage of social opportunities (being a "workaholic"). Commit to doing something "for fun" at least once a week.

In all these cases, you need to face the insecurity, hurt, and pessimism. You can indulge in feeling bad for a while, but then you have to work on the problem.

Working Out the Need for Time-Out

If you have underlying anger toward others for not loving you, then you need to love yourself. You must learn to be your own best date. Take yourself out on the perfect date. Listen to what you have to say with great interest and rapt attention. Compliment yourself on how you look. Tell yourself when you enter your house, "I had the best time with me tonight. I really enjoy my company!"

An Exercise for Going Beyond Loving Yourself

Go one step further than loving yourself, and *be* love. What does that mean? You could say it's an Eastern or Buddhist practice. Suspend any rational disbelief and do this exercise. Close your eyes and take a deep breath. Let the air fill your body and expand your being. Feel the air inside you nourishing every cell of you. Smile and imagine that you are sending love to every cell of your body. Feel energy rushing through you. Exhale and smile. Inhale again and think the word "love." Let that thought transform into a feeling throughout your body. Think, "I am love."

Getting Over Being Rejected

It's normal to feel dejected from being rejected, and healthy to want to protect yourself from being exposed to hurtful experiences. But this gets too extreme if you let yourself wallow in the feeling, to the point of withdrawing too long. The nature of dating is that it can entail rejections. It's like the careers that actors, musicians, artists, and performers face: Rejection comes with the territory. They don't get every break and every role. Directors, producers, and even fans can find fault and not give them a part or buy their product. But they have to pick themselves up and try again. Dating can be similar. Not everyone gets every lucky break and finds the perfect partner right away. Everyone gets hurt sometime. You're worthy even if someone else didn't appreciate your worth. You could even be philosophical and say that you are being saved for some better destiny. Check out Chapter 25 for good advice on how to deal constructively with rejection and get back up on your feet.

Reviving Belief in Men And Women

"I hate men and I'll never go out with another again," declared Delia after yet another disappointing dud date. "They never call like they say they will, they all expect me to bow down to them when they haven't done anything to please me, and I'm sick of all of them."

When dating woes make you so discouraged that you feel resentment and hatred toward people and the process, it's time to dig deeper into your past to see where an extra load of negativity has exaggerated the present reality, no matter how discouraging it may have been. This is where some deeper self-analysis can be helpful.

Try this exercise. Make a list of all the past men and women who have hurt you. Feel sorry for yourself over what happened and how you let them get the best of you. Get angry with them, even to the point of imagining them being prosecuted for hurting you, being found guilty and sentenced to life in jail without parole.

Delia found solace in reviewing in detail all the past dating duds she had suffered. Tracing them back in time, she cried and railed at her first real date in high school, and how the first boy she liked in elementary school ignored her. Then she realized the deeper source of her anger towards men when she remembered how her father left the family when she was only three and her mother said that men were no good.

Re-experiencing some of these past pains helped purge the extent of her hurt. And seeing how she had stockpiled all these upsets from men helped her to separate the past from her present experiences.

Facing the Great Escape

Taking a break from dating is fine. Escaping is not. Running toward a little relaxation is okay; running away from the whole situation is not. What are you trying to escape (fears of rejection, insecurities, or built-up resentments)? Identifying what you want to escape is the first step to conquering the need to run away. Avoiding any problem doesn't make it go away, it just gives you a false illusion that it doesn't exist.

Resisting Peer Pressure

At her best friend's wedding, everyone was joking about how it was Francine's turn next. The bride even looked over her shoulder when tossing the bouquet to make sure she tossed it into Francine's hands.

A bunch of his friends always had some girl or other to fix him up with, and Robert was fed up with blind dates but didn't know how to tell them "no" when they had such good intentions.

All of Raquel's girlfriends were going on the Internet, e-mailing guys, going on e-dates, and spending hours talking about nothing but their Internet dating. Raquel wasn't interested; she had other things on her mind, but felt there must be something wrong with her if she wasn't like her friends.

Francine, Robert, and Raquel all needed to resist their friends' pressure to date, or the pressure they put on themselves to do what everyone else was doing. Do what's right for you even if it displeases others or makes you feel different. Francine, Robert, and Raquel need to tell their friends gently but firmly that although they appreciate their concern, they do not like their friends' focusing on their being single. Nor do they want help right now.

Dr. Judy's Dating Do's

Avoid suffering from peer pressure by telling your friends that you do not share their intent on dating now, and enlist them in supporting you to focus on what is your priority at this time.

Achieving Balance in Your Life

We all have many roles and responsibilities to tend to—job, family, friends, hobbies, and perhaps children. At some point in time, going out on dates may be important, but at other times, it may take a back seat to all the other things that demand your attention. Allow yourself to shift these priorities.

For Raquel, getting her career on track was more important than going on the Internet, picking guys, chatting, and maybe making some dates. "I just don't want to do that now. I need to focus on doing well in the classes that I am taking that will help me get ahead in my career, so I can make money and take care of myself. It's more important that I have that secure base than that I look for a man to provide that base, or even distract myself from the work I have to do." Raquel was not avoiding dating; she was making a wise decision about what she needed to do in her life now. It was particularly difficult because all her girlfriends of her age had different priorities—finding a man—but Raquel had to accept that she is not like all her friends at this time, and that is okay. In fact, she is being constructive in what is right for her and building her life so she will be prepared when she is ready to get back in the dating scene.

Achieving "balance" in life has become a buzzword these days. Everyone feels pressured that they have to give equal time to work and personal life. Fine, but balance can shift, and it doesn't necessarily mean equal time for all. Sometimes work is more important than personal life and sometimes the opposite is true. You just have to be satisfied with the balance loading on one side sometimes, and on the other side at other times. Think of it as being on a seesaw.

Raquel was worried that if she didn't date her life wasn't balanced. "How can I be all work and no play?" I had to reassure her that balance for her meant that building her career was more important now. She had to trust that at another appropriate time, the balance will tip in the other direction.

The Benefits of Time-Out

I alluded earlier in this chapter to the benefits of taking a time-out from dating. Here they are. Pay particular attention to the last one, which is the best bonus of all:

- Taking a dating time-out gives you time to focus on other aspects of your life.
- It's an opportunity to discover new strengths and independence.

♦ You can approach relationships with the intention of building friendship, which is the best foundation for a good, lasting relationship anyway.

♦ You can get emotional distance from any "bad" experiences so you start afresh in a better frame of mind.

♦ You put yourself in the best frame of mind, which may draw someone to you unexpectedly.

Make your own choices about the role of dating in your life at any particular time and trust that this is right for you then, and that you may make another decision at another time.

Dr. Judy's Dating Do's

Have you ever heard that "when you stop wanting or looking for something, it often comes to you"? That is especially true in dating, because people are repelled by men and women who seem desperate for love, but drawn to those who are content with their lives and themselves.

Using Your Time-Out Constructively

Given the points I just made about the benefits of a dating time-out, there is much you can do while you're not in the game:

♦ Spend time with family. Many singles have told me they regret not spending time with a grandparent or aunt because they're just so busy; use the time you would be with a date to reconnect with your family.

♦ Deepen a relationship with a friend. Often when we're busy looking for love, we put our friends aside, even canceling time with them if a date calls, or only calling for consolation over a miserable date. I'm sure you've found yourself saying, "Friends are more important and last longer than going out on so many meaningless dates." Make an evening with a friend as special and planned as you would with a date.

♦ Take yourself out on a date. This is my favorite suggestion. Treating yourself as special as you would to impress a date builds your self-esteem.

♦ Take up a new hobby. There must be something you wish you could start if you had the time. Learning something will give you new energy and excitement, and something to talk about—when you date again.

♦ Catch up on your to-do list. Get to the things that you are always putting off. You'll feel terrific when you check off those items you always procrastinate.

The Least You Need to Know

◆ It is perfectly acceptable to take time out from dating. Giving yourself that permission can take so much pressure off you that it gives you a chance to rebuild your strength to want to date again.

◆ Be aware of and face potential reasons for dating abstinence that could present some deeper problems.

◆ Resist putting expectations on yourself or submitting to peer pressure from others to date when you don't want to; you are the best judge of what's good for you in this regard.

◆ Trust that there are advantages to dating time-outs and that you are capable of making wise decisions for yourself.

Part 5

Start the Fires Burning

What is this thing called "love" anyway? And how do you know if you're really in love, or just in love with the idea of being in love? And how can you tell if a person returns your feelings? Find the answers to these questions, and more, in this section.

Sex and love often get mixed up, so in these chapters, I'll help you sort it out. You'll find advice about when and how to say "yes" or "no" to sex, how to deal with fears of commitment and the "green-eyed monster," how to resolve disagreements, and how to stay safe. Best of all, you'll be able to recognize the essential components for a truly satisfying intimate relationship.

Chapter 21

What Is This Thing Called Love?

In This Chapter

♦ Essential characteristics of love and tests to prove it

♦ Can love at first sight work?

♦ The stages of love and when to say "I love you"

♦ When you can't choose between two lovers

In my years of experience hearing people's stories about love, not surprisingly, I have come up with some thoughts on the subject! For starters, I have come to recognize three essential factors for determining whether someone is really in love:

1. Do you have compatible needs for independence or togetherness? Some people need time alone or time for other responsibilities (like school, work); other people want to be with their lover all the time, or feel a passionate need to "merge" with another in order to feel whole. In my view, the healthiest relationship is when neither party is overly dependent or independent—when two people are interdependent.

2. Do you both have a strong desire to make your relationship work? Not all love comes naturally. The daily grind, arguments, outside pressures, and various other factors can get in the way of love, and test your commitment to one another. But almost all barriers can be overcome if you both want to make it work.

3. Do you experience the intermixing of physical love (sex) with emotional sharing and spiritual connection?

What Is Love?

Love—everyone craves it on some level. And we certainly date in an effort to "find" it. Without it, many people feel a gaping hole inside, their inner child crying out to be held, the adult longing to adore and be adored, to cherish and be cherished.

But we use the word "love" to describe our feelings for so many things. You can love your friend, parents, pet, movies, and even chocolate ice cream. We use it to describe the hormone-raging lust of teen years, but it also certainly applies to the comforting togetherness our grandparents experience in old age. In each case, we mean something a little different.

Who hasn't swooned after meeting someone and exclaimed, "I'm madly in love!" But this is a far different feeling from the deep connection one feels after being in a relationship with someone for years.

According to my definition, love entails the five C's: caring, communicating, compromising, commitment, and cheerleading. But true love also includes honesty, sacrifice, and sharing. And love can mean different things to different people. In an effort to get at your definition of love, start with the following exercises.

Love involves feeling love for others and being loved. Do this exercise to get a sense of that giving and receiving.

Exercise #1. List the top three things that come to mind when you think about what it means to love someone.

1. _____

2. _____

3. _____

Exercise #2. List the top three things that come to mind when you think about what it feels like to *be* loved by someone.

1. _____

2. _____

3. _____

Putting into words (in Exercise #1) how you feel when you are in love with someone makes it more real to you, and helps you focus on what's important to you. Expressing what it feels like to be loved (in Exercise #2) helps you experience the receiving end of love. Ultimately, both should merge, as giver and receiver become one. If one aspect is missing, work on that to understand more about why the relationship did not work out. Also answer the questions as you think your dates would, and notice if your experiences of love are similar.

Dating Data

In a landmark study of 500 passionate lovers, Dr. Dorothy Tennov listed a dozen components of strong romantic love. These included constantly thinking about the person you passionately desire, longing for reciprocation, the inability to act in love with more than one person at a time, and an "aching" in the heart when uncertain about your relationship.

Tests of Love

Is there a simple test to determine whether you are really in love? Of course not. But certainly there are questions you can ask yourself (and your mate) about your relationship. Here are some questions that may help you gauge your level of commitment:

- **The Mood Test.** Are you flowering in your relationship or dying on the vine (are you worried, threatened, criticized, and so on)?

- **The Sacrifice Test.** Remember the classic test: If the two of you were onboard a sinking ship with only one life vest, would you keep it for yourself or give it to your mate? A less drastic question might be: If you had something important to do, but your mate requested you to do something important for him, which would you do?

- **The Thoughtfulness Test.** Do you know your date's favorite treats? Do you go out of your way to indulge him in special ways? Does he do the same for you?

- ◆ **The Unconditional Love Test.** Would you love him no matter what he did for a living, or if she lost her looks? Do you feel your date is capable of loving you for who you are?

- ◆ **The Security Test.** When the two of you are apart, do you feel a sense of trust and security, or do you fear betrayal or loss?

While even true lovers will occasionally stumble on these tests (and be selfish, ill-tempered, thoughtless, demanding, or insecure), if you are basically happy, giving, thoughtful, accepting, and secure most of the time, you're well on your way to a rewarding love.

Love at First Sight

You see each other across a crowded room. Your eyes lock. Your hearts melt. Immediately you "know": You've found the one you've been searching for. It's "love at first sight"—the instant attraction people dream about. Love at first sight is possible (almost everyone has an anecdote to support the premise), but what is called "love at first sight" frequently turns out to be lust at first sight.

Surveys show that many people believe in love at first sight or want to believe it exists. On one TV show I did on the subject, half the audience at first said they believed in love at first sight. But by the end of the show, hearing horror stories of how some of these "fairy tales" turned out, most had changed their vote!

Looks undeniably play a part in such immediate attractions, and many times they matter too much. All too often , I hear young women exclaim that they are in love because "he's so good-looking," and guys say "she's so hot"—and yet they don't really know or care enough about who the person really is.

It takes time to determine how right or compatible a partner is for you. Real love develops slowly as you share and support one another through happy and sad times. My rule: Enjoy the initial thrill, but have at least six dates before you start seriously thinking he or she is really the "one." Even then, be cautious for the next six months as you observe your mate's character. Watch how he deals with family, friends, children, and colleagues. Is she caring and responsive? Does he tell the truth? Observe her in times of stress. Is he there for you in an emergency?

So how do you deal with the butterflies in your stomach? On the other hand, how do you know if something that doesn't give you an instant rush is worth pursuing? Here are some tips:

- Enjoy the excitement of being turned on by a stranger, but don't expect too much at first blush.

- Don't dismiss a relationship that doesn't provide instant thrills.

- Take time to let lust mature into more lasting compatibility.

Stages of Love

One thing is certain about love: It changes! Love comes in stages:

1. The first stage is not really love but attraction. If the attraction is accompanied by sexual thrills and excitement, we call it lust. In this "honeymoon" phase of blind bliss, you are usually obsessed with mystery and the desire to impress. You enter a fantasy world of idealizing the other person and imagining how perfect you are for one another.

2. The second stage is the testing period, where expectations are met—or not—and fears arise ("Is she really the one?" "Can this really last?"). You find out if you really enjoy the same things, if you can rely on one another, if you have the same level of commitment, and if you communicate on the same level.

If your relationship survives the testing period, you will enter a brief period of satisfaction where you'll feel that your fantasy of perfect love could indeed be fulfilled—until reality sets in. The more time you spend with your mate, the more opportunity you'll have to disagree with each other and see each other's flaws and imperfections. Inevitably, one of you might feel grumpy and disagreeable, or come down with some illness, providing a true test of your tolerance and ability to compromise.

Over time, you may also start to notice that his hair is thinning, her breasts are beginning to sag, she nags, or he spaces out in front of the television. In this testing period, you have to learn to compromise, accept imperfections, reduce your expectations, resolve your differences, and develop a realistic view of your life together—either that, or you'll throw in the towel.

If your relationship weathers the test of time, you'll end up with more intimacy and commitment, and with the resolve to make adjustments to "make it work." During this time, love deepens, but lust may fade. This creates another challenge—that you not take your relationship or each other for granted. Researchers call this "companionate" or "conjugal" love, which is where you'll find the warmth of a long-lasting relationship.

Woo Warning

Some people forget or don't realize that the excitement and passion of new love may not go on forever—it either gives way to something more permanent, or the relationship ends. This may come as a real letdown to someone who fears "He must not love me anymore" when the lust stage runs its course. This can be the reason some people hop from relationship to relationship—to try to recapture the initial excitement or challenge of falling in love.

Too Young for Love?

The feeling of being in love can happen at any age, although keep in mind that different cultures have different rules about commitment. Steve is 16 and wants to know, "I met this girl, and we want to spend the rest of our lives together. Should I dedicate my heart? Are we too young to know?"

Falling so madly in love that you think you want to spend the rest of your life together is a delicious experience. It can work, of course, even if you're young. You may marry your childhood sweetheart, but the chances are probably slender it will last. There's a lot of truth to the notion that you can't love someone else until you know and love yourself—and it is very hard for young people to truly know themselves. My advice to young people is to enjoy feeling love but don't act on it prematurely.

When to Say "I Love You" or Hold Your Tongue

I usually say that when you are in love, you should feel free to say *almost* anything: "If it's on your mind, let it be on your lips." But many of us feel anxious about telling someone that we love him or her—and there are some legitimate conditions and considerations.

When to Say I Love You

Yes, when:	Not:
It's true.	To force a return declaration.
You've been loyal.	When you're afraid feelings aren't returned.
You've been wanting to say it a long time.	To get something in return.
You feel overwhelmed with gratitude.	To convince yourself you feel it.
It seems appropriate in the heat of passion (and you know you're not just carried away, or saying what you think she wants to hear).	To prove you can say it.
You have your partner's full attention.	To get sex.
You know it's real.	Because you've always dreamed of saying it.
There is a chance it'll last.	When you're not sure.
You care deeply.	Because he's in love with someone else.
You've weathered storms together.	When you don't have full attention.
You feel it in your heart.	When you hardly know each other.
You've already told all your friends about your feelings.	You're having complicated feelings.

Three little words—"I love you"—whether whispered or shouted from the rooftop, have such impact and significance. Many of us have fears about uttering these three little words—fears of feeling silly, rejected, or misunderstood. But if you truly love someone, saying "I love you" is a risk you have to take. If you are concerned about what to say, start by expressing your appreciation or with a compliment: "I appreciate you for your support, (or strength, attentiveness, or thoughtfulness)." Then talk about your love in hypothetical terms: "If I could say I love you, without being afraid that you'd be scared to hear it, I'd say …" It's always a good idea to reassure the other person that you have no demands in return: "I want to say I love you, but it doesn't mean you have to say you love me back."

Dr. Judy's Dating Do's

Follow your comfort level and style in declaring love softly and slowly or passionately and exuberantly.

What if your mate has just told you he loves you? How should you respond? Obviously, with the truth. If you are not sure of your feelings, say, "That's wonderful. Let's take this slowly and see where it goes." If you are sure of your feelings, try, "I love you back" or tease, "I love you more." Express joy and appreciation: "Thank you for the beautiful gift of your love."

If you don't feel the same way, be delicate responding to "I love you." Your answer may have an impact for a very, very long time. Never say: "I wish you wouldn't say that," "I don't love you back," "That's a bad idea," or "It's too late for that." You can kindly say, "That's such a nice thing to say," or "What a nice feeling"—something that clearly doesn't return the feeling but acknowledges it.

Jumping the Gun

"What do you do when you think you love someone, but it might be too early to tell her?"

If the relationship is right, you won't need to play games—you'll be able to say what you feel. However, there is such a thing as jumping the gun. For instance, Eli had been seeing Rita for only two weeks when he told me, "I want to say 'I love you' to her. Is it too soon?" Of course, there is a chance that she feels the same way, in which case Eli's impulse would be welcome. But generally, two weeks is hardly enough time to get to know someone, much less love him. Early proclamations of love run the risk of making the other person suspicious of your intentions, burdened by your needs, and turned off by thinking of you (however unfairly) as insincere or desperate. It's safer to say, "I really like you a lot," "I feel tremendous affection for you at this moment," or "I'd really like to spend more time with you."

Examine what is behind your need to profess your love so soon (control, loneliness, or insecurity). Eli realized, "I don't have too many women notice me, so if one does, I have to say it to keep her because I'm afraid there won't be another." Eli needs instead to believe that the world is abundant—and that eventually the right person will come along.

Torn Between Two Lovers

I frequently hear from people who ask if it is possible to love two people at the same time. In almost every case, the person is asking for a specific reason—because of feeling torn between two lovers. For example, Mitch called my "LovePhones" radio show to say that he was dating a woman he really cared for—she had a terrific career, was wonderful with his family, and made him feel so comfortable. However, he still had feelings for his former girlfriend, and still slept with her on occasion—and found the sex much more satisfying. While he loved his fiancée, he couldn't stop lusting after his old flame.

Many men and women find themselves split—they are physically attracted to one type of person and emotionally attracted to another. While it is unreasonable to expect that one person will satisfy all of your needs, if you value monogamy, your happiness depends on finding a mate with whom you want to pledge exclusivity. It's a little tough if you're unable to merge these two competing sides of yourself (often referred to as the "Madonna-Whore Syndrome" for men, referring to the Virgin mother, not the sexy rock star; or the "Daddy-Don Juan Syndrome" for women). The trick lies in embracing and integrating your competing urges.

I encouraged Mitch to imagine his current girlfriend as being incredibly sexy, more of a "bad girl." She may also be looking for an opportunity or "permission" to express another side of herself. I also suggested to Mitch that he explain how he feels so she can help him solve the dilemma. If he couldn't work out his conflicts and integrate his competing desires, he might be wise to hold off on making any commitments or to look for someone who's a better mixture of what he wants.

Starved for Affection

Part of love is expressing affection. However, I often get calls from people who complain that their lover is not affectionate enough—or at all. People who think they are in love but feel deprived of affection are either so overly desperate and demanding that no one could possibly fulfill their needs, or, more likely, they sabotage themselves by getting into relationships that do not satisfy their need for affection. It's also possible that their styles are just different—one is more "touchy-feely," one more reserved.

But if you find yourself picking mates who withhold affection, it's time to ask yourself a few questions. Do you feel unworthy of love? Indeed, many women grow up with fathers who never hold them or say they love them. These women go on to choose men like their fathers and then try to change them as a way of repairing the early hurt. Learn to recognize when you are trapped in such dysfunctional attachment, misperceived as "love."

Dr. Judy's Dating Do's

To feel whole, you must truly love yourself. Then you will not feel needy, searching for someone to fill you up with what you lack. In tantra, this is called "becoming your own beloved." Enjoy being you; decide you want love but then stop looking. You do not have to "do" anything and you will attract the right person at the right time.

The Changing Face of Love

The beauty of love is that once you give yourself permission to feel it, you can experience it many times over—in different ways, perhaps, but in satisfying variations. You can always feel devotion, intense caring, trust, excitement, and spiritual connection.

Sophia recalled the first time she fell in love, with Rick: "I was the happiest girl on Earth. I felt I was doing exactly what I wanted, with the person I wanted." But they broke up, and for years afterward she didn't feel the same way about anyone.

Jerome found that he kept comparing all his new dates with his former beau Richardo. "I always wished they were different, more like Richardo," he said. Finally, years later, he met Bobby. While he did not feel that Bobby was as "perfect" for him as Richardo, by this time he had changed his priorities. He wasn't looking for perfection, but for someone to connect with on a deeper emotional level. Jerome called it "love" again, but the criteria and experience had changed.

The Least You Need to Know

- Our definition of love can change over time and with different experiences.

- Ask yourself important questions about honesty, loyalty, and thoughtfulness before determining whether you are really in love.

- Love at first sight may be only lust—but lust can sometimes develop into love.

- Love progresses through several phases and changes over time; accepting change is important for a lasting relationship.

22

Cold Feet and How to Warm Them Up

In This Chapter

- ◆ How to tell when it's serious
- ◆ Rules for commitment
- ◆ Recognizing and dealing with men and women with "cold feet"
- ◆ Overcoming fear of commitment
- ◆ What happens when you move too fast

I'm frequently asked, "How can I tell if she's the one? How do I know if this relationship will lead to marriage—or if I'm even ready for that step?" Commitment tends to progress in phases, but there are a number of clues that can tip you off as to where your relationship stands.

In the best case, you've both decided to dedicate yourselves to one another, to pledge your hearts for a lifetime. But what happens if your partner is not feeling exactly the same way? Or what happens if you're being pursued by someone, and you want to take things slower? Unfortunately, not everyone arrives at the commitment stage of a relationship at the same time. In this chapter, I talk about commitment, including how to spot "commitment phobes," and what to do if you're the one with cold feet.

You Know It's Serious When ...

Single men and women often ask me how to tell if they really care for someone and if they are ready to make a commitment. Basically, if you're asking the question, it means you're still not sure that this is "the one" or that you're ready. But here are some signs, in two stages, that can help you tell how serious you're getting. Keep in mind that these need to apply to both of you, for it to really work out.

Stage I. You know you're getting closer to making a commitment when ...

♦ You don't make many plans with your friends because you'd rather be with him.

♦ You start saying "we" instead of "I" or "you."

♦ You answer on her behalf (for example, the waiter asks what you'd both like to order for dinner, and you know exactly what she'll want).

♦ You start gravitating toward other couples instead of singles.

♦ You no longer keep track of all the single people you know or date.

♦ You find yourself more interested in romantic movies and love stories.

♦ You like hearing stories about others who have fallen in love.

♦ You have nothing to hide so you no longer panic about your date checking your answering machine or opening your closet to check for other people's belongings.

♦ You get tickets to some event and instantly think of taking her instead of your best buddy.

♦ You find yourself thinking of ways to please her instead of just yourself.

♦ You wonder about what furniture and belongings you'd both give up when you move in together.

Stage II. You know you're getting close to a proposal when ...

♦ You would rather be with her than with anyone or anywhere else.

♦ You say you're tired of the single life and really mean it.

♦ You think more in terms of your future: how and where you will live and work.

♦ You have a newfound interest in weddings.

♦ You consider money differently—with an eye toward buying a house, for instance.

♦ You expose secrets to each other that you wouldn't tell anyone else.

♦ You enjoy fantasizing about what your children will be like.

- You really want your families to get along.

- You picture yourselves growing old, sitting on some porch in rocking chairs together.

If the majority of these signs seem to apply to you, consider becoming comfortable with the idea that you are one step closer to settling down and making love work. Take the next step and discuss these signs with your mate to see where you each stand in your relationship.

Rules of Commitment

Here are a few simple rules about commitment that, if kept in mind, will help you avoid a lot of heartache and frustration:

- Believe it if he says he doesn't want to make a commitment.

- Believe it if she says she doesn't think she'll ever find Mr. Right. She's challenging you to try to fit the bill, but chances are you won't be "it" either. Do you really want to audition for this difficult role?

- Believe him if he says he doesn't like discussing his feelings. If you love to talk, you will be miserable in this relationship—and you're a fool if you think you can change him.

- Believe him if he says he doesn't want to change. Don't take pity or feel challenged, although it's tempting to think that you can show him a happier way.

Men with Cold Feet

"When it comes to commitment, a glacier moves faster than my boyfriend!"

"I have been with my boyfriend for three years and he refuses to discuss our future. I have asked him if we can talk marriage, but he simply won't. Am I wasting my time with him if he won't discuss the subject?"

If you are trying to catch someone who doesn't want to be caught, you better decide how long you can continue the pursuit. But think about this: If you truly want a commitment, you would probably be with someone who was more willing to commit! Keep in mind my "Mirror Law of Attraction": We are attracted to people who reflect a part of ourselves. Women who find themselves with noncommittal men frequently have some unconscious motivation not to commit themselves.

Fence-sitters rarely change until they have to—that is, until they are faced with the loss of something they truly value. If you're running out of patience with a noncommittal mate, an ultimatum will certainly put him to the test. But be careful—once you make an ultimatum, you have to follow through or you lose credibility.

Woo Warning

It's been a long-standing chief complaint of women: men who won't commit who have "cold feet," also called "Peter Pans" (because they won't grow up), who date around and are terrified of sticking with one person. While complaints about commitment seem to have leveled off, "commitment phobes" still abound.

When a pattern continues for many years, it is often difficult to change the relationship. As the partner, you may have to be the one to change—your expectations, that is. If you put up with a mate's continued ambivalence or distance, that's all you will get. The only way to find out what your mate's intentions are is to ask directly; and if you are reluctant to ask, you might ask yourself whether you really want to know.

Be wary if either of you turns love into a game of control. You'll know that's happening if one of you is pushing for a commitment, and the other resists because of feeling controlled. In that case, back off and give each other some time, until you can approach again out of true caring and not a need to control.

Women with Cold Feet

Men are typically pegged as the ones with commitment problems. But many women have cold feet, too. For example, Stephanie told me "As soon as a guy shows he cares about me, I brush him off." If you see yourself in Stephanie's shoes, think about why you back off when men advance. Some women with commitment problems have low self-esteem. Remember the cliché, "I don't want to belong to any club that would have me as a member." It's important to value the people who see your worth. By brushing off people who like you, you are devaluing their opinion, and yourself!

Dating Data

As men are becoming more comfortable making commitments these days, they are complaining more about women who don't commit. Women are realizing their own problems in this department, too.

Women with commitment problems may also be looking for a challenge. These women constantly need to test their attractiveness. If you fit this description, you have to start believing that you are desirable, and make the catch as valuable as the chase.

Finally, some women, like some men who have cold feet, are afraid of being suffocated. Certain "commitment phobes" were smothered by parents who made all their decisions and influenced all their choices. Sometimes a fear of commitment is really a fear of repeating the same scenario—having a mate who is too attached and too involved, just like their overbearing parents. If you see yourself in this example, resist repeating the pattern. Feel more secure in your independence. Go out only with people who have their own lives and who will not try to live through, or take over, yours.

Tips for Recognizing Cold Feet in Men and Women

Here are some signs that your love interest has commitment problems:

◆ He says outright he's not ready to settle down.

◆ She frequently complains there are no good men "out there." (Hint: There are, but she attracts those who aren't ready for a commitment because she's not ready herself.)

◆ He looks for—and finds—imperfections and faults in all the women he's gone out with.

◆ She tends to withdraw whenever she's pursued.

◆ He's a workaholic—too busy for a relationship.

◆ He breaks dates at the last minute—even with a convincing excuse.

◆ She says she wants a relationship, but her love history indicates that she doesn't.

◆ You're always doing the calling and pursuing. He never takes the initiative.

◆ When you give an invitation, he says he'd like to go but can't give you an answer yet.

◆ She doesn't reply to your message when you know she's online.

I Need My Space!

Having someone tell you "I need my space" is painful. It usually means that you want that person more than he or she wants you. But if you are the one demanding some space, you may be feeling suffocated by too much intimacy.

Remember I said that for any relationship to work, both people have to have similar needs for separateness or togetherness. If you and your partner are at different stages in your psychological development, you may have very different needs for intimacy—which can cause real problems in your relationship. If your partner is demanding "more space," get to the bottom of what he means. Does he really want to separate, or does he simply need a little breathing room? Sometimes, if you are able to leave him alone, his trapped feeling will subside, and he'll come back willingly.

For example, Diane had been dating Scott for nine months when he asked her for a little "space." She was devastated, because she really loved him with all her heart. Wisely, she stepped back and didn't call him. Within a few weeks, he called and the relationship got back on track.

"I've Got a Secret"

Some people run from commitment because they have a hidden shame or fear of rejection. Often this is the result of some secret (you never graduated from college; you have herpes; you once broke the law) that makes you feel as if you are just not good enough. What is the solution?

◆ Change your thinking, from "No one will love me if they know my secret" to get over your shame and fear, and decide that you deserve some happiness. If you do have a secret that will affect your partner, such as herpes, discuss it now! Remember, your partner has a right to know.

◆ Examine how you are using your secret or your shame to avoid or escape commitment.

◆ Trust your true love by showing him the real you—but only after you feel he's earned your trust and you know him well (after at least six months).

◆ Carefully select the right time to discuss your secret, and make sure your love understands you're revealing your secret out of concern for the relationship.

◆ Be prepared for possible disappointment or rejection. Not every one will be able to handle your secret.

Sabotaging Relationships

Along the road to commitment, many couples face dilemmas about faithfulness and other crises that sabotage the relationship. For example, Mike admitted, "I seem to have a problem staying faithful. Every time I have the opportunity to cheat with a beautiful woman, I can't stop myself." You will always be confronted by others you find attractive, but that doesn't mean you have to go after all of them (or any of them for that matter). It sounds as if Mike needs to feel that he can attract beautiful women—that his ego needs constant reassurance.

In John's case, his girlfriend is the one with the wandering eye. "My girl is always looking around, staring at attractive men. She compares it to admiring a piece of art. But I hate it, and I've told her that a million times. What should I do?"

Since John's girlfriend has heard and ignored his objections, there is not a lot he can do—except reassure himself that, after all, she is with him. Although looking is not the same as touching, if you've made your feelings known and they are being ignored, take heed. Chances are, she's gazing around for a reason (and it's not just art appreciation). She may not be ready to settle down, and is checking out other guys to see whether she's interested in pursuing someone else. If you're involved with someone who can't or won't stop looking around, despite your objections, take the hint and look for love elsewhere. You'll drive yourself crazy if you stay in the situation.

Constantly comparing a present love to an ex can be another way to sabotage your making a commitment. It's natural to compare your present lover to past loves. But remember, we often idealize old relationships, forgetting the pain, insincerity, and other flaws. While it's fine to indulge your private love history occasionally, don't overdo it. Put your energy and imagination into your current relationship—not into the past.

Overcoming a Fear of Commitment

If, in reading this chapter, you recognize yourself in any of the "commitment phobes," is there anything you can do to overcome your fears? The good news is yes, but as with any other significant change, overcoming your fear of commitment will take hard work—and a commitment to change! Here are some tips:

- **Face reality.** Realize that no one person will ever fulfill all of your needs (no one is perfect).

- **Re-prioritize.** Decide that focusing primary attention on your mate is something you value (rather than valuing playing around).

- **Control yourself.** If you have a wandering eye, stop yourself every time you turn to look at other women or men.

- **Examine your need to pursue others.** Whether it is for attention or proof of your desirability, get those needs satisfied in other ways.

- **Confront any anger or tension.** In your relationship, deal directly with your mate instead of escaping him by running to other relationships.

- **Create a different love script.** Replace the one of you as a swinging single with one of you as a committed partner.

Moving Too Fast

Before closing this chapter, I'd like to point out that not all commitment problems fall on the shoulders of the one resisting the commitment. In certain situations, one person in the relationship may be applying pressure too soon and may be trying to move the relationship along too quickly.

If your love interest is resisting your urge for commitment, examine whether you really are moving too fast. Think about whether you are truly in love, or are casting your mate in your love script without sensitivity to who he is or what he really wants.

Woo Warning

Ultimatums are risky. If you say to your partner, "Commit to me or it's good-bye," be prepared to leave if your terms aren't met. Crying "wolf" only tells your partner that your word means nothing and that you are easily manipulated.

Evaluate your pattern of choices. Do you constantly attract people who seem sensitive about commitment, who draw away, or who move too slowly? If you tend to move quickly in relationships, make this clear from the start. Explain, "If I really like someone, I tend to go fast." If your partner balks or seems to pull back, then you should pull back, too. Being sensitive to your own and your partner's needs for intimacy or separateness is the key to fulfilling both of you individually, and to finding a balance between you.

The Least You Need to Know

- Always believe it when someone tells you he or she has problems with or is unwilling to make commitments.

- Both women and men can have fears and resistance to commitment.

- Trying to change a "commitment phobe" is frustrating, if not downright impossible. Examine your need to attract these types of people.

- If you move too fast, wanting a commitment, you may not be truly in love but have a desperate need for attachment.

Chapter 23

Relationship Ruiners: Fighting and Jealousy

In This Chapter

- ◆ The 10 topics couples argue about most often
- ◆ Assessing your anger style
- ◆ Eight steps to stopping arguments
- ◆ Rating your jealousy meter and slaying the green-eyed monster

At some point in dating, you're bound to disagree—over simple things like which movie to see to more complex issues like handling finances. Believe it or not, disagreeing is part of any healthy relationship. It enables couples to pinpoint their individuality and determine what triggers each other's anger, as well as how to handle the anger and resolve differences. However, constant fighting can be a warning sign in dating. As the saying goes, anger is one letter away from "danger." If you can't agree early in your relationship, think of the trouble you'll have ahead, when life together gets more complicated.

Disagreeing disintegrates into chronic arguing or fights that can sabotage your relationship when you refuse to respect each other's point of view. Worse yet, you begin to resent each other, and go over the same points ad nauseum, in a stalemate.

Another element that can sabotage any relationship is that "green-eyed monster" we call jealousy. Jealousy can range from the superficial, for example, being envious of another person's body, job, or car, to the not-so-superficial—that your mate may leave you for someone more attractive or richer. However, one thing that all types of jealousy have in common is that they breed on your own fears and insecurities. As with any other emotion, you can learn to control it or slay the monster on the spot with lots of self-esteem and confidence.

Top 10 Topics Couples Fight About

Being prepared for the pitfalls in a relationship can help you work through them. As soon as you notice the following common sources of tension in your dating, realize that they're to be expected. Then focus on solutions in the sections that follow, rather than staying stuck in stalemates.

1. Timing togetherness: When and how often to see each other

2. Your level of commitment

3. Flirting with other people

4. Being late

5. Forgetting important dates (birthdays, anniversaries)

6. Being faithful

7. Who spends how much money and on what

8. How you spend time (watching too much TV, going out with friends)

9. The amount or type of sex you have

10. Family (when and whom to visit, their disapproval, stepchildren)

Woo Warning

If you're divorced and dating again, be prepared for other topics that can cause friction. These include child support, alimony, and seeing an ex-wife or ex-husband.

Anger Styles

Your style of handling anger and arguments can be explained by your communication style (see Chapter 16). Two common styles are withdrawing into the silent treatment ("He won't talk to me!"), or spilling it all out ("I have to get my feelings out to feel better"). Obviously, these two styles clash. Work on accepting each other's style and compromising, so both of you can have a chance to either cool off quietly or let off steam. Admit your style to each other, so you don't feel the other person is punishing or rejecting you (it's just their way). Then agree to take turns accommodating each other. (You can keep quiet for a while, and choose a time for a civilized discussion.)

Why You Fight

There's always a deeper issue fueling a fight. For example, all of the top 10 arguments listed earlier are smokescreens for other complaints, like, "You don't think about me enough," "You don't love me enough," or "I don't feel I can trust you." Once you recognize the real feeling and address that real need, you can move toward deeper intimacy.

Different Values

Joe had this complaint: "Because of an accident at work, I collected $45,000 in worker's compensation. My fiancé wants me to use the money as an investment in a house. But I bought a T-Bird and plan to use the rest of the money to purchase other "fun" things. Now we argue about it all the time and my fiancé even says that she's not sure she wants to be engaged to me anymore."

Joe and his fiancé obviously have different priorities but had to get to the deeper meaning of their disagreement. She wants him to buy a house as a sign that he's ready to settle down. His resistance and his types of expenditures may be a sign that he's just not ready to make that commitment. Instead of arguing about the "smokescreens" (what to spend the money on), they need to talk about each other's deeper needs and feelings, and differences over commitment.

Battles over Control

Many fights are really over whether who needs to be the boss—and make decisions. If you tend to argue over silly things, you are most likely competing over who gets his or her way. It would be a real breakthrough to just stop when you notice a fight over these repetitive, meaningless issues and admit, "I just need to feel in control right now."

Misunderstandings That Stem from the Past

Many times people argue because they both see a situation in a totally different way. We each wear our own special "glasses" through which we see the world. For example, Jim wants to simply go out with his friends and have a good time. Darla, his girlfriend, instead suspects that he's looking for another woman—something her ex-boyfriend did.

Before starting an argument, examine your own personal fears as well as events that happened in your past. Are you really mad at the person, or just scared that the past may be repeating itself?

Woo Warning

Some couples endure, or purposefully invite, the pain of fighting in order to enjoy the pleasure of making up. Arguing does stimulate physical arousal that can be channeled into sexual excitement. But beware of this motivation because it can erode your relationship. Find more constructive ways to spice up your passion for one another.

Getting Over Peeves

The best love is unconditional, such as the love mothers feel for their children. But when it comes to dating, you usually find some habit or other thing about your date that eventually bugs you. As Roseanne's TV sister Jackie admitted to her new beau in one episode of the TV sitcom, "I bite off my nails and spit them across the room!" Does she leave her shoes lined up on the floor? Does he leave the milk carton spout open or his dirty underwear lying around? Everybody has something—decide if you can deal with it!

Help keep others' habits from annoying you by concentrating on improving yourself. If you need to make a date feel "wrong," examine how you need to justify any self-defeating generalizations you might make about men or women (for example, that men never do anything to help out around the house or that women always nag about what men don't do). Focus on the behavior without blowing it out of proportion. Consider whether the behavior is worth bothering yourself about. Some things are just not worth your time and energy; put the peeves in proper perspective and concentrate on more important priorities.

Constant Complaining

Mike is upset because his girlfriend picks on him about everything. "She yells at me for silly things, like wearing gray socks with blue jeans, or not closing the door behind me. What's going on with her?"

Unrelenting nags and complainers are either copying the way their parents behaved, or are dissatisfied with their own lives and are taking it out on their mates. Keep in mind that naggers only keep nagging because they aren't stopped. Tell such arguers firmly that they'll have to speak to you respectfully or not at all, and to hold their tongues when they're about to start petty attacks. Ask them to examine how they can turn their own life around to fulfill their dreams so that they don't take their frustrations out on you. If naggers and complainers felt better about who they are and what they do, they wouldn't focus on your inadequacies.

How to Stop Fights

Arguments have a certain pattern that leads to an escalating cycle of unexpressed needs, unfulfilled needs, and misunderstandings. Brandon and Sue hadn't made love in three weeks. Brandon lost his sexual desire because he lost his job and felt miserable. This caused Sue to feel rejected and undesirable. At a party one night, when Sue noticed Brandon talking to a pretty woman, she immediately felt threatened, and nastily called him "a pig."

To stop these types of arguments and prevent them from occurring in the future …

- **Nip problems in the bud.** Mountains grow out of molehills. Sue was already building up weeks of resentment and hurt since Brandon had been neglecting her sexually. She was ready to blow her stack. Talk about your needs or complaints when you first notice them.

- **Clarify behavior.** Hold off blowing your stack until you get the facts. The truth is, Brandon knew the woman from work and she was married. He had no intention of going out with her. Sue jumped to conclusions, given the colored glasses of hurt she was wearing.

- **Explain how each other feels and ask for support when necessary.** Brandon withdrew from sex, and Sue, without letting her know how he was feeling—leaving her feeling insecure and vulnerable to losing her temper.

- **Get to the bottom of what the argument is really about.** Ask the question "What am I really upset about?" On the surface, people seem to be arguing about money, time, household tasks, or sex, but they're really arguing about deep emotional needs that are not being met. If your girlfriend complains that you spend more time with your friends, she's really trying to say, "I need to feel important."

- **Say what you want.** Don't be afraid to express the real need you have and ask for what you want. If Brandon had asked Sue for support and Sue had asked Brandon for reassurance, they wouldn't have had the misunderstanding that they did.

- **Exercise self-control.** Before exploding, take a deep breath and hesitate one moment. Purposefully do something else—walk away, smile, even say you feel you're about to explode but don't really want to.

   ◆ **Correct irrational or negative thoughts.** Don't assume the worst before you
      know the facts. Usually, the other person is not trying to do you in, humiliate,
      shame, or embarrass you; they're usually just trying to cope with their own
      problems.

   ◆ **Look for relationship patterns.** Are you getting revenge for what others in
      your life have done to you? Look at deeper issues: Do you feel insecure or
      deprived in life in general and are you taking it out on this person or situation?

Jealousy Barometer

Jealousy consumes self-esteem, sabotages your confidence, and ultimately scares any
potential good catches away. But, as with any other emotion, if you recognize it and
turn it around, you can harness it—for dating success!

The following quiz will help you gauge your potential for jealousy. For each question,
score yourself on a scale from 0 to 10, with 10 being the most true of you, and 0
being the least true of you. When you're done, add up your total score and record it
at the end of the list.

____ 1. I worry that others get better dates or more dates than I do.

____ 2. I compare what I have to others.

____ 3. I wish I were like some other woman/man who dates a lot.

____ 4. I feel better when I think I have something or someone that another person
        might want.

____ 5. I tend to wear clothes or use language to impress other people.

____ 6. I date people who I think my friends would admire or envy.

____ 7. I'm insecure about how much my love interests like me.

____ 8. I pout or scold if I think my date is looking at others.

____ 9. If my date flirts with somebody else, I freak out.

____ 10. As soon as I walk into a room, I gauge how I compare to others.

My total score: _____

If you scored *0–20*, you don't have to worry about killing the green-eyed monster—you've already learned to control it. Most of us compare ourselves to others once in a while. This is okay as long as you keep your eye on your own ball, feel good enough about who you are, and use others as examples to motivate you to be your best. Sometimes even a tiny bit of possessiveness can make your mate feel that extra spark of being prized. A score of *20–50* is a warning that comparisons are eroding your confidence and that competitiveness is blinding you from your own potential success. A score *over 50* is a danger sign. You are short-changing yourself by thinking you are less than others, comparing yourself to them, or copying them rather than being yourself. This makes you act irrationally out of fear and insecurity, which further sabotages your dating opportunities and damages your self-esteem.

Dr. Judy's Dating Do's

To overcome jealousy or envy, keep in mind the rule of the 12-step programs to overcome addictions: God grant me the serenity to accept the things I cannot change, the courage to change the things I can, and the wisdom to know the difference.

Slaying the Green-Eyed Monster

Most of the quiz questions deal with comparison. Your ultimate goal should be to be yourself—constant comparison will just keep you from achieving this. Of course, there are traits worth emulating, but they don't include having bigger breasts or a fancier car. Instead of focusing on superficial concerns, think about the following:

- **Work on developing confidence.** Often, what we envy in people is their confidence. What we admire in others is often what we want for ourselves. Don't waste your time focusing on things you can't change—your height, for example. Concentrate on things you can change—your assertiveness, attitude, or self-esteem. Even if you don't have his big bank account or her 34C bra size, walk around with the confidence as if you do; you can have the feeling of having what you want or simply be confident that what you have is great.

- **Recognize the roots of your jealousy.** Did your parents always compare you to your siblings ("Why don't you get good grades like your brother?" "Your sister never gave us any trouble.")? Resolve that you don't have to live with the ghosts of the past.

- **Trace your insecurity.** Tasha's mother went through three divorces—no wonder she doubted her traveling boyfriend's fidelity. Knowing the reason for your feeling gives you more control over it.

◆ **Refocus your thoughts.** When you feel pangs of jealousy, envy, or insecurity, refocus and snap your fingers (or use another action) to interrupt your train of destructive thought. Then let a new thought step in. Rather than obsessing that your date is attracted to another woman, turn your attention to what you can do to spark some energy between the two of you.

Developing Confidence

Jealousy stems from insecurity and low self-esteem while confidence slays the green-eyed monster. So if this is your problem, turn back to Chapters 7 and 8 to boost your self-esteem. Whenever you become flooded with doubts about your own self-worth, keep these tips in mind:

◆ **Do affirmations.** Immediately turn your mind to wonderful things about yourself even if you are not convinced about the truth of these good things at that moment. After all, "bad" or "critical" thoughts you have about yourself are no more true than positive ones (the brain, like a computer, only knows what you put in it). Like kicking a bad habit, force yourself to stop thinking destructive thoughts and to substitute constructive ones.

◆ **Make "life philosophy" corrections.** Instead of believing that others having more means you have less, believe that other people have special qualities, and so do you. The more abundance around you, the more resources available to you.

◆ **Practice imaging.** Picture yourself on a first date; everything is going beautifully—you're smiling, the two of you are chatting comfortably. Review these scenes as if you were watching a movie in your head. Most important, imagine being content and confident when you're on your own. The mental rehearsal makes it more likely that this will happen in real life.

◆ **Become the type of person you are jealous of.** Make the lifestyle for yourself that you envy in others. Tasha always feared that her boyfriend was going to cheat on her, and she imagined him having a fabulous time with any number of irresistible women. Deep down she wanted to be that "irresistible woman," desirable and leading an exciting life. Once she started concentrating on making that true of herself, she was more fulfilled in her relationship and herself.

Controlling the Green-Eyed Monster on the Spot

Questions 7 through 10 in the previous quiz evaluate how well you handle jealousy on a real-life date. If you are distracted by the idea that your date is about to leave you for someone else, or are convinced that you are not good enough to hold someone's attention, you will probably convince this person of the same thing. Yolanda, for example, is always comparing herself to other women, telling her boyfriend that so-

and-so is much more attractive, outgoing, and so on. Eventually she may convince her boyfriend that another girl is a better match—but more likely, she'll just push him away with her neediness and insecurity, and she'll lose him anyway.

Woo Warning

Allowing your jealousy to cloud common sense is destructive. You may think you are showing the extent of your passion, but in the final analysis, such theatricality only reveals insecurity. Do you enjoy losing control? Do you think it is an attractive quality? Will it get you what you want (attention, devotion)? Your answer to these questions should be "No."

There's also trouble brewing if you get so flooded with fury over a date's flirting that you fly off the handle. For example, Shaquira told me, "I spotted my man talking to another woman on the street and I stomped over and made a scene and dragged him away. The problem is, now he's not talking to me. What did I do wrong?"

If you feel yourself losing control, tap that stronger place inside yourself that communicates, "I feel deserving." Take a deep breath at the moment and calm yourself down. Distract yourself with something that makes you feel good (don't flirt with someone else in revenge). What is the worst thing that could happen (that your boyfriend or girlfriend will leave you)? Reassure yourself that you can deal with the outcome of this situation, whatever it may be (you are not going to fall apart). Then calmly, when the two of you are alone, tell your date what you saw and describe your concerns. Ask for an explanation of what was really happening (to see if you misperceived the situation) and describe how you felt. For example, you might say, "I was really upset when I saw you talking to that woman. I felt embarrassed, jealous, and was totally afraid of losing you. Can you tell me what was really happening?"

Jenine did it the right way. When she saw Brian flirting with another woman, she felt flushed with anger and fear. But instead of rushing over to interrupt, she waited until the next night when they were together and started the conversation on a positive note, "I love the way we are together." That allayed his defensiveness, reinforced her confidence, and set the tone for working out problems. Then in a more casual (non-accusatory) tone, Jenine reported what she'd seen, "The other night I noticed you were talking to someone else, and it seemed pretty cozy. I was wondering if you could tell me what was going on inside you so I really know and I won't jump to conclusions." Add reassurance, "I really want an honest answer. I don't want you to feel defensive or worry about my reaction."

When Brian admitted he found the other woman attractive, instead of flying off the handle, screaming, or throwing her glass of wine at him, Jenine said calmly, "That upsets me," and asked for more clarification, "What does that mean about our relationship?" That precipitated a conversation about their commitment and about how they both felt about fidelity.

While Jenine and Brian managed to have a useful conversation and work through the jealousy crisis, not all of discussions will work out this way. However, keep the following in mind: Communicate and clarify your feelings. Give each other reassurance, to help you grow individually and as a couple. And remember, knowing the truth is always better than being consumed by jealousy and imagining the worst.

Are You Jealous of the One You Love?

The phrase "penis envy"—coined by Sigmund Freud to refer to the feeling women have of being "less than" a man—has become politically incorrect and the concept has been challenged. Somewhere along the line, psychoanalysts conceded that men suffer from "breast envy" or "vagina envy"—feeling inferior to women because they lack the equipment to nurture and feed, or to receive pleasure through penetration. Critics have eschewed both concepts. But sexual characteristics aside, there's no doubt some men and women get hooked up with certain mates because they really wish they were them!

Rose is a prime example, as she told me: "My former lover was a personal trainer. I broke up with him because he was always flirting with the women he trained and I couldn't take it." "You're really jealous of him, aren't you?" I asked her. She was surprised to be "found out," and admitted it. He had a gorgeous body, all the girls drooled over him, and he was cocky and confident. Rose wanted all that for herself. It is not uncommon for women (and some men) to date people whom they want to be like—they feel that if they possess the person whom they so admire, then they can vicariously have that lifestyle or those qualities.

Do you complain that your date spends too much time doing things that don't involve you? Are you jealous of his friends? Have you tried to keep her from doing things that don't involve you? Do you try to involve yourself in everything he does? Do you criticize his work, yet think of him as perfect? Do you feel that he is "God's gift" but you are nearly invisible? Are you always imagining that others are trying to steal her away? If you've answered "yes" to any of these questions, read on!

Poisonous Possessiveness

Irrational jealousy over a date's friendships reveals your own insecurity. It is unreasonable to demand that a date drop friends or choose between friends and you. If your date is the jealous one, threatening to leave you if you don't drop your friends, ask her to examine why she feels threatened. Reassure her to the extent that it is possible, but then insist she back off. Tell her to stop living with ghosts of the past (past betrayals) and build self-esteem, or she may really lose you.

For instance, Laura was constantly telling her boyfriend to go out with other women, to get "experience." When he finally did as she asked, she screamed at him for betraying her. "But you made me do it," he protested. "I was testing you," she cried, "and you failed." Beware of such tests—they are unfair to the other person, who is blind to your motives and whose actions you may be quick to misinterpret. And they can backfire! Instead, ask directly for the reassurance you need.

Does Your Date Foster Your Green-Eyed Monster?

Is it possible that your jealousy is not self-perpetuated, but triggered by your date? Some people provoke others' jealousy out of insensitivity, thoughtlessness, hostility, or self-protection (hurting others before they get hurt themselves). For example, Paula's boyfriend told her, "My other girlfriends were much more energetic in bed. Why aren't you?" Such comparisons are bound to make someone feel insecure, and less likely to respond sexually! Mates should build, not break, your confidence. Point out how their behavior affects your feelings, and how you would like it to stop.

Refusing to Let the Green-Eyed Monster Die

Steve's girlfriend, Saundra, gives him the third degree whenever he walks in the house. Recently, an old flame called, and Saundra lost it, insisting that they were seeing each other behind her back. When Steve brought Saundra roses to express his love, she snapped, "What, did your other girlfriend turn them down?" If your jealousy is making you behave irrationally, take a big step back. You are going to alienate your lover by constantly putting him on the defensive.

Focus on your feelings. Why are you so insecure? Has your date given you any real reasons to doubt him? If so, why are you still involved in the relationship? Work on the problem so that it doesn't exist. Jealousy is unattractive, off-putting, irrational, and a surefire way of sabotaging all of your relationships. Rather than studying your mate for possible infidelity or petty indiscretions, work on your own self-esteem.

The Least You Need to Know

♦ All dating couples eventually have disagreements (they're usually called arguments or fights); think of them as "differences." It's how you resolve your differences that determines whether your relationship will last.

♦ Most arguments are smokescreens for the real complaints. Remember, deeper issues fuel a fight. Get to the real need and satisfy it; find the real problem and solve it.

♦ Jealousy eats you up; celebrate others' successes and grow under their glow.

♦ Turn envy into personal evolution—to become the best you can be.

Chapter 24

When Love and Sex Become Bedfellows

In This Chapter

♦ Deciding when and with whom to be intimate

♦ Can friends become lovers?

♦ Using sex to get love and love to get sex

♦ Playing it safe

♦ Keeping the fires burning

You've been on a few dates, and the two of you seem to "click." Now comes the tricky part: sex. No doubt about it, sex is complicated. For some people, sex is purely physical—for arousal, release, and pleasure. But for many others—men as well as women—sex means truly making love; they want a meaningful emotional connection, giving and receiving affection and sharing feelings.

Whether you're 15 or 50, think carefully before you introduce sex into a dating relationship. Having sex changes the dynamics. In this chapter, I'll help you sort out the complications so you can make healthy and wise decisions.

Making the Decision: The 10 Commandments

The decision to have sex is a personal one. Some people (however unwisely) still choose to have sex without any emotional commitment. Here are useful criteria to consider before making the decision. Wait until you …

1. Trust one another with your emotional and physical health.

2. Are able to communicate openly about your needs and desires and how you feel about each other.

3. Understand each other's attitudes toward dating and sex.

4. Know your physical, emotional, and sexual needs and how to meet them.

5. Spend time together nonsexually.

6. Observe how he or she treats other people.

7. Know how he or she behaves under pressure or in emergencies.

8. Understand the consequences of having sex.

9. Know how you'll feel afterwards.

10. Are responsible about birth control and safe sex.

Dating Data

New York dating coach Jim Sullivan, who runs workshops for homosexual men, says the stereotype of gay men rushing into sex still prevails, seeing a date–or themselves–as sex objects. In teaching the value of intimacy, he imposes a three-date moratorium on sex.

The First Time

Sharing yourself sexually for the first time is an important step that should not be taken lightly. You will likely remember this encounter forever, and it may influence your feelings about sex and love, so make sure it's a positive experience. As Rachel said, "I'm 26 and have never been sexually active. I have a fear of sleeping with the wrong person. I want it to be special." Her concern is warranted. Make sure your first lover is considerate, caring, thoughtful, and giving. Be proud of being a virgin until then.

Men also have first-time anxieties. Barry told me, "I'm 22 and still a virgin. I've met a girl who wants to have sex, but I'm really nervous. What should I do?" It's natural to feel silly, embarrassed, or ashamed about being inexperienced—especially when you think everyone else is sexually sophisticated. Don't try to pretend that you are experienced; share your nervousness and appreciate your naiveté. A caring partner will appreciate your honesty and the opportunity to teach you. If not, walk away—this is not a person to trust with your intimate feelings.

Agree to take it slow, and that things may not be as great as you both expect. Spend time enjoying each other's company and exploring your bodies through massage.

Too many men and women express regrets to me about their first time—that they felt pressured into having sex, that it wasn't special enough. Don't do it just to "get it (virginity) over with." Think before you act, so you'll have no regrets later.

Woo Warning

Many men these days still admit that if a girl submits to sex on the first date, he worries that she'll give in to other men, and even thinks of her in old pejorative terms as "slut" or "loose."

Increased Sexual Choices: More Are Saying "Yes" and "No"

Are singles having *more* or *less* sex? Both are true! Some surveys show that a majority of singles at colleges and younger ages have had sexual experiences. The Durex Global Sex Survey showed that men and women in the United States have their first sexual experience at a younger age than dozens of other countries. Other surveys show an opposite trend: More men and women—especially young people—are thinking twice about being sexually active. One survey by the Centers for Disease Control (CDC) found that more than half of young students believe that "love can wait" (saying no to sex), an increase from 10 years earlier. I hear from more older virgins who are less worried that there is something wrong with them.

What this means is that more men and women are exerting choice over their decisions about sex: They can say "yes" or "no." Being able to say "yes" or "no" is empowering, and the more empowered you feel (especially over sharing your intimate self), the higher your self-esteem. The higher your self-esteem, the more you love yourself, and are open to love from others.

It's essential in this new millennium to put an end to the fear of saying "no" to sex. It boils my blood when people feel pressured to have sex. This isn't just a problem for women—men often feel pressure, too. Don't worry about looking foolish, being embarrassed, or ruining spontaneity if you say "no." Be sure about such an important decision, so there are no misunderstandings or poor choices.

Valerie was so nervous about when to have sex, it kept her from dating: "I get nervous when guys ask me out. I keep thinking that somehow, sex will come up. It makes me so nervous that I never go out with anyone." Valerie has to realize that she has control over what happens. Her extreme nervousness implies some early trauma or bad experiences, but in any case, she can set boundaries. At the beginning of a date, if you feel any pressure, spell out your intentions. Say, "I find you attractive, and I want to go out with you, but I don't want to imply that I will jump into bed."

Don't put yourself in compromising situations. If you have doubts about a person, don't accept a date. Make your position clear. Bring up the subject of sex in a general way (mention that you saw something about casual sex on TV or on the Internet). Say, "I believe people should wait to have sex. They should care about each other. I'm simply not into casual sex." Discuss this even if you are dating online, to prevent disagreements and misunderstandings. If a date gets angry or loses interest, let him go. Someone who doesn't respect your feelings on such an intimate issue should not be treated with your heart, body, or soul.

Saying no can be difficult. Be clear if "no" is "no" or if you are leaving options open. Here are some phrases men and women have really used:

"I really like you, but I'm not ready for sex."

"I'm waiting for marriage."

"I like you so much, I'd like to take the time to get to know each other better."

"Being intimate is special to me, and I have to trust the person first."

Using Sex to Get Love and Vice Versa

So often women complain to me that they have sex with dates out of fear of losing the guy, and ask me if they should do it. For instance, Ally said, "I keep getting involved with men who sleep with me but then won't call. What am I doing wrong?"

Ally is choosing the wrong dates—those who don't match her values about sex. Hold off having sex until you really know someone and what he or she wants out of a relationship. You can't possibly know someone's true intentions early in dating. If you find yourself jumping into bed too soon, examine your self-esteem and deeper emotional needs. I'm heartened that more women are realizing themselves what I would tell them, "If he leaves you over that, he is not worth it." Too many people have sex when they are really looking for love. It's a mistake to have sex with someone you don't really know, with the expectation of receiving love, just as it's a mistake to mislead someone into thinking that you care when all you really want is sex.

Some people (admittedly more men than women) love the thrill of conquest and will "work" the relationship until they get what they want and then lose interest. It's easy to blame yourself if this happens to you, for not being interesting, sexy, or attractive enough. Instead, recognize you were being used, and prevent it from happening next time.

Anita called and told me about a man in her economics class. "This attractive guy flirted with me shamelessly and wrote 'I love you' on my notebook. He called me a few times and we had phone sex. After that, he stopped talking to me. What's up?" Anita should be glad this guy came and went quickly. I urged her to take responsibility for her own actions, instead of engaging in a sexual activity with someone she barely knew.

How Can You Tell if Someone Just Wants Sex?

A national opinion poll taken over a quarter century revealed that women still complain that men treat them as sex objects. How you can tell if someone likes you for *you* or is just interested in sex? Hold off on sex to see his reaction. If he disappears, you know his intentions. If he sticks around, talk about your fears of being wanted only for sex, how having sex changes the relationship for you, and how you need to know you're cared for. Spell out the qualities that you value: listening, giving, and communicating.

Be wary of dates who …

- Use persistent sexual innuendoes in the conversation.
- Don't listen.
- Have no history of long-term relationships.
- Make no references to the future (phone calls or dates).
- Feed you challenging lines such as "You're the only girl I ever felt anything for" or "You could be the one to finally make me change my ways."
- Only call at the last minute or in the middle of the night (for booty calls).
- Agree to meetings only on their terms or at their request.
- Leave you feeling used, empty, or frustrated.

Using Sex to Manipulate

Having sex just to please or keep another person not only damages your self-esteem but is manipulative and misleading. Sue is dating a guy who lives in another city. "When he comes to visit, we make love but I don't always feel comfortable about it," she explained. "But I don't want to do anything to make him think I'm seeing someone else. What should I do?" Sue should be honest. If he decides to dump her, the relationship was not on solid ground to begin with. Unless Sue expresses what she wants and needs, she'll never feel truly loved. Also, by not being honest with him, she is not giving him a chance to really please her.

Tara doesn't like certain positions in sex but explains, "I do it because I know my boyfriend likes it and if I don't I'm afraid that he will find another woman who will." Let him find another woman. Ultimately, the relationship is not going to work out because Tara's boyfriend will probably sense that she is desperate and willing to sacrifice her own self-esteem for his affection.

No Strings, Just Sex

I'm frequently asked, "Is it possible to have a purely sexual relationship without any strings attached?" Such arrangements are possible when both people feel the same way. Invariably, though, one person seeks more emotional attachment. In the current trend for "buddy sex," friends have sex without being in a committed or exclusive relationship. While these liaisons may start out as a convenient outlet for both, one person usually ends up wanting more involvement and gets hurt. Be clear about your needs, in the beginning of dating and as the relationship develops. If you go out with someone with the hope of having sex (and not much else), admit, "I'm not looking for a commitment, so please don't feel hurt if I don't end up calling you or giving you what you want. Sex may not mean as much to me as it does to you." This is a bit cold, but it's certainly a fair alert.

Woo Warning

If you're just starting a relationship, and the sex isn't satisfying, or you're already thinking about straying, you're setting yourself up for failure.

The best sex merges the physical act with an emotional and spiritual attachment. As one man put it, "She's the paint, I'm the painter, and the bed is our canvas, to create our beautiful painting of love." Take turns being the painter and the paint.

The Sex/Love Split

After years of counseling patients, running workshops, and fielding calls on the radio, I've heard a lot of people confused about sex and love. Here are two types of common questions, related to an important issue called "splitting":

1. "How come I can have great sex with a woman but, as soon as I start to develop feelings for her, I don't get turned on anymore?"

2. "I'm dating two men. One would be the perfect husband and father—the kind of guy that my parents would love—and the other is a real exciting 'bad boy.' I wish I could mesh them into one guy, but I can't. What can I do?"

Separating sex and love reflects a disturbing dilemma called the "Madonna-whore syndrome" (not the rock star but the Virginal mother figure) in men and the "Daddy-Don Juan syndrome" in women. The person splits lovers into either sweet, nice people or wild, sexy ones. Sex becomes desirable only with the latter, not the former.

While I frequently encounter this problem with married people, it also occurs with singles torn between two seemingly opposite lovers. Bill was enamored of Jill, a sweet, gentle woman, who had all the qualities he wanted in a long-term mate, and she adored him, wanted to marry and start a family. The problem was, he found her boring in bed. Bill was also seeing Liza, a woman who had few of the qualities he valued for a wife and mother of his children, but who really turned him on sexually. Liza was fond of Bill but wasn't interested in settling down. But every time Bill decided to totally devote himself to Jill, he ended up calling Liza for a "roll in the hay."

Dr. Judy's Dating Do's

Sex is not the only way of expressing love. Be creative; there are countless warm, emotionally satisfying ways of communicating and sharing. Keep in mind that lack of self-esteem, loneliness, or boredom won't be cured by sex.

Men like Bill are compelled to seek a challenge, and often devalue the very people who most value them. They think they are looking for the "perfect" person who combines all of the values they supposedly want with the sexual attraction they crave, but in reality, they can't let one person be everything to them.

If you recognize yourself in Bill's scenario, it's time to retrain your brain. Rather than separating sex and love, insist on having one with the other. If you stereotype men as either fathers or lovers, and women as either mothers or lovers, allow the other person to express both roles. Communicate all your fantasies, desires, wants, and needs (sexual and otherwise), and give the person a chance to fulfill your multiple needs. Admit that sex and love are both important, and possible to experience with one person. Discover that your lover is sweet but also a wild lover—these traits are not mutually exclusive!

Turning Friends into Lovers

It's a very common question I'm asked: "I like this person but how do I make him or her my boyfriend or girlfriend without ruining the friendship?" Friendship is the best basis for love, so I find it charming when people ask me how they can change a friendship into a romance. It can be tricky—you have to be willing to take a risk that might jeopardize your friendship. Most people would rather stay friends than risk losing what they have. But keep in mind that becoming romantic may not ruin the friendship; if you take the risk and your friend responds positively, it will strengthen your bond. If your friend does not reciprocate, at least you know where you stand and can direct your energies elsewhere. Ultimately, you have to gauge whether the potential rewards are worth the gamble—but I'd recommend going for it.

To get courage to broach attraction with a friend, remember the saying, "It is better to have loved and lost than never to have loved at all." One man told his female friend: "Our friendship is over," and then, after a pregnant pause during which she was confused and nervous, he added, "Now let's try being *more* than friends."

One of my interns at my radio show, Lee, had an inspiring story about turning a friend into a lover. She had been hanging out with a guy, shooting pool, watching videos, and hiking, for six months until one day while riding on a bus home from the movies, he leaned over after a stall in the conversation, took her face in his hands, and kissed her softly. Her first reaction was, "Oh my God," as he explained, "I've been wanting to do that for a really long time," to which she teased encouragingly, "Well, are you going to do it again?" His next kiss was deep, and months later he proposed. "The friendship was what made me love him," Lee told me, "because I learned I could really trust this guy and could tell him anything."

Woo Warning

If it looks like you can't turn the friendship into love, control your longing. As with any unrequited love or impossible situation, don't waste your energy wishing or hoping. As soon as the feeling overtakes you, switch your mind to planning or doing something for yourself. Figure out what you like about your friend and be open to someone else who possesses those qualities. Focus on finding someone who can be both friend and lover.

Who Makes the First Move?

As in asking for a date, more men today are relieved when a woman takes the initiative in sex. But men can also be a little intimidated by a sexually aggressive female. Tony was divorced four years ago and now is back in the dating game. "Are women really this fast now?" he asked me. "I like candlelit dinners, and they seem to want to get right to it!" At the end of Tony's date, the girl said outright she'd like to have sex. "I was so bowled over by such a bold female," he admitted, "that I was really worried about whether I could get it up for her."

While it may make you feel uncomfortable to know sex is expected of you on a date, not being approached can leave you feeling undesirable, frustrated, or confused. Cybil dated Howard six times but complained, "He was a perfect gentleman, but I was jumping out of my skin, wanting him to do something. I was wondering if he was gay, strange, or impotent, and what was wrong with me." Courtney also complained, "I've been seeing this guy for three months and he's only kissed me. I can't help feeling he doesn't want me. I also don't want to be the one who does everything first. What's up?" Find out from him whether he is shy, inexperienced, or afraid of getting hurt. Explain that you feel uncomfortable being the initiator.

If someone doesn't make a move, don't immediately assume you're not attractive enough. Find out what else is going on with that person (another relationship, inexperience, fear of rejection, embarrassment about themselves, their body, or sex). Take a risk and state your own interest. Cybil did the right thing. On her next date with Howard, she was open with him and said, "I've really enjoyed being with you, and I wonder why we haven't kissed because we've had a great time, and I wanted to kiss you." Thankfully, Howard was willing to be equally honest, and explained that he was afraid to move too quickly for fear Cybil would consider him too forward. Howard's openness about his fear, and Cybil's reassurance, were just the right triggers to give them permission for their first kiss.

> **Woo Warning**
>
> Inviting someone back to your home can be a set-up for a stay-over, so a date is bound to wonder whether this is an invitation—or expectation—for sex. A decline may be colored with a fear of such an expectation, so if you don't intend sex, be sure to be clear about that.

How Important Is Sex?

Couples often fall "out of love" when the sex that was once good falters. For instance, Darlene came to me for therapy because, as she said, "Sex with my boyfriend was great, but now it's so boring. I'm tempted to throw in the towel or at least to have a little fling. My boyfriend doesn't seem to mind that the passion has cooled."

Lust and passion do tend to cool over time, but it can be explained—and overcome. Find out the source. Causes of flagging sex interest are myriad, including stress, fears of intimacy and commitment, unresolved angers, physical problems, and unmet sexual desires. Anything can be resolved if you want to work on it.

Resist taking a date's sexual problem personally. For example, when a man is having erection problems, the woman may feel it's her fault, that she's not attractive enough. Or if a woman is having problems with orgasm, the man may feel inadequate as a lover.

Dating Data

Having sex with someone you love and feel loved by is emotionally and spiritually fulfilling. Research indicates that sex can also be good for health, as the body releases certain hormones and chemicals (including endorphins, the "pleasure chemical") that have immune-enhancing effects. These physical and psychological effects make the act even more rewarding and desirable—and make the choice of having sex and with whom much more important.

Different Sex Drives

Karen's boyfriend is ready for sex at any time, but she is not. She wonders, "Is there a chance for us?" Possibly. As with many couples, Karen and her boyfriend have different sex drives; no matter what's going on, he's ready, whereas her feelings are much more affected by her mood, the situation, how much time they have, and many other factors. Just as with other aspects of the relationship, decide how high a priority this part of your life is. Then, to make the relationship work, accept each other's differences and make compromises.

Some people have a naturally higher sex drive than others, but libido levels are related to many factors, both physical and psychological. This should reassure you that ups and downs are normal and do not signal the death knell of a relationship and that changes and adjustments can be made.

Sex drives are affected by hormone levels that themselves can be decreased (by illness or medication) or increased. Research has shown that women who make love weekly have twice as many circulating hormones as those who have sex sporadically or not at all. Also, certain foods are reported to boost hormone production, especially those that are high in vitamin B-12, vitamin K, and zinc.

Dating Data

The Trojan Shared Sensation Survey of 800 young lovers (aged 18 to 29) revealed that two thirds of couples said sexual pleasure should be equally shared. Men were less selfish than you might think (4 out of 10 men said pleasing their partner was more important than their own pleasure). Body rubs topped the list of shared activities. Three times as many unmarried couples as married couples shared bathing or showering, and more daters shared sexy e-mails than married couples. Women were more likely than men to question their partner's sexual past (asking about one-night stands, unprotected sex, HIV tests), but less likely to tell about their own.

Being Responsible About Pregnancy and STDs

In this day and age it is imperative that men and women be responsible in sex when dating—and well into a relationship. There is no excuse for not taking care of your own—and others'—health.

Learn all the options about preventing unwanted pregnancy and take necessary precautions. Consider which options work for your beliefs and lifestyle, including "abstinence only" (practicing tantric sex that intensifies intimate connections without genital contact being necessary can be a terrific technique!). Beware of so-called natural methods (rhythm, withdrawal) as these are highly ineffective. Keep up-to-date about new developments in the field of contraception. Women need to be equally prepared as men.

You'd think everyone would be wiser—and safer—by now, but epidemics of sexually transmitted diseases (STDs) persist. Statistics from the American Social Health Association warn about gonorrhea, chlamydia, herpes, and newer strains of Hepatitis C (which ex-Baywatch Babe Pam Anderson admitted having). And while new drugs for HIV/ AIDS are life-saving, the threat has not gone away. Because people travel extensively, STDs can spread around the world.

The heartening news is that more people are aware of these diseases. And there are more over-the-counter screening tests, as well as new medical treatments. But pay attention to your health, and make careful decisions about with whom to have sex. Traveling singles have to be particularly on the alert. Talk honestly about your sexual history, never take risks, and find ways to be intimate other than through sex.

Sex in the Age of Terrorism

Living in an age of terrorism affects every aspect of life, including dating and sex. Fears, depression, and anxieties that result can make you withdraw from sex. But those experiences can also do the opposite, making you want to affirm life though love and sex. Threats of terrorism after September 11th spurred reports about an increase in affairs and casual sex—called "terror sex," "apocalyptic sex," or "end of the world sex." Faced with the thought that life could end any minute, some singles threw caution to the wind, immediately gratifying sexual urges and even disregarding precautions about STDs and pregnancy. As one single woman said, "If I only have one day left to live, I might as well have the best time of my life, whether buying clothes or bedding men."

Confronted with death, it is natural to want to reaffirm life by indulging in pleasurable activities like sex. I call it the "Anne Frank Syndrome," reminiscent of the teen who had her first sexual experience when facing discovery by the Nazis. In the film, and Broadway show, *The Summer of '42*, a woman who finds out about her husband's death finds renewed desire to live and has an affair with a younger man. In more extreme cases, overindulgence in sex, as in drugs or alcohol, represents an effort to bury painful feelings. It is important to recognize how these fears affect your sexual decisions.

Battles over Control

Roman says, "The girl I'm dating acts like a drill sergeant. She bosses me around and doesn't listen. During sex, she tells me faster, harder. It's all for her. When she's finished, she rolls over and leaves me there." Roman's girlfriend is behaving selfishly. But Roman needs to ask himself if he is looking for someone to control him, perhaps because he is afraid of being controlling himself. I suggested that he make control a deliberate game—that they take turns, where he can be commander-in-chief for a change. Playing the extremes can be a helpful technique for couples to reach middle ground, and to help each understand how it feels to be in each role.

Over the years, as the world has become more complex and daily life more stressful, more and more people tell me about their interest in sex acts involving dominance and submission. Playing "master and slave"—where one person is in control and the other takes orders—can be constructive ways to take turns expressing power, but extreme forms of this behavior—sadomasochism, in which partners derive satisfaction from inflicting and enduring pain—reveals a serious inability to experience love, intimacy, and vulnerability. Terrified to reveal needs for nurturing, people mask their needs with aggression, and inflict or experience pain in a desperate attempt to feel *something*. Many defend their indulgence in such activities, but need professional help to release themselves to love.

Afterburn or Afterglow?

Many people, especially women, have complicated intense reactions after having sex. Some fall into what I call "after-sex addiction"—becoming intensely attached to someone after having sex, even if she didn't care all that much for the person before. The experience of "giving her body" makes her feel more invested in the relationship.

At the other end of the spectrum are people who retreat after sex, as Carla found out. "After dating Ken for a short while, we had sex. The next day, he didn't even want to talk to me. What's his problem?" A person who retreats after intimacy is either not interested, not ready for a relationship, or frightened and withdraws to protect intense, uncomfortable feelings. Be prepared to let the relationship go if your needs are not equal or are not being met.

Just as I mentioned about dating in general earlier in this book, having sex is an opportunity to learn about yourself and people. Always get feedback. Ask your partner, "What did our relationship mean to you? How do you feel now? How do my actions affect how you feel? What did I do to affect how you acted?" Ask without implied criticism or demands. This means a magical combination of what I call "nondemand dating" (not expecting any response) and "informed dating" (learning from your experience). Your mate may be too immature, inarticulate, or inexperienced to answer you honestly, or he may not have insight into his own motives or feelings. But at least you know you've tried.

Spicing Up Your Sex Life

When the flame seems to fizzle, you can fire things up. Identify your love script, from Chapter 2, and see if your date fits into the scenario of your dating ideal. What also helps: romance, massage, sharing feelings, having fun. Recreate what worked to create the thrill in the first place. Read my book, *The Complete Idiot's Guide to a Healthy Relationship* (see Appendix A), for lots of good tips on bringing back the excitement.

> **Dating Data** _____
>
> To heighten your capacity for love (instead of having sex for sex's sake), practice tantra, the ancient art of love, through meditation, sexual healing, energy exchanges, and new ways of touching. You can learn plenty of exciting ways to achieve these higher states of ecstasy and enlightenment by following the exercises in my book, *The Complete Idiot's Guide to Tantric Sex* (see Appendix A).

The Least You Need to Know

- Ideal sex is with someone you love, fulfilling both physical and emotional needs.

- Clarify your intentions and expectations about sex and love so that neither person is misled or disappointed.

- Feel confident about saying "yes" or "no" to sex.

- Understanding and good communication is essential for good sex.

- Accept your sexual urges, feelings, and desires; self-love is important for happiness within yourself and when choosing a partner.

Part 6

Throwing Your Hat Back in the Ring

Being rejected is never easy—no matter which end of it you are on. Nor is dating after a long spell alone, or a relationship that ended. Read the chapters in this section for extremely helpful steps on how to get "no" and let go, and come out of it feeling complete and whole again.

After you've been out of the dating world for a while, it's not always easy to get back into the game. But with the right attitude—and steps to take—you can start dating again, and find fulfilling relationships. In this section, I'll tell you how to do that!

25

Handling Rejection: When to Hold or Fold

In This Chapter

- ◆ Know when it's over by watching the Dating Traffic Light
- ◆ The "frightful five" blow-offs
- ◆ The do's and don'ts of dumping
- ◆ The nine phases of dealing with rejection
- ◆ How to let go
- ◆ Patching things up

Now that you've learned how to get a relationship going and make it work, it's time to deal with the flipside: getting out without falling apart. Rejection is difficult for the one who feels "dumped," but also for the one who wants it over. In this chapter, I'll go over how to deal with "no" and let go, or as the famous Kenny Rogers song (using a poker game analogy) goes, "Know when to hold 'em, know when to fold 'em."

"My boyfriend told me he loved me," Denise wailed, "so how can he turn around the next week and say he needs his space?" Easy. He meant he cared at one moment, but that didn't mean it would last forever. While it's never easy, and always disappointing, you must learn to move on when love ends for your lover but not for you.

The first and most important question you should ask yourself after a rejection is: "Why waste myself on someone who doesn't want me?" And if you are the one initiating the breakup, why waste time and energy for both of you? If you thought you were wild about someone, but are now having doubts, what do you do? What's the best way of disentangling yourself, while being both firm and kind? Read on for those answers.

Deciding to Stay or Go: The Dating Traffic Light

In at least one relationship you'll have in your life, inevitably the day will come when you ask yourself, "Is this working?" or "How long should I keep at this before it's really over?" or "When's the right time to break this off?" Only you can determine your limits of tolerance for working on a relationship. Some people look for instant gratification, and as soon as their needs aren't being met, they're out the door. Others hang on forever, hoping and praying things will get better. Neither approach is ideal, but it helps to know where you and your partner fit along this continuum.

As I first mentioned in Chapter 13, think of dating as a long road punctuated by traffic lights. Red lights signal danger, yellow lights require caution, and green lights mean keep going (but proceed cautiously, since you never know when a car might run a red light!). Take a look at the following lists and check off what statements apply to you and to your date.

You're at a *green light* if your mate …

❑ Has positive, close relationships with family, friends, and co-workers.

❑ Is responsible and trustworthy.

❑ Is a good communicator (listens and empathizes).

❑ Is open to commitment.

❑ Expresses feelings.

❑ Shows respect for self and others.

❑ Wants to be intimate.

❑ Pays attention.

❑ Has values that are similar to yours.

❑ Tells you the truth.

You're at a *yellow light* when ...

❑ He's cheated before.

❑ Friends repeat negative rumors (that might not be true).

❑ She always falls in love too fast.

❑ He always talks about ex-partners.

❑ You "hang out" without ever doing anything meaningful.

❑ He cancels or forgets dates.

❑ She sends "mixed signals"—one minute you're great, the next you're ignored.

❑ You feel deprived and unfulfilled.

❑ He ignores intimate talk.

❑ She sends fewer e-mails and leaves fewer belongings at your house.

You're at a *red light* when ...

❑ You're sad all the time.

❑ She betrays you or cheats on you.

❑ He keeps secrets (like not revealing a home phone number or never inviting you over).

❑ She constantly blames, criticizes, or denigrates you or others.

❑ Either of you has deep unresolved anger toward the same or opposite sex.

❑ There is a clear reluctance to commit (saying "Marriage is a disaster" or "I'll never settle down").

❑ He is overly controlling or obsessed with sex.

❑ Friends warn you with evidence you refuse to believe (unlike you, they're not wearing "love blinders").

❑ You're being mentally, physically, or sexually abused.

❑ His life is dangerous (involves drugs, illegal acts, or guns).

Excuses: Holding on When You Know You Should Let Go

Even when trouble is obvious, it can be tough to let go. I hear lots of excuses from people who are unable or unwilling to leave a relationship, including …

◆ **"We've been together a long time."** For instance, Adriana told me: "My boyfriend's cheating, and now he says he doesn't want to be with me as much as before, but I don't want to break up. We've been together for five years." It's natural to get attached to people, but consider "reframing" the way you view the situation. Instead of regretting all of those "lost years" if you gave the relationship up, think of how many more years you'd be investing in being miserable if you stayed; consider that you've learned valuable lessons and need to move on for a better future.

◆ **"He was my first."** As Pam told me, "It's not working out with this guy I'm seeing, but I'm having a hard time letting go because he was my first." You'll probably always feel a special attachment to your "first," but you can't sacrifice happiness for sentimentality. You've probably become dependent on each other; have courage to face new independence and the unknown.

◆ **"But I still love him."** Kiesha explained, "I know I should stop going out with him—he cheats and treats me bad—but I still love him." Love yourself more, and treat yourself to someone who treats you well. You can always love the person, but that doesn't mean you have to be together.

◆ **"I gave her everything."** I recently talked to a guy who told me: "I really liked this girl and bought her lots of things like a $50 sweater, and the next day she broke up with me! What can I do to get her back?" Save your money and your self-esteem and let an ungrateful and unwilling mate go. If someone clearly doesn't want you, regardless of your gifts, you're trying to buy love, a sign that you may be low on self-esteem. The result is disappointing anyway, as the other person usually ends up loving you less.

Sometimes we need a kick in the pants to get out of a really bad relationship. Laura told me, "My boyfriend drinks too much and has been unfaithful. When I tell him I want to leave him, he says he'll never let me go. He tells me that the problem is that I'm unhappy with my life, and I'm blaming him. Is it my problem?" Laura's problem is that she is putting up with this man's psychological abuse and manipulation. His drinking, cheating, blaming, and threatening are sure signs that *he* is the one who is desperate, disturbed, and in need of help.

Dr. Judy's Dating Do's _____

Don't allow someone else's threats to intimidate and paralyze you. Life is too precious to spend another minute being miserable and treated poorly. Be firm about your complaints, expectations, and intentions. Take action—get legal counsel or an order of protection if necessary. Insist that a troubled partner get counseling, and get support for yourself (from friends, a therapist, or a 12-step program for people in relationships with addicts). If nothing changes, bless the person and go on your way for a healthier life. _____

Reading the Warning Signs

Most of us can tell if a relationship is going sour, but often we want to ignore even the most obvious clues. Trust your instincts. Re-read the yellow and red light statements to see if the relationship has run its course. When you're smitten, it's easy to ignore signals that a relationship is not progressing. And it's natural to want to make the one you love return your feelings—especially if that person is hard to catch. Cathy's is a typical story. "I've been seeing this guy who lately has been rather indifferent and mean. I've also heard he's been seeing another woman. But I don't want to lose him. How can I get him to see that I'm the right one for him?"

Imagine hitting your head against the wall. Does it hurt yet? If it doesn't, would you hit it harder? When will it hurt so much that you'll be forced to stop banging it against the wall? Consider emotional pain like that physical pain: When will your heart hurt so bad that you stop running after people who make you unhappy? Imagine that every time your heart is broken, your heart muscle gets chipped and torn. Be as protective with your emotions as you would be with your body.

Finally, I'm frequently asked if bad sex is a good reason to end a relationship. Yes and no. Bad sex is often just a smokescreen for other problems: lack of communication, lack of attention, unresolved hurt or anger, lack of trust, and more. Before condemning a relationship because of bad sex; carefully explore the reasons behind it. But having no sex can be a warning sign that something is wrong, since it can mean a withdrawal from closeness, intimacy, and sharing.

Be Prepared: The "Frightful Five" Blow-Offs

If the handwriting is on the wall—you sense it's over though you're not ready to admit it—how can you prepare yourself? For starters, ask for feedback. Be sensitive but blunt; ask if the signals you think you are detecting are the ones that he wants to be sending. If you have to force the conversation, you probably have your answer right there.

Prepare yourself for being alone by rekindling those friendships that you may have neglected during your relationship. Also, make an effort to make new friends that have no connection to the two of you. Protect yourself from constant reminders of your ex. If you and your soon-to-be-former lover have "your" special places, try going there with other friends to establish a new association in your mind. It's easy to become sentimental about the restaurants, movie houses, and hang-outs where you used to meet. "Detoxify" these places, or after a few relationships you may find your-self without any place to go!

If you are handed one of the "frightful five" blow-offs that follow, don't beg or plead. Accept that he or she wants the relationship to be over. You can ask for more explana-tion, but really what you want is to know it was once real, you once were loved, and you still can be lovable. Hopefully you'll get some reassurance, but even if you don't, remember that you *are* still lovable. In any case, accept the end and move on.

"I love you but I'm not 'in love' with you."

"I thought we both knew it wasn't going anywhere/was just sex."

"There's no chemistry."

"Let's just be friends."

"I met someone else."

Disappointing Dating Scripts: Making the Best of It

Bree was really excited about her date with Jason. She had her hair and nails done, bought a new outfit, and even bought some new things for her bedroom. She had been looking forward to the evening for weeks and was sure they would end up in bed. They started the evening at the movies, where Bree put her hand on Jason's knee. When he didn't respond or return her touch, she began to worry. Outside, after the movie, he told her that his stomach was bothering him and he thought he'd just go home. Bree was disappointed and felt foolish. Was Jason really feeling bad, or had she misread his flirting with her so heavily when they'd first met? Whatever the case, Bree realized that her expectations had led to disappointment. Bree had fallen into a common trap: "writing a script" for an evening without really considering the actual role of the other person. We write their part without thinking about their needs, expectations, moods, or plans. Bree wrote a script for romance with Jason, and when the evening didn't go as planned, she felt horribly let down.

It's impossible to script every experience in life, because people are unpredictable. If things don't turn out as you plan, make the new events work for you. Instead of bemoaning Jason's unresponsiveness, Bree decided to welcome that Jason went home; it gave her free time and inspiration to start writing the novel she'd been thinking about for two years. See how you can "reframe" what happens—no matter what someone else does, you can turn it into something personally fulfilling.

When You Are the One to End It: Do's and Don'ts of Dumping

Most of us know what it feels like to be dumped: the pain, humiliation, anger, and hurt. But the time may also come when you must do the dumping. Is it possible to minimize the other person's pain? Are there rules for breaking up?

Consider this scenario. As Zak described, "I've been dating Lindelle for a few months, and I really like her—as a friend. I recently met a woman I feel passionately about. Lindelle is terrific, and I know she loves me. What can I say or do to let her down easy?"

Dr. Judy's Dating Do's

Remember the Golden Rule: "Do unto others as you would have them do unto you." This is a good time to put that rule into action.

If you have ever been on the other side of the fence, like Zak, you will probably be sensitive to the following "Do's" and "Don'ts" for breaking up with someone:

- ◆ DO take responsibility for your actions.

- ◆ DO talk about splitting as a mutual benefit ("It's right for both of us") so the rejectee doesn't feel so out of control.

- ◆ DO be respectful (give her the opportunity to work through feelings).

- ◆ DO reaffirm that there was something good between you (to reassure the "dumpee" that the relationship was real).

- ◆ DO remind the dumpee of wonderful aspects of himself (to boost his self-esteem).

- ◆ DO point out your own resistance ("I'm not ready for a commitment," "I can't be true to someone yet").

- ◆ DO be sure about what you're doing.

- ◆ DO spell out the terms of the separation clearly ("We shouldn't call each other") to avoid misunderstanding.

♦ DO be firm. Leaving the door open even a crack invites efforts to change your mind.

♦ DON'T break up over the phone (it's too impersonal).

♦ DON'T break up before an important date such as a holiday or anniversary (the date will be ruined forever).

♦ DON'T blame or criticize what he did or did not do.

♦ DON'T use a "frightful five" blow-off (which can linger painfully).

♦ DON'T let guilt change your mind.k

♦ DON'T hit below the belt ("I just don't find you exciting anymore").

♦ DON'T accept being the "bad guy" (both people generally contribute to a breakup).

Dating Data

While women think that men have an easier time after a breakup, research shows that men may actually suffer more. When men get involved in an intimate relationship, they share otherwise repressed emotions. When they break up, they tend to keep their pain hidden, which often leads to physical complaints (fatigue, headaches, and so forth). Women, in comparison, are more open about suffering, and tend to surround themselves with friends and family to help ease their pain.

Dealing with Rejection: The Nine Phases

If you are the one who is being dumped, be prepared for the "stages" of rejection. While the pain may be awful, each stage is part of the healing process. The stages generally follow the sequence described in the following list, but the steps can alternate with each other. Dealing with rejection is a lot like dealing with other kinds of loss, even death (the end of a relationship is a death of sorts). The stages are similar:

1. **THE DENIAL PHASE:** "This can't be happening." During this stage you may find yourself waiting for the phone to ring, not believing that the relationship is actually over.

   SOLUTION: Acknowledge reality and acknowledge your feelings about it. Accept but do not dwell on shame and embarrassment, and all the "shoulda/woulda/coulda's" ("I should have known better," "I could have been sexier").

2. **THE BARGAINING PHASE:** Driving yourself crazy, thinking that "If I get my hair cut," or "If I just let him have sex more often," or "If I don't call him for a week," he will change his mind.

   SOLUTION: There's only one solution: Accept that it's over.

3. **THE LONELINESS PHASE:** Feeling as if no one understands or cares.

   SOLUTION: Surround yourself with people who do care, and who openly say so. Remind yourself often that you are loved—and that you love yourself, too.

4. **THE HEARTBREAK PHASE:** Feeling like your heart is really breaking. You may even feel pain in your chest, or want to throw up when you think of that person or if you see your ex with someone else.

   SOLUTION: You *can* go on. Rub your hand over your heart to soothe it. Talk with a friend for consolation and hugs (hugs heal). If you are feeling really bad, snap your fingers to interrupt the thought, and fixate on something that makes you happy. Do not drive yourself crazy with thoughts that your ex is blissfully happy while you're miserable. Only your experience counts, and only your efforts can make you happy.

5. **THE BLAME PHASE:** Pointing the finger at yourself or your ex for what each of you did wrong.

   SOLUTION: Decide that neither of you is at fault, but both of you are responsible for the breakup.

6. **THE DEPRESSION PHASE:** Feeling sad, worthless, and foolish. You may have trouble eating and sleeping, and you may imagine that you'll never find anyone to love again.

   SOLUTION: Allow yourself to feel and express your pain. Write out the events and your feelings. Listen to sad songs and cry. But do not wallow in self-pity. Keep busy with exercise or projects.

7. **THE ANGER PHASE:** Feeling furious for being rejected.

   SOLUTION: Allow yourself to experience the anger, but don't exaggerate it, or tack it onto all your past hurts. Don't let yourself become bitter.

8. **THE ACCEPTANCE PHASE:** Finally believing it's over. You no longer expect your ex to call, and you begin to feel at peace. Now you can have fun and enjoy your new freedom.

9. **THE HEALING PHASE:** Getting your life back. You are now ready to go out with friends and to meet new people, and you are no longer dwelling on your ex.

Eighteen Tips for Letting Go

Christina's is a typical story: "I've been dating Chuck for two years, and I really love him. A month ago he broke up with me, saying that he wanted to date other women, but I can't seem to move on. I can't picture myself with anyone else. He says he loves me, but that he'll never treat me the way I deserve. He keeps encouraging me to go out with other guys. What does all this mean? How can I get him back? He wants to be friends, but I only want to see him if I can get him back. How can I stop thinking about him all the time and get my life back?" It's time for Christina to let go, in order to move on to a healthier life.

Time heals all wounds, though it's hard to accept this when you're in the midst of the pain. Meanwhile, the following list gives you some tips and exercises that can help with the process:

1. **Practice thought-stopping.** It's normal to have recurring thoughts about your ex. One way to wean yourself is to decide on a specific time of day where you will give yourself over to the thoughts (such as nine o'clock at night, for 10 minutes). If you find yourself obsessing at other times, force yourself to "change the channel" in your brain, or pick yourself up and do something constructive—take a walk, water the plants, clean out a closet.

   Try this exercise: Think about your ex. Now think about being in love with someone else. Now think about your ex. Now think about getting a raise at work. Now think about laughing with a new friend. Now think about a pink elephant. See how you can control your thoughts?

> **Dating Data**
>
> In Japanese Morita therapy, you do not wallow in your feelings; you simply do what you have to do each day to function—and concentrate on those actions. You brush your teeth in the morning, you get dressed for work, and you talk to new potential mates. It's that simple.

2. **Recognize the quality that you miss in your ex and find a substitute for it.** Focus on the qualities you liked in your ex. Was he funny? Great in bed? A good listener? Realize that these aren't such unusual traits—they do come along in other people, and you will encounter them more than once in a lifetime. Enjoy those qualities in other people or find other ways to enjoy them. Go to funny movies, or take up a sport yourself.

3. **Instead of bemoaning the end, celebrate new possibilities.** Ask friends to join you. In this technique, called "paradoxical intention," you wish the very opposite of what you think you prefer. Put on some music, uncork the champagne, jump up and down, and yell "Good riddance to bad rubbish!" Then honor your time alone.

4. **Be your own cheerleader.** Remind yourself of all the good things about you. Make a list of those qualities and reread the list.

5. **Call all your friends and have them reinflate your deflated ego.** Get your pals on the phone and ask them to remind you of all your wonderful traits. Let them take your side. When Georgette was dumped, she called her best friend, who reminded her, "You are beautiful and smart and funny and fun to be with."

6. **Understand the situation realistically.** Dee was devastated when her boyfriend decided not to leave his wife for her. He said he loved her, but was worried about his kids, his business, and his wife. If she had looked at the situation realistically from the beginning, she may not have been as devastated. While she shouldn't punish herself, she should have been prepared for the possibility.

Woo Warning

Some people are so distraught over a break-up that they talk or think about killing themselves or someone else. No one person holds the key to your self-worth. If your hurt and rage are this severe, or if your ex is threatening to hurt himself or you, get professional help immediately.

7. **Be realistic about dating in general.** While I certainly feel that you should pump yourself up, don't expect that everybody will love you.

8. **Accept your responsibility, not as a way of blaming yourself, but to learn.** Go over all the sides of the story. Was he mean, cruel, insensitive? Blame him, and then face up to the fact that you pick men like that.

9. **Reaffirm that you deserve to be treated well.** Remember how you would treat a child or best friend—you would be loving, protective, and reassuring. Treat yourself that way.

10. **Do a "relationship review."** Recognize the patterns in your past relationships to prevent the same problems in the future. What type of person do you go for? What happened at every stage—who started the relationship, who made the decisions, what was the tone of the relationship (fun, sharing feelings, fighting), what did you do together (music, art, ideas, books, movies), who ended it? If you see a pattern that displeases you—you're always the caregiver, you try to "buy" love, or you're frequently attracted to people who are already involved—make it a point to make changes.

11. **Indulge in pleasure.** Make a list of things that make you feel good: getting a massage, listening to music, taking a walk. Indulge in one of these pleasures every day.

12. **Keep a sense of humor.** Research has shown that laughter strengthens the immune system and leads to better functioning after a loss. On this basis, seeing the lighter side of your situation is a positive step in your healing process. Imagine your ex in a silly situation, or go see a funny movie.

13. **Feel empowered.** Consider that you chose for the relationship to be over. Even if you think he dumped you, consider that your energy helped create the outcome. Decide "I wanted it over." This is no more real or unreal than any other explanation.

14. **Do deeper work.** Help the little child inside who is still hurting from past losses. Imagine yourself as this little child, and also imagine yourself as an adult protecting this child from being hurt, holding and comforting her.

15. **Purge your anger.** Write your ex a letter, pouring out your hurt, disappointment, and anger—but instead of sending it, rip it up or burn it as a way to release feelings and dissipate anger.

16. **Rebuild trust.** Resist generalizing; not all men or women are alike. See each person as an individual. Practice forgiveness—a high state of being. In another technique, imagine putting all those who have hurt you in the past into a computer file and clicking them into the recycle bin. Now you have a clean slate. Of course, trust gets shattered after you're hurt, but try to put the past aside. If you live in fear, imagining that people are not trustworthy, this is the reality that you will create. Accept the challenge of tuning your love antennae to people who are more trustworthy.

Dating Data

Researchers at a Midwestern university helped women who were depressed over lost loves to use their dreams to heal their pain. All the women were having recurrent dreams of bumping into their ex and feeling devastated by the experience. The researchers trained the women to put a new ending on the dream, one where they walked away from the encounter smiling and feeling happy. Some women imagined they were with another man, others pictured being happy on their own. The women were told to review the script before going to bed, to set the story in their mind. All the women felt better about coping with their loss using this technique, and the majority reported recovering sooner than they expected.

17. **Welcome your dreams.** As Brenda asked, "It's been seven months since my relationship ended, and I have constant dreams about the situation. What can I do to stop them?" Instead of seeing your dreams as obsessions, believe that your mind is trying to work through the pain on a deeper level. Trust that something better is on its way.

18. **Repair your self-esteem.** Amanda's cry is typical: "My boyfriend left after two years. What's wrong with me?" Nothing. Not everyone can appreciate your value, but you need to continue to do so.

Revenge

It's natural to want to anger, humiliate, and hurt the one who has hurt you. "I'd like to make her life hell, and make her suffer like I'm suffering," said Pete after he was dumped by Liz. "I'll get him for hurting me," Kaetlin vowed after Jorge cheated on her.

Don't waste your energy on revenge. As much as your ex might deserve your wrath, you are standing in the way of your own happiness by not letting go. To purge yourself of these feelings, tell your ex how mad and disappointed you are. But then take responsibility for yourself and move on. Be glad that the person is out of your life, and that you endured a bad relationship for three months instead of four.

Moving on can be especially difficult if you've helped a lover through a particularly bad time, only to have him leave you when his life got back on track. Try to be glad that this person's well-being is no longer your concern.

Look for patterns in your own life: Are you always the caretaker? Are you always on hand to "save" a lost soul? If so, be grateful that you've gotten this out of your system.

It's okay to indulge in fantasies of revenge (for a short while, anyway), as long as you don't act on them. Don't dwell on your ex. It is better to bless him, spread white light around you, and get on with your life. Remember, "Living well is the best revenge." Comic Jerry Seinfeld says, "A lot of people say that living well is the best revenge. That doesn't work for a guy like Charles Bronson, after his whole family is wiped out by a street gang. 'Charles, you don't need a 9mm, what you need is a custom suit and a convertible. That'll show 'em.'"

Dating Data

Taking an Eastern view, you can separate without incurring further "debts" or karma to each other so you can start a new relationship afresh.

When Your Ex Refuses to Get the Message

Suppose you've done all the right things—leveled with your ex, telling her that your heart isn't in this relationship, and that it's over. What if she refuses to get the message? Is it possible that you're sending the wrong signal? Maybe she's in shock and needs explanations for closure. Be as considerate as possible even if you don't relish going over it.

Some people become obsessed when rejected. For example, John's girlfriend continued to call up to five times a day for months after they broke up. When he didn't return her calls, she would show up at his house. John asked, "How do I get her off my back? I feel like joining the witness protection program."

It's very disturbing, and often frightening, to be pursued obsessively. Clearly, John ex's attachment to him went far deeper than their actual relationship, probably mirroring something in her family. Such an obsessive lover needs to be told she is a good person and cared for, but that your closeness is over, and that pursuing you is not acceptable. Insist that she get counseling. If such behavior persists, go to the police for an order of protection (some states have anti-stalking laws). Be firm. Don't give in and get back together because of feelings of guilt. Any inconsistency in your behavior will be interpreted as a sign that you don't really want out.

Woo Warning

If you truly want to end the relationship, don't be tempted to sleep with the person "one last time." Having sex will only make the breakup harder.

On the other hand, what if the lover who recently left you calls and says she wants to see you? Be cautious. If she was so sure that the relationship was over, what has happened to change her mind? Is it loneliness, boredom, or a true change of heart? Proceed slowly to find out what she wants. When it comes to sex, be especially slow and cautious. Sometimes sex with an ex is good because you're free of commitment or problems, but a roll in the hay won't get you the love you want. Watch out for "yo-yo" lovers—the kind who vacillate between wanting you and wanting freedom.

"Why is sex always better after breaking up?" Sometimes it's easier for couples to have great sex when their commitment and relationship problems (arguments, miscommunications, angers) are put aside, and when they have dropped any expectations. Also, the tension of a breakup can seem to intensify passion, like the popular song goes: "The best part of breaking up is making up." But as I described in Chapter 23, beware of starting arguments just to fuel your passion.

Not Fully Cutting the Cord

"Is it okay to keep in touch with an ex-boyfriend of three years if I'm now seeing someone else?"

"Is it normal to still have feelings for an ex?"

Both situations are "normal." Some people can totally sever a relationship and never see an ex again. Usually this happens if the relationship was fraught with pain and anger. But if you truly cared, you will always have a soft spot for that person, remembering when you hear "your song" or see "your restaurant." Past lovers are a part of your life and your personal history. In fact, at certain times in your life, you may feel an urgent need to get in touch. Often during major transitions (marriage, divorce, death of a parent or spouse, kids leaving the nest), people want to contact ex-lovers to be reminded of good times, or to resolve some issues. This connection can make you feel vital and acknowledged.

But before picking up the phone, think about what you are looking for. Review the relationship and what the person actually means to you. How did that person make you feel? What is he symbolic of? What were you going through in your life at the time (college days, your first job, junior year abroad, the prom)? Then, consider the other person. It might be that your call is the last thing that person needs right now.

Repairing the Hurt

What makes breaking up so traumatic? Often, there are many unresolved emotions and unfinished business. If you see an ex too soon, you risk triggering those unresolved feelings and fantasies, which will prevent you from moving on. But when the time is right, such reunions can also be a valuable opportunity to work through some unfinished business. Sometimes you'll discover that all of the feelings of unworthiness or rejection that you've been harboring are overblown. Such realizations allow you to move on to new relationships.

Don't rush a reunion with your ex—give yourself plenty of time for the wounds to heal. When you are both ready, get together and review what happened. Explain the things that hurt you, what you wanted, what you feared, and what you miss. With distance and a fresh perspective, any lingering pain may ease, and a new love may emerge.

Many of us entertain the fantasy of seeing an ex and having him or her say, "You were right all along. Take me back!" This would restore your feeling that you—and your love—mattered to that person (your love always matters, even if unrequited)! It is possible for this to happen.

It happened for Didi. Didi had been very much in love with Kirk when he left her. While she'd gotten on with her life, she still had feelings for him and always wondered "What if …?" Ten years passed, and after a serendipitous meeting, Kirk called. They got together and talked about their lives. He explained that he and his wife were "just friends." Their sexual relationship had long since died, even though the marriage was intact. Hearing this, Didi realized that the longing she felt for Kirk all those years was suddenly gone.

Dating Data

Research has shown that it can take half the time of the relationship to get over losing it, and even then 10 percent of the pain remains. But it's different for everybody, and if you find yourself in turmoil after a year, or if you can't function (eat, sleep, work, and so on), get professional help.

When Kirk left her years before, he gave Didi one of the "frightful five" blow-offs, saying, "I love you but I'm not in love with you." Soon after their breakup, he fell "madly in love" with someone else. Now he was telling her that this love, too, had died, and his sex life was barren. It seemed like poetic justice to Didi. Kirk went on to apologize for hurting her, and to express his feelings of remorse. Kirk's apology and expressions of regret were what Didi needed to deal with her residual pain. It helped her realize that she hadn't imagined his feelings for her, and that she was probably better off having Kirk as part of her past than part of her present.

Can't We Patch This Thing Up?

More often than not, when things go really sour, it's better not to look back. Getting back together will only work if both of you have worked on the problems that caused the relationship to flounder. If you decide to give it another go, you both must also express your commitment to giving it a fresh start. Only under those conditions is it worth trying to patch things up.

Wanting to reconcile is a common dilemma: "When my boyfriend broke up with me I kept begging him to take me back. Why isn't he listening?"

You must already know from previous chapters in this book that I'm no advocate of game-playing. Instead, I encourage you to express your needs and feelings. But I do think there is one time when you should hold back—when your emotional needs are out of proportion to the reality of the relationship. There's a big difference between saying, "I don't want to break up, I love you" and "I can't go on without you." The latter, acting desperate, pitiful, and "clingy," will only drive your lover away, since such desperation tends to trigger contempt and disgust (often because the person fears that your desperation may trigger his own). Your desperation also sends a clear signal that you are hanging on for your own needs—it is less about your true love for him than about your need to prevent feeling abandoned, and to play out your "love script."

Dating Data

Some lovers later find out an ex-partner had really been more attracted to the same sex, so the relationship was not meant to be, anyway.

Even if you have strong feelings for your ex, don't go crazy or make a scene. Imagine yourself surrounded by white light, being happy without the person. You can suggest reconciling, saying something like, "It would be nice to get back together." But don't put your life on hold, just leave the door open. Then pull yourself together, look your best, go out, and have fun. Your patience may pay off.

In letting your ex know you still care, don't make demands. People have to choose to be with you freely, not out of guilt, loneliness, or sentimentality. If your ex is asking you to do things as friends, take the bait only if you can control yourself. If you can't, keep your distance. As painful as it may be to say no, it will be less painful in the long run.

The Least You Need to Know

- Everyone faces rejection at some point in life.
- Someone may not love you, but *you* must always love you.
- There are predictable stages of dealing with loss.
- It's better to leave a bad relationship and get on with your life.
- You will survive any breakup, no matter how painful.
- It is possible to reconcile with an ex if both people are willing, and if both of you work to resolve the problems that plagued the relationship.

Chapter 26

Getting Back in the Saddle

In This Chapter

- Changing from old views to the new you
- Dating when you have kids
- Finding love in the senior years
- Dating after the death of a spouse

Each year, 1.2 million marriages end in divorce. That means 2.4 million people reenter the singles life again. Most have been married for about 10 years, and about 70 percent will marry again.

But making it work the second (or third) time around depends on how much you've learned from past mistakes and how well you've reassessed yourself and your needs.

The New You!

You deserve a life again! Being alone doesn't have to mean being lonely. Allow yourself to feel passion and give yourself permission to love again. Use the following guide to change your way of thinking.

Old Way of Thinking	New Way of Thinking
Restrictive: Dating is not for me	**Permission:** All possibilities are open to me
Punitive: I have no right to go out	**Supportive:** I have a right to enjoy myself
Fearful: I'm afraid to commit, get hurt	**Confident:** I can risk again, I won't make the same mistakes
Excuses: I have no time to go out	**Freeing:** I can figure out how to make love work

Saying Good-Bye to the Old and Hello to the New

One big reason why newly single people resist reentering the dating world is that they are stuck in past relationships. My favorite technique to help people get past this is called "completing unfinished business." Because there are many things that have gone unsaid in such a relationship, in this technique you have an imaginary conversation with your ex or departed one, saying all the things you wish you could have said to the person. Imagine asking for, and receiving, permission to go on with your life.

Simply the experience of getting things off your chest can free you from the weight that you have been carrying. The more mired you are in the past, the more you will simply not "see" something good that will come your way. Freeing yourself from thoughts and letting go of the past enable you to be more open and receptive to the new opportunities that are bound to come your way.

The loss or death of a spouse/lover is traumatic under any conditions, especially if the relationship has in many ways been good. Some divorced and widowed men and women feel so spiritually attached to their partner that they cannot move on to date others. Death is particularly traumatic because it can happen so suddenly. But it is important—and possible—to accept the pain of the loss and resolve to move on with your life.

Rebuilding Self-Esteem

Being out of the dating world for a long time can make you feel insecure, frightened, and hesitant. "I've been out of that scene so long," Jack said, "I have no idea what people do!" Many people struggle with guilt and feelings of being a failure. Take Leila, for example: "I couldn't make it work with Greg, so I'm really frightened to try again with someone else."

It is especially important for people who carry a lot of emotional baggage from the past to be aware of those feelings and try to prevent them from spilling into their new relationships. Recognize your fears and remind yourself that the past does not have to repeat itself. Reevaluate all your strong points (your character and your experience). Trust that there will be people whose company you will enjoy and vice versa.

Single-Parent Dating

Alone again, you are entitled—when you're ready—to get back in the dating scene. Inevitably, you will have some practical concerns, and many fears and confused feelings: "When am I going to have time to date when I have children to take care of?" or "How am I supposed to be an example to my teenage kids when I'm also playing the field?" You may even experience guilty feelings: "Will it upset my kids if I start dating again?" These fears and feelings are all normal, and knowing that you're not the only one to feel this way can ease some of the pressure.

Parents negotiating child support and custody may have particular emotional conflicts (confusion, frustration, sadness, or anger) at this time. Professionals have become particularly aware of the "father depression" that some men suffer from when they are saddled with child-support bills, but deprived of being with their children.

Dr. Judy's Dating Do's

Single parents using an online dating service should always ask specifically if a person has children or welcomes dating someone who has children.

A Ready-Made Family in the Deal

With divorce rates high and an escalating number of young women having babies without marrying, there are large numbers of single parents in this new age on the dating market. Despite being more accepting of single life on their own (I've mentioned how one major survey showed more than one third of single women no longer feel desperate to have a man in order to have a baby), most single parents would like to find a loving partner with whom to raise their family. Fortunately, some singles welcome the idea of an instant family by marrying a single parent. Others (especially never-married singles) may resist the idea. Be prepared for such reactions and how you will cope with them.

If you're about to date a single parent, but have never been married or had kids yourself, be prepared for differences in responsibilities and attitudes. Some couples adjust easily: Garth, a never-married man, was ecstatic that dating Barbara included a "ready-made" family with her two young children. Others face problems: Sue became resentful that her boyfriend spent time with his ex-wife and little girl every other weekend, and felt threatened and left out. Unfortunately, if Sue wanted to continue dating her boyfriend, there was nothing she could do but accept her boyfriend's package: ex-wife and child. If you're in this situation, it's important to discuss your feelings with your partner and get the reassurance you need. Also, don't waste time worrying about the ex; switch that energy to making your own relationship work. In addition, share time just with the child, so the two of you form a bond.

Tell a new date about your family situation at the beginning of your relationship. Recognize some initial resistance that could be based on fears, jealousy, or competition (he's upset you spend more time with your kids than with him, she's worried you spend more money on your kids than on hers). These issues can be resolved by talking them through and making compromises. But if a new partner is unwilling to work out these realistic problems, sabotages your parenting, or rejects your responsibilities and their role in parenting, consider passing up the relationship. Even if you love the person, the potential arguments and resentments that will arise over time will erode your relationship and create havoc in your family.

What About the Kids?

Of course you want to be a good parent. But consider yourself, too. Realize that your happiness will spill over into how you treat your kids and what example you set for them. It is important, however, to be prepared for all the feelings that your children may have in reaction to your dating.

Keep in mind that your children will probably always be upset about the new love in your life no matter how much they like him or her. Deep inside, children want their family back together again. Any newcomer is bound to be perceived, even subconsciously, as a stranger who is sabotaging this fantasy. It is crucial to understand this dynamic and recognize why your children may resent the new person in your life.

Dr. Judy's Dating Do's

Ask about your child's feelings: "What do you think about (the person you're dating)?" or "How do you feel about me dating/having a relationship?" It's important to show that you respect your child's feelings, but do not let those feelings interfere with or rule your dating. Show that you are considerate of, but not controlled by, your child.

One way to deal with this is to introduce your kids only to someone who really matters to you; casual dates may only confuse them. Also, put feelings into words for children who may be afraid or unable to express themselves: "I know how disappointed you are that your father and I are not together, and I understand why you may dislike my new boyfriend." Or simply affirm the child's feelings: "It is normal to feel angry at me and my new girlfriend." You should also share some of your own feelings: "This is a difficult adjustment for me, too." And, reassure your child: "No one will replace your mother," or "No matter what, know I love you."

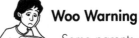

Woo Warning

Some parents avoid the difficulties of dating by immersing themselves in their children. While this can be a welcome relief and offer joy and needed attention, such escape and living vicariously through children—or over-absorption in them—can be unhealthy for all concerned.

When a New Lover Meets Your Child

When you decide that it's time to introduce your new mate to your child, refer to your paramour in casual terms at first. For example, you might say, "I'd like you to meet a good friend of mine." Try planning a fun activity together; for example, go to a baseball or basketball game, shopping, or to the movies. Do something together in neutral territory first, outside of the child's home. This lessens the chances of the child feeling invaded or imposed upon at home. Doing something with the child not only makes the child feel included, it also dilutes the anxiety of a face-to-face meeting.

Most kids become anxious about their parents dating. Their distress can range from worrying about being displaced in their home to being replaced by their parent's new-found love. Children might also be very judgmental of whom their parent is dating, and simply not "approve." When 13-year-old Ben called me, he was distressed that his mother was dating a much younger man (not much older than his older brother). He also didn't like watching this person order his mother around. He feared that his mother might be sexually and financially used, and he was afraid that she would be hurt badly. I encouraged Ben to talk with his mother abut his fears and concerns, while reminding her that he loves her and has her best interests in mind. I also told him he might have to accept her decision whether or not he likes it, but that he should also reflect on how his mother's choice was reflecting his own anxieties about dating, as he was at that age to start thinking about mates, and probably fears repeating his mother's problems.

Sleepovers should be reserved only for serious relationships and only after your child has had opportunities to get used to your suitor's presence. Your child should also be told first that your relationship has taken a more significant turn. This shows respect for your child's feelings, and portrays sex as a very serious step in a relationship.

What Others Say

Friends, family members, and co-workers will always have their own judgments and opinions about you dating again. Some may sound ominous and scary: "You shouldn't be going out so fast, give yourself time to recover" or "No one's going to want someone with the baggage of kids." These opinions are just that—opinions. Remember, what others say is only a reflection of their own fears or experiences and does not have to be true for you. Take such advice with a grain of salt.

Where to Meet People

Review all the suggestions in Chapter 4 on where to meet people. However, pay special attention to places that would draw other divorced people or divorcees with kids. Meeting people in the same situation is just as important as meeting people with the same interests. This is especially true if you both have children, since each of you will understand responsibilities and limitations that being a parent places on dating. Keep in mind that you can bring your child to any of the "hunting grounds." Children can serve as both company and icebreakers for starting up a conversation.

Divorced men and women can find many clubs and organized activities especially for divorced people listed in specialty newsletters and community newspapers. Local religious centers are also a good resource. Playgrounds are particularly good places to meet other single parents, as the environment is conducive to playfulness and feeling at ease. Watching others play with their kids also gives you the opportunity to observe their kindness, thoughtfulness, and generosity. Other resources include children's events and activities (many are listed in local newspapers), school groups, and single-parent clubs.

Seniors: Making the Most of the Golden Years

Age can affect all the issues concerning reentering the dating world. These include social stereotypes, personal attitudes, fears, and proscriptions that are often a carry-over from youth. I invite—and implore—you to keep my overriding rule in mind:

You never have to retire from love! You are never too old to date and enjoy the companionship and intimacy that being with a romantic interest can provide. To reinforce that rule, keep in mind that:

◆ Romantic interests boost your self-esteem and joy in life.

◆ You are entitled to love.

◆ There are always opportunities to meet people and find new love. Seniors can even enjoy the fun of online dating—to meet new people, have fun, and feel renewed interest in relating.

Recognize your resistance to being open to new love, in order to prevent it from paralyzing you. In this day and age when so much value is placed on youth, it's crucial to boost your self-esteem, so follow the suggestions in Chapters 7 and 8 to feel good about yourself. Change your thoughts from "I'm too old" to "I'm full of life and new interests." Take a deep breath and project feeling happy, open, and available. Discard self-defeating lessons you may have grown up with, such as women should not approach men or that it's shameful to place a personal ad. Instead of focusing on your diminished strength, energy, or physical abilities, appreciate the wisdom about life and people that comes only from age, telling yourself that you can only enjoy this stage of life having been through whatever you have experienced. Reframe your defeatist attitude, from "I'll never find anyone" to "There is always someone who will cross my path who will see how wonderful I am." Every time you think "I can't ..." rephrase it to "I can" or "I will." Remind yourself that dating enriches your life and keeps you active and alert to explore new avenues of enjoyment and growth.

Dating Data

Research shows that people's eligibility criteria change as they get older. Whereas physical attraction is high on the attraction list for younger people, companionship, shared interests, and compatibility play a bigger role in relationships as people age. This is reassuring to those who fear waning physical beauty.

Getting Out and About

The adage "You won't meet anyone sitting home alone" becomes even more pressing for older singles, who can have a tendency to stay at home. Getting out of the house is crucial to increase your chances of meeting someone. If you cannot get motivated, ask friends to consistently call to encourage you and insist you come out to join them. Accept invitations to get out and about even if you are not eager to go. Once you get there, you will be surprised at what a good time you can have.

You may become "set in your ways," or develop anxieties about certain situations, or be rigid in your habits (eating, bedtime, TV watching). Yet, in order to adapt to dating, you need to remain flexible and open to change. In reality, the maturity and security of older age can afford you the wisdom to be able to accept the idiosyncrasies of others, and make compromises that are necessary to any new, or good, relationship. While at 25 years of age you might never have considered a man shorter than you, or a woman who does not look like Claudia Schiffer or Demi Moore, at 55 you may have a different set of values. Change can be just what you need to give you a renewed excitement about life. Being secure about who you are can allow you to consider going off your beaten path, without fear that something drastic will happen.

Woo Warning

As your financial status becomes more set as you get older, it is that much more important to clarify how dating costs will be handled. It takes courage to discuss who treats, but clarification is important to avoid confusion or upset.

Dating during the retirement years has potential advantages. Freedom from work or family responsibilities can give you more energy, free time and attention, more clarity about financial resources, and more opportunities to take advantage of events and places to meet people. In fact, this can be the time for you to take up those hobbies, or learn those skills, that you never had the time to do before, like joining a gym, or taking courses at the local "Y."

Seniors and Sex

Just as I said earlier about love: "You never have to retire from sex." Research supports this view that continued sexual desire and behavior can be a sign of psychological, as well as physical, well-being. Sexual interest and activity result in a self-supporting cycle, between a positive self-image and outlook on life, and physical benefits from increased blood flow, stimulation of body chemicals and heart rate, and muscle exercise.

Since body image greatly affects sexual desire, it is that much more important as you age to keep yourself looking as good as you can. Choose hairdos and clothing styles that flatter you. Treat yourself to a makeover if that would make you feel good. Physical fitness is also important. Follow an exercise program tailored for particular age groups, for safety and appropriate motions targeted at body types and physical ability.

Feeling good about yourself is a precursor to feeling open to another (and the ultimate quality of sex appeal). Self-pleasuring can be extremely useful in the interim when a partner is not available. Research has proven the physical benefits of such activity, including less atrophy of tissues, and fewer genital problems in those who remain active, compared to those who do not engage in such behavior. While often shrouded in silence and shame, solitary pleasure throughout the lifespan is more common than you may think. Surveys show that up to a third of older men and women continue to enjoy some self-pleasuring.

The golden years can indeed be golden! Replace fear with a challenge to find new interests and excitement in life, to be open to new people and experiences, and to feel good about yourself. Men and women over 50 are looking better, staying fit, and thus emanating more sex appeal.

 **Dating Data**

Many older men and women fear for their sexual potency as they age. While changes certainly occur in both sexes (men need more time to get aroused, and women need added lubrication after menopause), sex drive can remain high and performance adequate. In some cases, sex drive increases with reduced fears of pregnancy and increased self-acceptance.

When a Spouse Has Died

Losing a spouse or lover is traumatic, and requires mourning and adjustment. Some widows and widowers find themselves open to another relationship, falling in love again as a way to heal the hurt and loss. Others find themselves unable, or even resolved, never to fall in love again.

If you were blessed to have enjoyed a long and pleasurable union, it is certainly sad to lose that connection. You can of course decide that there will never be anyone else for you and you have no desire to date again. But some loving spouses deep down would like to find love again, especially knowing how wonderful it once was. Appreciate your blessings, but also respect your desire to continue enjoying such an experience.

The death of a spouse creates certain idiosyncratic conditions when compared to separation or divorce. Self-blame or guilt may be less (associated with "What did I do wrong?" or "How was I not good enough?"), considering that you were not the cause of the loss. Finality of the loss through death also eliminates the stage of mourning where you try to get the lover back, or feel pained if he or she is with someone else.

Yet some widows and widowers feel so attached to their partner, they cannot move on to date others. Friends may try to fix you up, but you insist there can be no one else in your life. Or you feel that to fall in love with someone else would betray your beloved. Certainly your choice is entirely personal. Decide what truly makes you happy. But if you want to date again but cannot due to fear or other resistance, there is a way to help get over this hurdle.

Woo Warning

Statistics show that sexually transmitted diseases of all kinds are predominant in older age groups. Protection is therefore warranted at whatever age.

A useful technique for widows is the "set me free" exercise. Imagine your spouse in the room, pledge your love, and ask permission to move on to love someone else in this life. Really see your ex in your mind's eye smiling at you, acknowledging the love between you, and cutting the cord between you, detaching to allow you to get on with your life on this earth and to be open to be with someone else should the opportunity arise. If it makes you feel better, you can even agree to meet in an afterlife!

The Least You Need to Know

- You're entitled to date and love again—at any age or under any circumstances.

- Having children does not make it impossible to find dates, but make sure that new partners understand your situation.

- Kids will always want the family to be whole again—recognize this so you can understand your child's behavior regarding your dating.

- Friends, family members, and co-workers will have their own judgments about you dating again. Remember, what matters most is what you think and feel.

- After losing a loved one, resolve that you *can* love again.

- You never have to retire from love—or loving yourself—at any age.

A Final Word

Wow! Have we been through the world of finding love! I've put my heart and soul and everything I know into this new edition, and I'm sure you've equally put your heart and soul into reading it. Thank you for that. Keep it handy, and go back over sections when the issues arise for you. Do the exercises over time, too, and see how your answers change. After all, it's been my hope in this book to inspire you to always be growing! Review parts with friends and with your current (or future) partners.

When you find a certain special someone, do get a copy of the next in this series that I wrote, *The Complete Idiot's Guide to a Healthy Relationship*, since that was really an outgrowth of this book. And then, be sure to read *The Complete Idiot's Guide to Tantric Sex* not just because I wrote it, but because I genuinely know you will love it, and discover many new joys for yourself alone or with a partner. It's a blending of ancient and new ideas in my unique format that really is an exploding new phenomenon. Be on the cusp of what's "new" in love!

I've tried to think of everything, making this tome an encyclopedia of sorts, but if you have something you'd like to add, e-mail me or write to me at the address given at the bottom of the order sheet in the back of this book.

Thanks for being aboard—and keep on reading for some helpful info in the appendixes.

Blessings to you from me.

Appendix A

Resources

Dating Services

Ask details about different methods, services, and process of making matches. Some are franchised businesses with local or regional headquarters. Others are web-based services, with no personalized interviews. And some are "good old-fashioned matchmakers" that give one-on-one, totally personalized service.

Internet-Based Services

www.match.com

www.matchmaker.com

www.jdate.com

www.Udate.com

www.italmatch.com

www.personals.yahoo.com

www.nerve.com

www.lavalife.com

Franchised Services

Together
www.togetherdating.com or info@togetherdating.com
Regional California office: (310) 279-3300
Franchised introduction service with over 80 offices around the country (and London, Toronto, and the Netherlands) serving half a million singles since 1974. Members are 53 percent female, 47 percent male, 60 percent between ages 30–44 (range 21–87), 66 percent white collar, one third earn over $50,000. Fill out a "compatibility profile" and personality tests, and get assigned to a personalized matchmaker. Small picture, no video. Matches are guaranteed. Several membership packages, starting at about $2,000.

Great Expectations
www.great-expectations.net
(972) 448-7900
Offices in about 50 cities (not including New York). Choices made by viewing videotapes of clients. Costs about $1,000 to $2,500 per year.

Speed Dating Variations

On the Internet, two sites to check out are www.8minutedating.com and www.HurryDate.com.

Matchmakers or "Marriage Brokers"

Fields Exclusive Dating Service
317 Madison Avenue, New York, NY 10017
(212) 391-2233
American and worldwide clients. A grandfather-handed-down-to-grandson service, in business 70 years, arranging marriages for all ages (16 to 85), professions, and religions, "the old-fashioned way." They work seven days a week. No gimmicks, no computers. Members sit with family owners and go through files. Fee starts at $100 for several names and depends on the level of service.

Visual Preference
297-101 Kinderkamack Road, P.O. Box 310, Oradell, NJ 07601
(800) 533-1712
Tri-state area of New York, New Jersey, and Connecticut only. In business 30 years, matches made after personal interviews about your needs and criteria, filling out preference descriptions and personality profile. Photo and information sent to your home. Consultations for image arranged. Cost based on individualized program. Unlimited referrals. Fees start at $599 for five-month program, up to several thousand for longer.

There are also various love brokers with personalized service. You can find their advertisements in the personals sections of major magazines, or surf the Internet. Search the innumerable dating sites to familiarize yourself with the entire world of services, but then always get referrals. Individual operators in business a long time include Denise Winston, by appointment only at (310) 276-0072 or (212) 935-9350.

Clubs and Organizations

Single Gourmet
510 Madison Avenue, New York, NY 10022
(212) 980-8788
www.singlegourmetny.com
e-mail: info@singlegourmet.com
Dining clubs available in about 18 cities in the United States and Canada; contact local directory assistance or website. Offers dining events with mingling opportunities, often mixed with various outings such as theater, sporting events, or trips, especially on major holidays, locally or to foreign countries. Costs include membership fee (initial $85, renewal $45, includes newsletter and reciprocal membership in Single Gourmet clubs) plus cost of dinner or event.

Parents Without Partners
1650 South Dixie Highway, Suite 510, Boca Raton, FL 33432
(800) 637-7974
e-mail: pwp@jti.net
www.parentswithoutpartners.org
National organization with local chapters around the country. Offers social activities, classes, study groups, and other help for single parents of all ages with children. Membership fees (for example, $30) plus fees for some activities (for example, picnic, $3).

12-Step Programs
Nationally available, contact your local directory assistance. Based on the famed 12-step addiction model, these self-help groups offer frequent group support meetings for people with similar life issues ranging from alcohol or drug abuse (AA or DA) to overeating (OA) and love and sex addictions (LSA).

UJA-Federation
130 East 59th Street, New York, NY 10022
www.ujafedny.org
National organization with local affiliates in various cities offering events, trips, and courses; for example, Business and Professional Singles, Resource Line.

Christian Singles Organization
www.christianmatchmaker.com (for national network) or www.4step.orge-mail:
nj3singlechristian@yahoo.com (in the Northeast area)
Offers singles groups, events, and online community catering to those of Christian faith.

Book and Music Stores

Book and music superstores such as Borders Books and Music Stores and Barnes &
Noble Bookstores offer opportunities for meeting singles as you browse or enjoy a
latte. Check local listings for locations.

Restaurant Chains

Check local listings for theme restaurants such as Planet Hollywood, Hard Rock
Café, and All Star (sports) café. Also, check out chain restaurants that have entertainment complexes such as ESPN Zone (www.ESPNZone.com) and Dave and Busters
(www.DaveandBusters.com).

Expos and Courses

New Life Expo
168 West Park Avenue, Long Beach, NY 11561
(800) 928-6208
www.newlifeexpo.com
Has a magazine and holds three-day symposiums/expos in cities around the country,
consisting of hundreds of lectures, workshops, and exhibits on "a smorgasbord of
body, mind, spirit issues," like holistic health, alternative medicine, spirituality, meta-
physics, human potential, psychic phenomena, and the environment. Admission
$15–$25 for exhibit hall and free lectures, extra fees for other workshops. Well worth
a day of shopping, eating, learning, and meeting like-minded people.

The Open Center
83 Spring Street, New York, NY 10012
(212) 219-2527
e-mail: infop@opencenter.org
www.opencenter.org
Offers over 600 events (including lectures, workshops, conferences, and retreats, each
year) centered around holistic learning and culture, and led by world-renowned experts.
For example: classes in Buddhism (drawing large crowds with equal numbers of men
and women) and conferences on alchemy in Prague and the Holy Grail in Wales.

Learning Annex

www.learningannex.com

Adult education organization founded in 1980, offering nearly 8,000 short, inexpensive courses a year on a wide variety of subjects, like personal growth, business and career opportunities, showbiz and media, health and healing, sports and fitness, spirituality, relationships, high tech, and many other subjects. Schools in New York, Los Angeles, San Francisco, San Diego and Toronto, as well as a video and audio library. Speakers include inspirational best-selling authors and celebrities.

YMCA/YWCA and YMHA/YWHA

Local chapters in various cities around the country. Contact local directory assistance. Offers support groups, courses, and activities on various themes from "How to Flirt" to "Letting Go and Moving On." Cost of events varies from $2 and up.

Books and Magazines

You can obtain copies of my books through your local bookstore, on amazon.com, or send an e-mail to APOLL143@aol.com for ordering information.

Berkowitz, Bob. *What Men Won't Tell You but Women Need to Know.* HarperCollins, 1991.

Brockway, Rev. Laurie Sue. *A Goddess is a Girl's Best Friend: A Divine Guide to Finding Love, Success and Happiness.* Perigree Books, 2002.

Farrell, Warren. *The Myth of Male Power.* Berkeley Publishers, 2001.

Gabriel, Bonnie. *The Fine Art of Erotic Talk.* Bantam Books, 1995.

Gray, John. *Men Are from Mars, Women Are from Venus.* HarperCollins, 1992.

Hatcher, R.A., S. Colestock, E. Pluhar, and C. Thrasher. *Sexual Etiquette 101 and More, Third Edition.* Bridging the Gap Communications, Inc., 2001.

Kuriansky, Dr. Judy. *How to Love a Nice Guy.* Doubleday, 1990.

———. *The Complete Idiot's Guide to a Healthy Relationship, Second Edition.* Alpha Books, 2002.

———. *The Complete Idiot's Guide to Tantric Sex.* Alpha Books, 2002.

———. *Generation Sex.* Harper, 1996.

———. *Sex, Now That I've Got Your Attention, Let Me Answer Your Questions.* Putnam, 1986.

Moore, Myreah, and Jodie Gould. *Date Like a Man.* HarperCollins, 2000.

Tannen, Deborah. *You Just Don't Understand.* HarperCollins, 2001.

Stone, Merlin. *When God Was a Woman.* Harcourt Publishers, 1978.

Sullivan, Jim. *Boyfriend 101.* Villard, 2003. A how-to gay guy's guide to dating, romance, and finding true love. www.boyfriend101.com.

Local city magazines, like *New York Magazine* and *Los Angeles Magazine*, can be found at newsstands and in hotels. Check event listings and personals. For a list of city magazines for over 50 cities, see www.fourbnetworks.com.

Travel Services

Club Med
40 West 57th Street, New York, NY 10019
(800) CLUB MED
www.clubmed.com
All-inclusive vacation packages at villages around the world offering varied sports and activities. Many travelers are single, median age is 35, and two thirds are professionals. Membership fee, plus cost of trip (week-long, over $1,000).

Hedonism
Book through travel agent for good prices. All-inclusive vacation package to Jamaica, known for its almost entirely single patronage and uninhibited atmosphere. Search the Internet for Hedonism I, II, and III in Jamaica.

Outdoor Bound
18 Stuyvesant Oval, New York, NY 10009
(212) 505-1020
www.outdoorbound.com
Outdoors and travel club offering various trips with varied activities from rafting to camping. About 10,000 people are on the mailing list. Membership fee of $30. Also look up the famous Outward Bound site (www.outwardbound.com) for adventure trips.

Information on Health Issues

Social Phobia/Social Anxiety Association (www.socialphobia.org)
Nonprofit organization that provides information, free moderated mailing list of resources and a forum about therapies for social anxiety disorder.

ASHA (The American Social Health Association)
P.O. Box 13827, Research Triangle Park, NC 27709
(800) 230-6039
www.ashastd.org

National STD and AIDS hotline (Center for Disease Control)
(800) 227-8922 or (800) 342-2437
www.cdc.gov (then search STDs)
Answers to questions available 24 hours, seven days a week, by live person.

SIECUS (Sexuality Information and Education Council of the United States)
130 West 42nd Street, Suite 350, New York, NY 10036
(212) 819-9770
Fax: (212) 819-9776
For AOL members: siecusinc@aol.com
For other service members: siecus@ibm.net
www.siecus.org

Planned Parenthood Federation of America
810 7th Avenue, New York, NY 10019
(800) 230-PLAN or (212) 261-4300
www.ppfa.org

Alan Guttmacher Institute
120 Wall Street, New York, NY 10005
(212) 248-1111
Fax: (212) 248-1951
www.agi-usa.org

GMHC Hotline
1-800-AIDS-NYC (1-800-243-7692)
In New York City: (212) 807-6655
www.gmhc.org

Dating Quiz

Take this test to see how good you are in the dating game and how to improve your dating skills. The answers to this quiz can be found at the end of this section, including my advice and also the responses of men and women from the many surveys that I have done over the years.

Ask your dates these questions, to start interesting conversation:

1. What are the top three things that men say attract them to a woman?

   _____

2. What are the top three things that women say attract them to a man?

   _____

3. Which of the five senses is the most powerful in attraction? Circle one:

   Sight   Smell   Hearing   Taste   Touch

4. If you were going to whisper sweet nothings in someone's ear, which ear would you whisper in? Circle one:

   Right ear   Left ear

5. What are the two phrases that women most want to hear?

   _____

6. What are the words that men most want to hear?

   _____

7. What do both men and women (according to surveys) most want to hear?

   _____

8. What is the best way to "pick up" someone?

   _____

9. Where is the best place to go to meet someone?

   _____

10. How many approaches should you make before you give up on a dating prospect? Fill in number: _____

11. What's the best way to show someone you're interested?

    _____

12. How do you know someone's interested in you?

    _____

13. How much eye contact should you engage in when you're interested in someone?

    _____

14. What are two good ways of dealing with rejection?

    _____

15. Who should be your "best" date?

    _____

16. How many dates are recommended before you know someone is "it"? Fill in number: _____

17. What is a good test of true love?

    _____

18. What are three qualities that make for the best-lasting relationship?

    _____

19. What is the most important rule about using a condom?

    _____

20. Why do some men roll over and go to sleep after sex?

    _____

Answers to Dating Quiz

1. For the top three things that men say attract them to a woman, you'd be right if you mentioned looks first, and then qualities like a good personality, intelligence, and sense of humor. A lot of men, like women, say "eyes."

2. For the top three things that women say attract them to a man, you'd be right if you said personality (warmth, caring), trustworthiness (honesty), intelligence, and sense of humor. A lot of women, like men, say "eyes." When women get to talking about the subject in more detail, they mention money.

3. Smell is the most powerful sense in attraction because the messages go straight, and therefore quickly, from the olfactory bulb to the brain. In my surveys, a majority of people say "sight."

4. Whisper sweet nothings in the left ear to connect to the right (romantic) side of the brain. People more often answer the "right" ear.

5. Women most want to hear the words "I love you" and "You're beautiful." In my surveys, women joke about money; for example, they want to hear something like, "My credit card is platinum."

6. Men most want to hear how good they are, including in bed. Some survey answers include, "Let's get naked," "I don't want a commitment," "The football game is on!" and "Let me pay!"

7. Both men and women (according to surveys) most want to hear "I love you" and their name.

8. The best way to "pick up" someone is to be natural and be yourself. Survey answers include to make conversation, look and listen, and smile (that works!).

9. The best place to go to meet someone is where you feel comfortable, so you will shine. Other good choices: where energy is alive (sporting events, amusement parks, concerts). Many people in my surveys give answers like through a friend (good answer!), or at classes, a bar, the beach, or church.

10. Make three approaches before you give up on a dating prospect.

11. Show someone you're interested by admitting it, complimenting him or her, and making eye contact. In surveys people rightfully say to smile!

12. Assess someone's interest from his or her body language, especially eye contact, and whether they want to talk to you.

13. Make eye contact at least 60 percent of the time.

14. Deal with rejection by switching attention to what makes you feel good, and realizing that one hit in three is a good batting average (and many people who find love start out with an even lower batting average).

15. *You* are your own best date.

16. Follow a six-date minimum.

17. A good test of true love is going through crises together.

18. Qualities of best-lasting relationships include commitment, communication, and caring.

19. Condom-sense means using protection every time you have sex.

20. Men don't *have* to roll over and go to sleep after sex; they're tired, or have trained themselves that way, or they may want to escape intimacy.

Index

FOR MORE from Dr. Judy!!!

Over the years there have been many requests for personal advice to individual questions, private sessions, or copies of various articles or tapes of my work. I am happy to provide these for you now. Contact me for any of the following, including for that special personal session to answer your questions, further information, being on the mailing list, etc. Thank you, and I look forward to hearing from you and fulfilling your requests and interests.

Meanwhile, make sure to get your copy of my books, some of which are only available by personal order. Order the following books directly from me: E-mail PlanetLove411@aol.com or call (718) 761-6910, or write Planet Love, 59 Commerce Street, Staten Island, New York 10314.

- *How to Love a Nice Guy.* A "must have" excellent and timely 10-step program that is highly effective to help you stop falling for the wrong person and get the love you really need! This is the best guide of its kind and essential for every dating woman and man today! ($9.95)

- *Generation Sex.* America's hottest sex therapist answers the hottest questions about sex. Another "must have" book, with thousands of questions you won't find anywhere else, plus advice from celebrity guests. A "must" for every LovePhones radio show fan, and everyone else, with amazing answers to thousands of sometimes outrageous but always heartfelt honest questions. Fans say it is the best book they ever bought— and keep it by their bedside and read it with their friends! ($5.99)

- *Sex, Now That I've Got Your Attention Let Me Answer Your Questions.* Dr. Judy answers interesting questions about sex, plus quizzes about sexual power and others! ($9.95)

- *Sex in China.* A one-of-a-kind view into the sexual problems of Chinese men and women. (In Chinese, $2.95)

- *Hello My Happiness, Goodbye My Troubles.* An inside look into issues from America to Japan about relationships. (In Japanese, $4.95)

Order the following books by Dr. Judy from your local bookstore (Borders or Barnes & Noble) or through Amazon.com:

- *The Complete Idiot's Guide to a Healthy Relationship.* The best guide to a loving, lasting and passionate relationship.

- *The Complete Idiot's Guide to Tantric Sex.* An awesome guide to enlightenment and ecstasy.

Send e-mail to PlanetLove411@aol.com, call (718) 761-6910, or write Planet Love, 59 Commerce Street, Staten Island, New York 10314, if you would like the following:

___ A personal consultation with Dr. Judy (in person, by phone, or via e-mail).

___ Dr. Judy giving a speech, keynote address, seminar, workshop, or other presentation, acting as spokesperson, or hosting your organization.

___ Dr. Judy's consultation or help for your public affairs campaign or marketing events.

___ Proposing cooperation with Dr. Judy on your committee or project.

___ To be put on the mailing list.

___ To receive information. Specify: _____

___ Order any items checked below.

___ Other. Specify: _____

E-mail: _____

Name: _____

Address: _____

City _____   State _____   ZIP _____

Country _____

Telephone (Daytime) _____   (Evening) _____

Fax: _____

By popular request, the following items are available. To order, check the items that you want to receive:

Articles by Dr. Judy (each copy $1.00; include self-addressed mailing envelope):

__ P10 "Love At First Sight: Is It Possible?"
__ P11 "Psychic Sex and Psychic Massage"
__ P12 "The ABC's of Sex Hot Spots" (G Spot, AFE Zone, and others)
__ P13 "Exercise and Sex"
__ P14 "Panic Attacks"
__ P15 "Sexual Compatibility"
__ P16 "Too Tired for Sex"
__ P17 "The Sensuous Supper"
__ P18 "Pillow Talk—What Loving Couples Say in Bed"
__ P19 "Are you Soul Mates?"
__ P20 "Good Judgment: Making Wise Choices"

Item Description	Number of Copies	Price Each	Total
Color photos (5x7 for $3.95, 8x10 for $5.95):			
P10 Autographed photo of Dr. Judy in radio station, personalized to you			
P11 Autographed photo of Dr. Judy with rock star at music festival, personalized to you			
Audiotapes ($6.95 each):			
A11 Best of "LovePhones" I (collection of the deemed "best" of calls to the classic LovePhones radio show)			
A12 Best of "LovePhones" II			
A13 Advice from Dr. Judy on dating			
A14 Advice from Dr. Judy on sex			
CDs:			
C11 Best of "LovePhones" I (collection of the deemed "best" of calls to the classic LovePhones radio show ($6.95)			
C12 Best of "LovePhones" II ($6.95)			
C21 Dr. Judy endorsed music for love I ($15.95)			
C22 Dr. Judy endorsed music for love II ($15.95)			
C23 "Towers of Light," an original song of healing after 9/11 terror attacks, written and co-produced by Russell Daisey and Dr. Judy ($5.95)			
T-Shirts autographed and personalized by request ($15.00 each):			
T1 Generation Sex T-shirt			
T2 T-shirt with photo of Dr. Judy and Jagger3			
Videotapes ($16.95 each):			
V11 Video of lecture on love			
V12 Video of college lecture on sex			
V20 Video of Dr. Judy and Jagger at rock festivals			
Booklets ($7.95 each):			
"The Best of 'LovePhones'" (including calls, transcripts of celebrity interviews, "LovePhones" facts, jokes, e-mails, and "LovePhones" dictionary)			

SHIPPING & HANDLING CHARGES	
Up to $20	$4.75
$20.01 to $30	$5.75
$30.01 to $40	$6.98
$40.01 to $50	$7.98
$50.01 to $75	$10.75
$75.01 to $100	$12.75
$100.01 to $150	$14.98
Over $150	$15.98

Merchandise Total	
Sales Tax (New York State residents pay 8.25%)	
Shipping & Handling (use table to left)	
Total	

Call (718)-761-6910 for e-mail instructions or send this form, along with a check or money order, to:

**Planet Love
59 Commerce Street
Staten Island, New York 10314**

Discount for multiple orders. Please allow 4–6 weeks for delivery. Payment to be made in U.S. funds. Price(s) and availability subject to change without notice.